Fides and Secularity

Fides and Secularity
Beyond Charles Taylor's Open Faith

by
EMILIO DI SOMMA

Foreword by
PHILIP G. ZIEGLER

☙PICKWICK Publications • Eugene, Oregon

FIDES AND SECULARITY
Beyond Charles Taylor's Open Faith

Copyright © 2018 Emilio Di Somma. All rights reserved. Except for brief quotations in critical publications or reviews, no part of this book may be reproduced in any manner without prior written permission from the publisher. Write: Permissions, Wipf and Stock Publishers, 199 W. 8th Ave., Suite 3, Eugene, OR 97401.

Pickwick Publications
An Imprint of Wipf and Stock Publishers
199 W. 8th Ave., Suite 3
Eugene, OR 97401

www.wipfandstock.com

PAPERBACK ISBN: 978-1-5326-4943-1
HARDCOVER ISBN: 978-1-5326-4944-8
EBOOK ISBN: 978-1-5326-4945-5

Cataloguing-in-Publication data:

Names: Di Somma, Emilio, author. | Ziegler, Philip Gordon, foreword.

Title: Fides and secularity : beyond Charles Taylor's open faith / Emilio Di Somma ; foreword by Philip G. Ziegler.

Description: Eugene, OR : Pickwick Publications, 2018 | Includes bibliographical references.

Identifiers: ISBN 978-1-5326-4943-1 (paperback) | ISBN 978-1-5326-4944-8 (hardcover) | ISBN 978-1-5326-4945-5 (ebook)

Subjects: LCSH: Taylor, Charles, 1931–. | Secularism. | Religion and culture.

Classification: BL2747.8 .D55 2018 (paperback) | BL2747.8 .D55 (ebook)

Manufactured in the U.S.A.   11/14/18

To my Father, Vito
And my Mother, Lucia

Contents

Foreword by Philip G. Ziegler | ix
Preface | xi

    Introduction | 1
1   Faith and Religion: Against Their Identification | 19
2   Secularity and Religion: The *Status Quaestionis* | 58
3   Hegelian and Post-Hegelian Approaches | 102
4   Between *Secular* and *Religious:* A Theological Perspective | 150
5   Secular Faiths Today | 190
    Conclusion: Faith and *Weltanschauung*, the Need for a New Theoretical Framework | 211

Bibliography | 217

Foreword

CHARLES TAYLOR'S SIGNAL CONTRIBUTIONS to contemporary rethinking of the question of secularity and the secularization of Western societies continue to stimulate debate. In this work, Emilio Di Somma undertakes a searching reconsideration of the conceptual terrain at the heart of such debates. As the title of the work—*Fides and Secularity*—indicates, Di Somma's wide-ranging study looks to think again about the way in which the concept of faith is deployed in contemporary thinking about religion, religious life, and modern "secular" societies. Working up from historical insight into the ancient unity of faith and social life—argued at length in the opening chapter—he goes on to cultivate the idea that faith is a fundamental structure of human existence, the nature of which ought to efface the hard boundary between religion and secularity that commonly marks contemporary debates. The argument unfolds by way of an extended engagement with Taylor's work—especially *A Secular Age*—and involves insightful, critical, and creative use of a range of theological and philosophical interlocutors including Carl Schmitt, Benedetto Croce, H. Richard Niebuhr, Joseph Ratzinger, Johann Baptist Metz, and Ernesto De Martino among many others.

On display throughout this volume is Di Somma's marked gift for synthetic, interdisciplinary thinking and his drive to hold the normative concepts of our age firmly within their formative history. One of the great merits of this study is the constructive introduction of Italian theoretical materials into a discussion which is often unhelpfully dominated by English-language thinkers and texts in translation. Also at work here is Di Somma's tenacious conviction that something of fundamental political and humane importance is at stake in critically overcoming the operative religion/secular schema. For conceiving of the "expanded sphere of faith" in this way affords us more discerning insight into—and critical purchase upon—those fundamental forms of consciousness at work in our contemporary social and political life the significance of which can otherwise be occluded.

This is an ambitious work of contemporary theorizing in a field where the stakes are high. And it is one that merits our close attention. For Di Somma wagers that our contemporary concepts of religion and secularity can and must themselves be placed back into the discursive histories to which they rightly belong, for only in this way can they be responsibly interpreted and responsibly inhabited. And how can we really come to terms with the nature of our secular age apart from recognition of the myriad ways in which the abiding demand of human faith to search out the meaning of our world and to invest its social structures with sense has and continues to play itself out?

Philip G. Ziegler

Preface

IT IS NEVER EASY to develop a book of philosophy, especially when you are a young scholar and your main interlocutor is one of the major contemporary political philosophers and ethicists like Charles Taylor. It becomes even harder when the theme you wish to address is as controversial as the concept of religion, especially when discussed within the framework of contemporary political and social debates.

However, as a young scholar hailing from Naples, I take inspiration from one of the most relevant Neapolitan philosophers of the twentieth century, Benedetto Croce. According to Croce, to engage meaningfully with a philosopher means to develop a critique of his philosophical work. For this reason, in the course of my research for my PhD, I have found that the most promising way to develop my philosophical engagement with Charles Taylor was to develop a reasoned and careful critique of his work, using Croce's philosophy (together with other authors) as a support for my arguments.

However, why write an academic book about the concept of *faith*? The concept of faith has interested many theologians and philosophers, some of which are explicitly quoted in the course of the book. At a first sight, another book on the concept of faith may seem redundant. After all, has not faith been one of the core concepts of Christianity and religions in general? Has not political philosophy of the last century also discussed faith in secular and political contexts? Both questions have a positive answer. Faith certainly has been discussed in its religious and political value. However, I am of the opinion that contemporary scholarly debates have not addressed faith in its *anthropological* value. We have always been led to use the concept of faith to denote a specific attitude towards reality that we could define as *religious*. An irrational posture, a *belief* in some things for which we do not have certain proof, an anticipatory stance toward things in which we *have to believe*. Even in those instances in which the concept of faith has been used *outside* the religious sphere, it has always been an *extension* of the field of religion and never an attempt to escape the category at all. In those cases in which faith has been discussed in political/secular ideologies, it has always been an attempt to extend the *irrationality* attributed to religions to other movements. In this sense, faith is always haunted by a penumbra of irrationality; with the dawn of modernity, faith has become the attribute of a *lesser, irrational* humanity, while modern humans are described as being *reasonable* beings who do not rely on faith to sustain their own ideas.

The driving force behind my research work was, and still is, the will to criticize this prejudice and free the concept of faith from its presupposition of irrationality. Instead, it is my wish to discuss faith in its anthropological value. What does this mean, however, anthropological value? To answer this question, I have to take inspiration from the other great figure who inspired my work, another philosopher (and anthropologist) from Naples, Ernesto De Martino. Ernesto De Martino investigated, in his research in culture and religion, how human beings, in the creation of their own civilizational and historical narratives, commit to *ontological operations*. Whenever we see the development of a culture, of a history, we are also seeing the development of another *world*, with its own ontological qualities and hypostases. De Martino used this assumption to criticize naturalistic anthropologists who, in their studies of indigenous cultures, quickly subsumed their beliefs and traditions (especially regarding magic and rituals) to *superstition*. De Martino, without falling into spiritualism (like many anthropologists of the nineteenth century) still wished to criticize what he believed to be a case of *cultural pride*. Modern, scientific, naturalist anthropologists are committed to the ontological operation of *world-making* as much as a shaman is negotiating the ontology of his own tribe. For De Martino, the difference of the outcome did not subtract to the validity of this assumption. The modern scientist was able to discover the rules of naturalistic causes and effect only *after* that the fundamental ontology of the world was changed. Modernity, in this sense, was the historical moment in which, quite literally, a world *died* and a new world was created in its place. In this sense, De Martino warned us, modernity is not a final stage of history, as much bad contemporary philosophy would lead us to believe; it is merely *a* stage of human history among many, and a very culturally and geographically localized one at that. Nothing promises that the modern human being will not lose itself in the future, or be able to preserve its own ontological framework.

The consequence that flows naturally from this assumption is that there is not a *good* framework to experience reality in an objective way; every cultural framework substantially constitutes its own ontological experience of the world. Having this assumption in mind, I threw myself into this analysis of faith, not anymore as a *religious* attitude toward reality, but as an anthropological one. Faith represents this activity of world-building that precedes any successive act of knowledge; in this sense, then, it is not possible to discuss faith just within the sphere of religion; we need, instead, a new framework of philosophical and theological discussion. These were the motivations which inspired my research in this direction. As for the results, I hope that the reader of this book will look at my proposal as an invitation to escape from old and, in my opinion, useless categories of philosophical and academic discourse, without prejudice. It is my opinion that a new outlook on concepts such as *faith* and *ontology* will bring much benefit to the self-understanding of our contemporary culture.

As a final remark, I wish to thank all the people that supported my research for three years. To the department of Divinity and Religious Studies at the University of Aberdeen, for sponsoring my research and for providing a great environment for research and learning. Special mention is deserved by Professor Philip Ziegler and Professor Christopher Brittain, to whom I am most grateful for supporting my research and for being great mentors and wonderful persons. I also wish to thank Dr. Charlie Collier at Pickwick for the editorial work that has been dedicated to the publication of this book.

Introduction

RECENT YEARS HAVE SEEN an increasing number of scholars in religion and secularity beginning to question the general assumption of *secularization theory*. This assumption states that religion is a phenomenon due to disappear as society becomes increasingly secular. Examples of works that put into question this assumption can be found in the scholarly production of authors like Jose Casanova, William T. Cavanaugh, and Charles Taylor. They wish to propose a new interpretation of the existing relation between the secular sphere and the religious sphere. Even sociologists previously strongly committed to secularization theory have started to question the claim of the disappearance of religion as unsupported by evidence. For example, Peter Berger, on a talk given to the University of Massachusetts on September 12, 2013, affirmed that secularization theory has been proved wrong by empirical evidence. Religion not only has not disappeared, it is even on the rise in some parts of the world.[1]

My main interest in this, still ongoing, debate focuses on the categories through which scholars develop their arguments. From the first moment a scholar tries to address arguments about secularity and religion, he immediately faces what I believe is a common prejudice that has to this

---

1. Berger, *Heretical Imperative*. In this work, Peter Berger addressed the crisis into which modernity has plunged religion. Such crisis is, according to Berger, that of pluralism. Modern society is dominated by a plurality of institutions, while modern consciousness by a plurality of choices. With this plurality of institutions and choices comes uncertainty. With this, we begin to believe unstable, in-cohesive and unreliable the foundational plausibility structures of our societies, which are the means by which institutions are legitimized. This affected most notably the plausibility structures of religion. Religion itself becomes a matter of choice. Of necessary choices, insofar there are few taken-for-granted religious facts to fall back upon, but not more necessary from the moment those facts are disputed. This crisis, according to Berger, was inescapable. It would have led to the all-encompassing secularization of the world.

However, as he affirmed later at the University of Massachusetts, his analysis regarding secularization theory and its future success has been proven incorrect.

point influenced the field of studies as a whole. The prejudice is that the two phenomena of secularity and religion are distinctively separable, almost two *genera* through which is possible to categorize with extreme precision two very distinct ways of being in the world. It is as if an individual in a religious framework possesses a different *form of consciousness* than an individual in a secular framework. Having revealed my main interest on the argument, I believe we are already in need of a clarification about the nature of this prejudice. The first important thing to be said is that, in speaking about this prejudice, I am not criticizing the historical distinction between religion and secularity. Clearly, secular structures and authorities are different historical facts than religious ones. Modernity as well, despite being historically connected with the previous eras and events, is also its own historical event and developed its own rules.[2] The problem does not lie in the historical distinction or definition between secularity and religion. We need a theoretical framework that is able to distinguish between secular and religious authorities and between secular and religious societies. In the same way, we also need a definition that preserves the specificity of concepts like *religion* and *secularity*.

However, the prejudice is connected to this distinction. It is true that we can, and we must, make a historical distinction between modernity and premodernity, between religious authorities and secular authorities. However, the prejudice pushes this distinction further, and almost identifies secularity and religion as two inherently different ways of being in the world.[3] This prejudice creates the impression that the secular individual and the religious individual experience different modes of existence relating to different forms of consciousness. In this way, we have the construction of the modern, secular individual, who interacts with the world through rationality and immanence. The secular individual is believed to possess a scientific mind. In his interaction with the world there is no space for superstition, mysticism and, in general, any form of connection that escapes the laws of causality. For these reasons, he is believed to possess a higher degree of objectivity in his judgments about the world. The religious individual, instead, is believed to interact with the world through beliefs and

---

2. Rules that are, in any case, historical and historically contingent. Unlike those scholars that claim the supposed exceptionality of Modernity, like Charles Taylor and Hans Blumenberg, which I will address in the course of the book, I do not share such enthusiasm in evaluating Modernity. Of course, to deny that modernity is a special event is not equivalent to deny that modernity is also its own historical specific event.

3. This expression should be understood in the sense intended by Heidegger, as conscience *in the world*, existence, or *Dasein*. For a proper explanation of Heidegger's *Dasein*, see Heidegger, *Being and Time*, 67–90. Also Gelven, *Commentary on Heidegger's Being and Time*, 47–74.

transcendence. He elaborates his experience of the world through mysticism and religious authorities. His belief in the presence of God is enough to question his adherence to science and a strong causal relation between phenomena. For this reason, his capacity to develop objective judgments is considered impaired.

While it is true that the examples I have proposed may be interpreted as *ideal types*, at the same time it cannot be denied that, in contemporary public space, religious claims are often undervalued, when not openly ostracized. Religion is interpreted as something belonging purely to the private sphere of beliefs. Therefore, it should not have place in public discourse about the policies and political structures of the community. Its language and its contents are considered unacceptable, as they are considered divisive, when not openly violent, by secular authorities, that, instead, are believed to be neutral. To bring religious claims into the public/political discourse is a contested practice. This is the first obstacle that this study will have to overcome. The debate is structured around functional definitions of the concept of religion and secularity. In this way, they are distinguished and differentiated in public spaces and scholarly studies. To find a widely accepted definition of the concept of religion is not an easy task, as will be shown in the course of this book. Ernst Feil, in "The Problem of Defining and Demarcating "Religion,'" questions whether it is even possible to obtain a functional definition of religion for the sake of social studies. The purpose of this book, however, is not to reach a final definition of religion, or secularity. Instead, the purpose is to enlighten what are believed to be anthropological features that the two share on a social level.

For the sake of this argument, then, I wish to express a preliminary statement that will clarify how the concepts of religion and secularity will be interpreted from now on. In this study, both religions and secular ideologies are defined as being, fundamentally, *Weltanschauung*. Comprehensive worldviews that provide the people embedded in them with the fundamental social/existential tools through which individuals can structure their own social/moral/political and physical existence. Both categories, in their being comprehensive worldviews, find their distinction in their specific historical features, the main one being that religions refer, usually, to a divine or quasi-divine sphere, while secular ideologies refer to alternative sources of legitimization. It has to be said that this definition of religion and secularity may not be applicable to all historical facts worldwide.[4] However, it is not the purpose of this book to investigate the distinction between secularity and religion on a global level, but merely to address the consequences of this distinction in Western cultures and societies.

4. The example of Buddhism is the first one that comes to mind.

In this sense, the distinction I have described, at first sight, reveals nothing new. The belief in a divine figure is, usually, the first feature that, in Western societies, identifies a social structure as religious. However, the consequences of this distinction are relevant and worthy of study. The first consequence is that, by focusing on the historical differences between religions and secular ideologies, an inability to see what is similar between them has been imbued in our sensibility. This, I believe, is a direct consequence of the prejudice I have described earlier. To be clear, and avoid possible criticism in this direction, it is not my intention to deny that secularity and religion involve different experiences of the world. After all, the belief or nonbelief in the existence of one God (or more gods) does have an influence on how we experience and structure our lives. What I want to question, however, is the source of these experiences. There are anthropological features, constants, in the history of Western civilization, which both religious and secular frameworks share. It is for this reason that I consider an analysis of Charles Taylor's work an obligatory starting point for this study. Faced with the secular reaction against religion in the public space, Taylor shows the will to speak in defense of religious values and transcendence. In addition, he is able to offer an extremely good historical narrative about the origins of secularism and modernity in Western civilization. However, as I will present in the following pages, Taylor's argument reveals how the current frame of the debate understands the concept of religion and secularity according to the prejudice that I have introduced in the previous pages; even in the case of thinkers like Taylor, who wish to speak "on behalf" of religion.

Taylor's philosophical work is focused on understanding how the features of modern identity developed historically and socially. I am of the opinion that his attempt is one of the best efforts to reconstruct and analyze the historical and social processes that allowed the modern individual and modern societies to structure themselves in the forms we know them today. I find the particular position Taylor wishes to reach with his work worthy of attention. This position can be described by way of a general schematization.[5] Let us describe the main actors in the debate between religion and secularity as belonging to two main categories. We have those authors who are critical of secularism, of which they attack its perceived limitations and shortcomings.[6] Then we have the supporters of secularism[7] who, instead,

5. I acknowledge this schematization may be superficial, but it allows conveying my understanding of Taylor's philosophical position.

6. I believe this position is represented well by postliberal theologians. Great examples for this side of the controversy are: Hauerwas, *Against the Nations*; Milbank, *Theology and Social Theory*.

7. Very good examples for this side of the controversy are: Stout, *Democracy and Tradition*; Connolly, *Identity/Difference*.

claim that secular structures of society are the best neutral ground possible for intercultural and intersocial debates. Taylor seems to locate himself precisely at the center of this controversy, still advocating for a kind of resolution between secularism and religion. He is searching for a third option that could create a synthesis between the two different positions so that the best features of both could be retained.[8]

My analysis starts with Charles Taylor's book *A Secular Age*. I find the work a masterpiece of historical and sociological analysis concerning how modernity and secularism could be developed from the crises that hit religious authorities in the sixteenth and seventeenth centuries. The main purpose of the work is to question a narrative of modernity as a process of subtraction, as a gradual disappearance of religion from the public space and focuses, instead, on those positive and creative social processes that allowed secularity to spread as the new main framework of Western societies. The final aim of the work is to allow for the construction of a synthesis between secular and religious social forms. It aims to look for those territories in which some kind of connections can be created and tries to show how both religious and secular spheres are important features of our contemporary moral life. In this way, the intended outcome of the work is to preserve the best features of secular and religious positions, in order to propose moral and political arguments to develop peaceful and cohesive communities in our Western context.

Of course, such a project has received both appreciations and criticism. José Casanova, for example, in his essay "A Secular Age: Dawn or Twilight?," affirms that Taylor "offers the best analytical, phenomenological, and genealogical account we have of our modern, secular condition."[9] Nonetheless, he still argues that Taylor has overlooked the fact that even secularism in itself is not a homogeneous social phenomenon. It develops in different forms according to the different cultural spheres and contexts.[10] In a different vein, Michael L. Morgan, in his essay "Religion, History and Moral Discourse," suggests that Taylor's philosophical work must be interpreted as an attempt to combine a pluralist and nonexclusive view to a traditional religious heritage so to illuminate both religion's role in our moral lives, and how the divine-human relationship figures into our moral understanding.[11]

---

8. In affirming this, I am making also the claim that he is a Hegelian philosopher and that his Hegelianism has heavily affected his conclusions, as I will argue in the course of the book.

9. Casanova, "Secular Age," 265.

10. Casanova finds problematic Taylor's assumption that groups the entire North Atlantic world under the same definition of secularism, while there are clearly differences between European and American religious/secular phenomena.

11. Morgan, *Religion, History and Moral Discourse*, 53–55.

Critics of Taylor's work, by contrast, focus on his ambiguity in dealing with the opposite sides of the debate about modernity. They also criticize his implicit, but stern, refusal of secular language (and values) as well as the lack of strength in his claims. Justin D. Klassen, for example, affirms that, although remarkable, Taylor's proposal is, at its best, a recommendation to put our linguistic determinations *at a distance*.[12] Ian Angus, instead, calls into question the very possibility of the Hegelian reconciliation that Taylor seeks.[13]

However, I have found the most interesting criticisms of Taylor's proposal in William Connolly's work *Identity/Difference*. Through this criticism is possible to understand what is at stake in the secularism/religion controversy. Connolly describes Taylor's account as a form of civic liberalism.[14] A form of political thinking that tries to find a harmonization between the space given to rights and individualities and the juridical and communal side of politics. In particular, Connolly affirms that Taylor's theory "proceeds from a rhetoric of self-realization within community, through a rhetoric of communal realization through harmonization of the diverse parts of an ongoing culture, to a rhetoric of progressive attunement to a harmonious direction in being. The latter is a requirement of his theory."[15]

The critical point of this theoretical movement, Connolly says, is reached when it is realized that, even if such *direction in being* to ground a community would be needed, it still would be impossible to prove how such direction would be available to us.[16] Therefore, Connolly accuses Taylor of still being, inherently, an Augustinian philosopher who is unable to prove his theory through particular arguments and has to rely on textual tropes that presuppose the availability of such direction.[17] From Connolly's criti-

---

12. Klassen, "Affirmation of Existential Life," 37.

13. Angus, "Recovery of Meaning?," 253–54.

14. Connolly, *Identity/Difference*, 89. In addition, Connolly affirms that it is an exemplary one for the category as a whole.

15. Ibid., 89.

16. Ibid., 89.

17. Ibid., 90. Connolly, who seeks a solution to the paradox of identity and difference, finds Taylor's concept of community and politics extremely faulty, because:

> The gentle rhetoric of articulation, realization, community, purpose, attunement, fulfilment, integration, and harmonization significantly reinscribes the common life, obligating people and institutions to reform and consolidate themselves in ways that may be arbitrary, cruel, destructive, and dangerous if the pursuit of consensus and commonality are not supported by a harmonious direction in being. The gentle rhetoric of harmonization must be ambiguated and coarsened by those who have not had its faith breathed into their souls, particularly those moved by nontheistic reverence for the rich ambiguity of existence. (ibid., 90)

cism, I can identify my main interest in Taylor's work. Taylor advocates for a direction in being,[18] precisely because he does not see such a direction in the secular movement. We could say then, that Taylor tries to develop his position in a conciliatory movement that, through Hegelian dialectic, tries to take the best from both sides of the controversy to achieve a synthesis that could satisfy the largest number of people possible.[19] However, precisely because of this dialectic movement, Taylor relies on the prejudice I believe still determines the whole debate. I will propose the interpretation that Taylor's position further exacerbates the sense of difference between secularity and religion, precisely because he sees the need for a Hegelian synthesis between secularity and religion. The result of Taylor's proposal is that a human being, embedded in a secular framework, relies on a different form of consciousness than a human being embedded in a religious framework does.

In this sense then, it would be interesting to compare Taylor's work with Jeffrey Stout's work *Democracy and Tradition*. Stout's proposal is the specular opposition to Taylor. Stout, in fact, starts from the immanent side of the problem to decline it in a conciliatory way to make possible a peaceful coexistence between the different cultural groups of the same society.[20] Stout tries to develop his argument in a way that gives birth to an interpretation of democracy as tradition. He identifies that the main problem, for liberal democracy, in the eyes of traditionalists (especially Augustinian ones), is that such a democracy totally levels the basis on which the virtuous common life is held to depend (be it called tradition, culture, civilization, community etc.). Such a democracy's characteristic form of moral discourse

18. Ibid., 89.

19. At the same time, Taylor's Hegelian movement is eminently Hegelian in the sense that is unable to achieve a true synthesis and just manages to achieve the empowerment of one of the two sides of the controversy. This problem will be discussed in the third chapter.

20. Stout, *Democracy and Tradition*, ch. 3. Stout affirms that he is unconvinced by the argument of people like Rawls or Rorty. Rawls's argument is unconvincing in the measure its account of reasonableness cut out, paradoxically, any one that, for any personal commitment, should disagree with Rawls's understanding of social contract. It would cut out any space for religious commitment in the public debate.

In addition, Stout declares, Rawls seems too focused in idealizing an impossible act of reasoning, while ignoring completely the important role that immanent criticism and candid expression actually play in democratic states. In the end, Rawls's argument for restraint when talking religious language is, paradoxically, a moralistic one. Rorty's argument, Stout claims, is extremely different from Rawls. Rorty adopts a pragmatic stance by claiming that religious arguments are a conversation-stopper and are, therefore, unsuitable for political debate. Stout replies that the true conversation-stopper is, more than religious claims, faith claims. This, however, leads to two important conclusions; first, not all religious arguments are faith claims. Second, there are political/social claim that rely on faith claims without being specifically religious.

is an assertion and counter-assertion of individual rights, without reflection on and cultivation of the virtues. Even democratic tradition considers values and piety important.[21] According to Stout, then, the first issue to solve is establishing what piety means. A traditional interpretation of the term would be an act of deference toward the hierarchical power. Of course, Stout rejects such a narrow interpretation. For a democratic individual piety is a social virtue that concerns just or fitting acknowledgments of the sources of our existence and progress through life. In this sense, the modern democratic individual does not need a traditionalist piety. He does not need priests.[22] The problem would be to identify the characters of democratic piety. Stout follows Dewey's and Emerson's work to show how even the democratic tradition has its own worries about public virtues so that the political community can properly execute its function and not be corrupted by personal vices. What should be maintained is an attitude of respect between the different supporters of different kinds of piety. If the traditionalist cannot impose religious belief on anyone, then at the same time secular democrats should avoid a stance of absolute atheism, that is rejection and mockery of every kind of source of life or piety, as it is unable to provide any content to a healthy democratic community.[23]

Through this short comparison, we can point out the main consequence of the prejudice regarding the separation between religion and secularity. The main problem, for the authors presented so far, is ethical in its essence. Is secularism able to sustain consistent ethical claims? For Taylor, the answer is *partially*. Secularity needs to rediscover the positive influences and importance of religion for moral life. For Stout and Connolly, instead, the answer is positive. Secularism is able to sustain its own moral claims and does represent a neutral ground in which all the different views can join in a peaceful dialogue.[24] What I want to focus on, however, is how the

21. Ibid., 19–28.

22. Ibid., 29–31. In quoting Withman, Stout affirms that the democratic individual does not need precisely a hierarchical figure of reference and take matter of acknowledgment of the sources of his life in his own hands. Priests do not disappear physically. Instead, their authoritative role is stripped of power. In this sense, Stout says that Withman's remarks have been prophetically true and that this is (mostly) the condition of modern democracy.

23 Stout, *Democracy and Tradition*, 31–41.

24. Stout acknowledges that modern secular claims also depend on a tradition of their own and, as all historical product, can be falsified and misled; however he still affirms that modern democratic individuals are entitled to their own claims and that, if properly used, can lead to a better society (ibid., 287–91).

Connolly, as well, while admitting that liberal individualism may as well be a form of forced normalization, of identification of evil within a society, like theological

source of ethics has been described. I believe that the current frame of the debate, in which we describe secularism and religion as inherently different, is unhelpful to address the problem of the source of our ethical/political claims. Taylor tries to describe secularism as the alternative developed by Western societies when the previous religious framework became unable to guarantee consistently a *sense of fullness*. However, as I will propose through the book, his historical interpretation transforms secularism in an antithesis of religion. Taylor can advocate for a synthesis between them precisely because he describes secularity and religion, today, as radically different and thus not contesting for the same positions in the social sphere.[25]

However, this specific frame of the argument is not a trait belonging only to Taylor; instead, they influence the debate as a whole. The current categories of interpretation of the problem understand our experience of the world as being filtered and modified by our social/historical framework. In this sense, there would be a neutral world, a neutral reality, which our framework then allows us to experience in a more or less precise way. A great example of this account would be Slavoj Zizek's documentary *The Pervert's Guide to Ideology*. In the documentary, Zizek takes inspiration from the movie *They Live*, in which the protagonists, using special glasses, uncover the real world masked by the illusion created by a race of alien overlords. For Zizek, the glasses are like a critique of any ideological framework, criticism that unmasks a reality that is still out there, ready to be experienced as it is.

In the context of our problem, Taylor sees that the secular framework, being the modern and most rational one, would offer, unlike the religious one, a more accurate experience of the world. In this sense, the disenchantment of the world was a necessary step to be free of naïve faith and be able to retain only the most positive features of religion. After modernity, we see the world as it is. The only problem remaining for an ethicist would be to identify the correct moral sources and the correct way to inscribe them in society. This is an understanding of the problem with which I disagree. I reject the assumption that secularity and religion rely on different forms of consciousness. I also reject the idea that it would be possible to put on a *pair of glasses* to see a supposed neutral reality, that could be the basis for

---

mechanisms, is deeply convinced that liberal individuality, free of theological dogmas, represents a deep appreciation of existence as such (Connolly, *Identity/Difference*, 75–80).

25. After all, the dialectical conflict is never a conflict of positions and always a conflict of reciprocal empowerment and improvement through the synthesis. Taylor shows clearly this theoretical structure of reasoning in his separation of secularism as *immanent* from religion as *transcendent*, as I will show in the second chapter of this work.

truthful ethical claims. I strongly believe that our experiences of the world are not just filtered through the framework, but are constituted by it for a great measure.

At a first glance, this distinction may not seem relevant, and offers, functionally, very scarce material to work with. However, the consequences of such difference of interpretation generate different expectations once we try to address our categories of analysis at a scholarly level. I believe that Taylor works with an interpretation of experience and framework in the first sense. This allows him to develop a progressivist account of modernity and secularity, in which it is possible to develop a better social framework to interpret reality and is possible to obtain a more truthful representation of the world.[26] Instead, to believe that the framework, the *Weltanschauung*, constitutes ontologically our experiences of the world means to give up on any expectation on the improvement of the framework. If the framework does not just register and filter the ontology of the world, but constitutes the ontology in itself, then there would not be a neutral reality ready to be truthfully experienced once we improve the quality of our framework, or when we criticize the ineffectiveness of other frameworks

To make myself clear, I should give also more details about what I mean when I speak about reality. When I say *reality*, I mean *historical reality*. Any kind of hypothesis, theory or description about reality, secular or religious, is always a human historical product and is always influenced by historical conditions.[27] Here is the central point I want to make. Any kind of claim about our historical reality, particularly ethical/social/political claims, always imply an *ontological hypostasis*. Every time we see a claim about an ethical approach, a given form of government, a specific organization of society, I believe we are also in the presence of an implicit understanding about what the world *really is*.

---

26. We transit from a naïve faith to a responsible faith. Alternatively, we move from an enchanted world to a disenchanted one.

27. Of course, someone could interpret this statement as a criticism of hard sciences. Hard sciences, it could be claimed, do not operate historically; they look for patterns and causal relations that are independent from historical conditions. However, I would say, if any progress has been possible even in hard sciences as well, this has happened because the historical conditions have changed. Science is, in any case, an historical product and, therefore, even its own conclusions can be interpreted only historically.

An example, in this sense, could be the year-long Liebig-Pasteur controversy: Pasteur was convinced that fermentation of alcohol was a biological process; Liebig, instead, believed that it was only a chemical process. Liebig's conclusion was clearly influenced by his historical conditions, which allowed him to address the matter from a very specific point of view. Pasteur's experiment of fermentation did not only represent a change in the scientific mentality of the time, but also a change of the historical conditions of all successive scientific considerations.

What does a term like ontological hypostasis mean? With this term, I am indicating an implicit understanding about reality that allows a society to structure itself. Whenever we are involved socially/historically with other human beings, we share not only ethical/moral/social conventions, we also structure those conventions through an implicit understanding on the nature of the world in itself; the *Weltanschauung* provides us with fundamental ontological statements about reality that become the source and ground of any future engagement. Certain things make sense, socially, because the world in itself is structured in a certain way. It is a silent conspiracy, a hidden establishment about the grain of the universe, a presupposition of reality that allows for all the things that make sense to us to actually have sense.

A good example to represent better what I wish to describe can be found in a thought experiment from quantum physics theory, the paradox of Schrödinger's cat. In this thought-experiment, Schrödinger imagined that a cat was closed in a box with a hellish machine and a decaying radioactive element. At an unspecified point in time, the radiation would trigger the machine to open a poison flask and kill the cat. Schrödinger's paradox affirms that, until an observer opens the box to confirm the state of the poor animal, we have to consider the cat both alive and dead at the same time.[28] This thought experiment, which caused quite a stir in the debate about quantum physics, possesses a great potential to represent what happens, at an epistemological-existential level, in socio-historical structures. What we consider, at first sight, an open choice (the cat is either alive or dead) that we confirm with our actions (to open the box) is already the result of a restriction obtained through the given ontology of the world, the *Weltanschauung*. In this way, to have a given idea of the cat, of the box and of the hellish machine already restricts the possible outcomes that we expect to happen from their interaction. We can only obtain either a dead or an alive cat, we do not have access to *other* options, to other experiences. On a socio-historical level, I believe, a similar process happens. Through the *Weltanschauung*, we already possess given fundamental ideas about the reality of the world, such ontology directs and determines the amount of possible interactions we can create with the world around us. That is the reason behind my argument that the *framework constitutes the experience*. Because any kind of claim, idea, hypothesis expressed through the social/historical framework has to rely on a very specific idea of the world and the relations established within it. It is not just an altered experience through the framework, the framework, in part, creates the experience. In this sense, then, we could

---

28. Regarding the value of the paradox of Schroedinger's cat for ethical and theological studies, I have found useful the following source: Holder, "Quantum Theory and Theology."

say that two different historical frameworks can be considered as *living in two different worlds*. It is not productive to discuss better frameworks, as we would simply be switching from one ontological hypostasis to another.[29] To paraphrase Nietzsche: *There are no facts, only interpretations*,[30] but then *interpretations become facts*.

However, to acknowledge this fundamental ontological difference between frameworks does not imply that different frameworks require the single subject/society to operate through different forms of consciousness. Instead, it calls for considerations on the fundamental human attitude required to structure the world ontologically, the anthropological constant on our historical activity of world-making. In the moment in which the subject faces the world and has to construct his relation with it, through the framework, I believe he is appealing to the same forms of consciousness. This would happen independently from the framework within which he is embedded. In this sense, a secular individual and a religious individual would appeal to a fundamental human attitude to structure ontologically the world they live in. The quality of their experiences, then, is altered by the historical/social/cultural conditions, that can be religious or secular.[31] In this sense, then, a conflict between frameworks is always also a *conflict between worlds*.

These are the reasons behind the title of this work, *Fides and Secularity*. It should not be interpreted as the already executed attempt to discuss *fides* (faith, belief) as something distinct and outside the field of secularity. I believe, instead, that faith has to be considered as the fundamental human feature that allows human subjects, embedded in a framework, to structure their world not only socially and/or morally, but ontologically as well. To have faith, then, would not just be a namely religious attitude, but a fundamental ontological/existential posture toward the world. Faith is to believe in a given structure of reality, structure that allows all the explicit values and sources of meaning to be sustainable. My attempt, with this book, is to propose a way in which we can see these two concepts, faith and secularity, as being related to each other, instead of being distinct and separated. Is it possible, in secular social forms, to observe something that we can define as faith? What form of consciousness the concept of faith describes? The

---

29. Of course, this process of change and exchange of ontological hypostases does happen historically. More will be said in the course of the study.

30. Nietzsche, *Writings from the Late Notebooks*, 115–16.

31. To be clear, I am not denying the subjective power of historical action, as if the subject is only at the receiving end of the framework. The subject is always in a reciprocal relation with the framework in which he is embedded. In this sense, the possibility for the transformation of the framework is always an historical possibility.

driving assumption of this work, then, is to consider faith not as a parochial religious concept, but as the fundamental form of relation through which human beings establish existential and ethical relations with their world and people around them; both in an immanent and transcendental sense, and obtain, in this way, a substantiation for their ethical/existential claims.

Of course, I also recognize the critical exposure of my argument. If we were to consider every framework as also an ontological constitution of the world, then any claim of the alleged neutrality of the secular public space would sound less convincing. After all, we would not be speaking about a better understanding of the world, just of a different one. In this sense, the separation between the secular and the religious sphere that the modern framework has built in the last two centuries would reveal itself in all its contingency and non-necessity. Still, I believe it is worthwhile to push this interpretation of the problem. I believe that for too long secularism has donned the mask of *rationality*, leaving to the religious the realm of the *belief, transcendence*, and *mysticism*. This is also the reason why this work is an analysis of Charles Taylor's work, and yet also an attempt to go beyond such analysis. Through an analysis of Taylor's work, I will show how the fundamental prejudice that understands secularism and religion as relying on different forms of consciousness exercises a strong influence in his work, despite his best attempt to resolve the debate in a positive manner. At the same time, through the proposal of a short analysis of the phenomenon of faith, I will propose a possible alternative way to understand the problem as a whole, thus going beyond a simple analysis of Taylor's work.

To develop this argument, the first chapter will propose a brief analysis of the history of the concepts of faith and religions. I will suggest that in ancient traditions starting from the Greeks, the concept of faith possessed a more social/existential meaning, than a religious one. More than referring to the divine sphere, or to specific gods, the concept of faith, in the Greek and Roman tradition, indicated those reciprocal relations of trust, loyalty and credibility that were considered the fundamental prepolitical values on which it was possible to build a stable political community. Even in those instances in which the concept of faith was used in reference to the gods, the meaning was always that of a guarantee for a promise, a vow that had value only between fellow citizens, of which the God was not an active enforcer, but the formal guarantor. I believe, only in a few cases we do find the concept of faith in relation to something that we can consider as *transcendent*. However, even in those cases, the reference was not toward a religious or divine sphere, as we understand it today. In the cases in which faith was used to indicate a superior order, a higher harmony of the universe, faith denoted the relation of trust and commitment a Greco-Roman citizen showed toward social structures as representation of this higher order. The Greco-Roman socio-political structures made sense, and were considered worthy of trust, because they represented, on a political level, the grain of the universe, the fundamental ontological hypostasis through which the world itself was constituted. It was the comprehensive Greco-Roman worldview that allowed the social structures/customs/laws to make sense. Through the work of Jacob Taubes, I will suggest that the *nomos*, the *law*, was the fundamental hypostasis of the Greco-Roman tradition and discuss how it entered into contact with the Jewish sensibility. This relation between different cultures, with a different understanding of the concept of faith, introduced the divine figure in the relation of faith. This intertwining represented the first step of the historical evolution of the concept that led to an interpretation of faith as a religious concept the way we understand it today.

From this encounter, the Christian sensibility could be born. Paul's attempt to establish the foundations of the Christian church were also an attempt to shake the very ontological foundation in which the imperial order found its own legitimization. I believe it was for this reason that Christianity, unlike the Jewish religion, could not be integrated in the social structures of the empire, and had to face persecutions. However, even when the Christian understanding of the world became the dominant one, this did not lead to the disappearance of the previous understanding of faith. Through the work of Piet Fransen on the concepts of *fides et mores*, I will propose a philological interpretation according to which faith continued to be understood more in a social and ontological sense even in the early Christian and medieval period. More than indicating a form of mystical enlightenment given from God, faith indicated the relation that tied the Christian to the church and to God. This relation found its legitimization in the grain of the universe that was developed around the figure of the one God as "existence" *par excellence*. Only after the Council of Trent, the concept of faith is understood in a mystical sense and opposed to *ratio*. The first chapter will also allow me to introduce the theoretical background and the studies which inspired my current argument and motivated my criticism of Charles Taylor's work in first place.

In the second chapter, I will begin my analysis on Charles Taylor's interpretation of the theory of secularization. I will argue that Taylor, despite his attempt to develop a positive theory, still has to rely on a negative understanding of the process of secularization. He has to rely on the disappearance of religion (or, as he says, the transcendent) as a contradiction to secularity, to be able to structure his proposal. In this sense, Taylor's proposal is similar to Hans Blumenberg's historical narrative. Both develop an understanding of modernity as an absolute historical event. As an alternative to

Taylor's narrative on the process of secularization, I will propose a critical comparison with Carl Schmitt. Particularly, one of the main sources for this comparison will be his work *Political Theology*, and the debate Schmitt developed with Blumenberg after its publication. My aim is to expand Schmitt's concept of political theology to identify this fundamental relational attitude of faith, which provides legitimacy to the social structure, to see if it can be useful to understand what is truly at stake in the controversy between secularism and religion. Particularly, Schmitt's assumption—that, in a society, there is an accordance between political structures and a metaphysical understanding of the world—convinced me that a comparison of Taylor's work with Schmitt's analysis is fruitful and worthwhile.

In the third chapter, I will focus on Taylor's *Hegelianism*. I will argue that Taylor's historical account relies on a strict understanding of Hegel's dialectic. For example, the Hegelian concepts of *Sittlichkeit* and *Objective Spirit* have been central for Taylor's philosophical work. Taylor's Hegelianism is one of the major causes of the limitations of his historical/sociological analysis. As a possible integration, I will show how a post-Hegelian criticism of Hegelian dialectics provides us with useful tool to develop a better historical/sociological analysis. I will apply Benedetto Croce's criticism against the Hegelian process of *thesis-antithesis* to Taylor's historical analysis. Through Croce's *dialectics of distinct concepts* and his theory of the *degrees of categories* that are connected through processes of *implication*, it is possible to conceive a different understanding of historical events within a Hegelian sensibility. Through this argument, I will also show how Croce possessed a sensibility that allowed him to use the concept of faith in nonreligious contexts. In this sense, he understood the concept of religion in a more liberal way than the common modern understanding usually allows. As a conclusion of the second chapter, I will also introduce an anthropological application of Croce's sensibility through the comparison between Taylor's concept of *buffered self* and the work of Ernesto De Martino, an Italian anthropologist and student of Benedetto Croce. De Martino affirms, with his concept of *culturally conditioned nature*, the existence of the fundamental ontological hypostasis I have described at the beginning of this introduction. The focus of his anthropological studies has been, in fact, to investigate how the *Weltanchauung* constitutes the world ontologically.

In the fourth chapter, I will develop my argument against Taylor, and its application to the *religion/secularity* binary, through thoughts gathered from Christian theology. I will argue that there is, on the Catholic side of the controversy, a stern criticism of the secular claim about rationality and neutrality. This criticism goes together with the implication of the existence of this attitude of faith, this hidden irrationality, in secular social structures. In particular, I will explore the thought of Joseph Ratzinger and Johan Baptist Metz on the subject. Ratzinger understands the relation between secularity and religion in a more complex way than the current debate allows, one that escapes Taylor's Hegelian categories. In addition I will show how he describes faith as something that should not be tied narrowly to historical religion, but, instead, as a general attitude through which human beings relate to their values and their societies. With the thought of Johann Baptist Metz, on the other hand, I will argue that this religious sentiment is understood politically/ideologically. Metz uses categories that allow understanding of political/social ideologies as tied to deeply irrational *foundational values*. In this sense, Metz's category of *middle-class religion* or *alternative religion* is a useful tool, albeit one that I do not appreciate entirely, that reveals the similarities between secular and religious historical structures. This will demonstrate that a theoretical separation between them does not serve social and historical analyses. In the second part of the fourth chapter, I will develop a viable description of what entails an attitude of faith. To do so, I will rely on the work of H. Richard Niebuhr. Niebuhr has demonstrated a sensibility regarding the concept of faith that allows him to use the concept in relation to secular sources of values, not just religious ones. If we understand the attitude of faith as the attitude of loyalty, fidelity and commitment, then religions are not the only social structures in which we see faith. Instead, secular social forms (like nationalisms, ideologies, economic structures) reveal the same attitude of faith that the modern sensibility has relegated to the realm of the religious and of the transcendent. In this sense, Niebuhr's work will allow me to free the concept of faith from a restrictive interpretation of religious attitude and make viable its use in nonreligious contexts. At the same time, Niebuhr's elaboration of the concept of faith as commitment and loyalty will reveal a feature of the concept to which Taylor has not dedicated enough attention, that is, an active pursuit of the enforcement and spreading of the value we consider meaningful.

In the last chapter, building on the arguments developed in previous ones, and as a way of going beyond Taylor, I will propose a thought-experiment. What would happen if we were to consider "faith" in a nonreligious sense? I will focus on proposing contemporary examples of political ideologies, economic theories, and philosophical narratives, in which an attitude of faith is required to access to them and enforce them at a social level. I will consider that faith is something related more to our *realm of meanings*, especially to their ontological value, their interpretation of the world as such, their worldview. In this way, the question becomes: *can we find this attitude of faith, this ontological construction of the world, alongside ethical/political claims, in modern and contemporary social forms?*

The proposed examples from economy, politics, and philosophy are meant to show how it is worthwhile to use a language of faith, as an ontological relation to reality, to define secular social phenomenon. In this sense, my main point of reference, for economy, will be Giorgio Agamben's considerations on the existing relation between theology and liberalism. Followed by considerations of Milton Friedman's discourse *Free Market for Free Man*, given at the University of Chicago in the 1970's. For politics, I will focus on studies of American Cold War propaganda. I will concentrate my attention particularly on studies regarding the radio station Voice of America and on the United States Information Agency to analyze their political and social language. For the philosophical sphere, instead, I will offer a short analysis of Francis Fukuyama's work *The End of History and the Last Man*, to show how, even in philosophical language, we can consider the existence of this attitude of faith as a fundamental support for ethical and political claims. The purpose of these examples will be to show how very different forms of languages (economics, politics, philosophy) share this fundamental attitude of faith interpreted not only as a *mystical knowledge* about an higher truth, but also as a *presupposition of reality*. This implicit acceptance of a fundamental ontological hypostasis, a grain of the universe, gives stability and substance to further ethical claims. I propose, through our thought experiment, that any meaningful social/political claim has to rely, implicitly, on a sense of reality, a worldview that is in equal parts ontological and social. To say that free market, democracy, or liberalism are the inevitable outcomes of human societies is also to say that the world, and human beings, are structured in a certain way.

Before concluding this introduction, there is a final point that, I would like to elucidate. First, on my last chapter, as contemporary examples for our thought experiment, a careful reader will notice that I have focused on very specific examples of Western social/cultural forms. I admit that there would have been other, equally viable, options (Communism and Nazism are some examples). I focus on those specific examples purely for historical reasons. By historical reasons, I mean that I believe it cannot be denied that those social forms have been, at the present state, the winners of our history. They have been able, for various reasons that cannot be presented in this work, to overcome all the alternative social/political structures and impose themselves as the correct interpretation of our social reality, or the right side of history. It is precisely for this reason that I have not considered other examples, those alternative forms can be considered the current losers of our historical path, and it would be all too easy to create a sense of distance between our social forms and theirs. My attempt, instead, is to propose that there are social/ethical processes happening even in our actual framework, which many people would like to consider as *better* than those alternative examples. I want to show precisely that there are forms of consciousness, in the human relation with the world, that keep their influence and action even in our contemporary context.

1

Faith and Religion
Against Their Identification

AFTER A PERIOD IN which it seemed that Western societies had given away with "religion" as an issue, both socially and politically, recent years have seen the topic return in our social, political and economic frameworks. Not only the wars that have plagued the world since the start of the new century seem strongly tied with "religious" issues; but also economic debates since the economic crisis of the 2008 have started to rely more and more on a "theological vocabulary." In an attempt to understand the causes and reasons for the failure of "free market" and the inability of economic "experts" to foresee and react to such a crisis.

Although not tied exclusively to a specific religion (even though attempts in this direction have been taken by media and political discourse), religion as a phenomena has again, by force we could almost say, taken his spot in social struggles and debates. Of course, such an upheaval sparks the interest of many scholars, both in matters of philosophy and theology. On one hand, this has led the academic debate to put into question the so-called *secularization theory*, to the point that there are scholars that openly talk about a *postsecular* world. On the other, there has been also a development of the academic debate about the concept of religion itself, in an attempt to redefine it and to understand what this concept does really denote. Charles Taylor's philosophical work, especially his most exhaustive work *A Secular Age*, is an attempt to move in both these fields. It is an attempt to understand what *secularization* is, and how Western civilization was able to achieve it historically and culturally but it is also an attempt to understand what *religion* is, and why it is, allegedly, a necessary component of our lives.

As I already presented in the introduction, my aim, in this book, is to engage with Charles Taylor on both these issues. While my purpose is, certainly, to present the most important arguments of Taylor's philosophy in the most detailed way possible, my aim is also to use such engagement to add something new to the ongoing debate about religion and secularity, especially concerning a concept that is central to the debate: the concept of "faith." However, before proceeding to the main argument of this work, I wish to introduce the reader to the analyses and thoughts that have inspired this engagement in the first place. The pages that follows present considerations and material I gathered and developed in the first months I was engaging philosophically with Charles Taylor, and are the theoretical inspiration of the argument I will be making in the following chapters of this work. These considerations focus, of course, on the concept of faith and on the history of such a concept within the Western tradition.

There are, mainly, two reasons for giving start to this work with such a step: the first is that, as I already mentioned in the introduction, I am quite dissatisfied with how the contemporary philosophical debate has fossilized the concept of "faith" within the religious framework. I believe that Taylor follows in this path as well, as I will argue in the successive chapters. My aim is, then, to clear the field of this misconception and highlight the complexity inherent to the concept of faith itself, to free its use in a wider meaning than just the *religious* one. This will show how, historically, the narrow interpretation of the term, as something related solely to religion, is a recent development and how, instead, in its premodern contexts faith possessed a "larger" scope of meaning. The second reason lies in the fact that, by introducing now the concept that, later, will develop in the main argument of the book, I will be able to present it as a coherent whole. While the successive chapters will allow me to touch specific features of the concept according to the specific questions in Taylor's philosophy I will be addressing.

For this reason, this chapter should also not be considered merely an attempt to review the literature regarding the linguistic uses of "faith" within the Western tradition, or as an attempt at philosophy of language. My aim, instead, is to point out how the concept, in Western tradition, has not only been given a meaning that cannot be restricted simply to the religious field. I wish also to stress how faith, as an anthropological attitude towards reality, has much to do with how human beings and societies constructs their own *ontology*, than just an indication of a human-divine or human-human relation. As Teresa Morgan has pointed out in her work, *Roman Faith and Christian Faith*, the concept of "faith" was used, in the Greek and Roman traditions,[1] to mean a plurality of realities, which spaced from the economic to the legal ones, in which religion occupied a reduced, and rather secondary, space.[2] According to Morgan, this, in turn, revealed the extreme fragility of the relations of faith, to which Greek and Roman societies reacted with the development of rules, code of laws and ritual actions, in an attempt to reinforce the inherent fragility of an act of *trust* toward another human being. I do agree with this interpretation, however, I also believe that more can be said on faith from a cultural and an anthropological interpretation. Particularly, and this will be an argument I will be constantly defending throughout the scope if this work, I support the idea that a relation of faith is not only a hidden understanding about "how things should go," but also about "how things are" on an ontological ground.

In this sense, Faith is the acknowledgment about a fundamental structure present in the universe, which allows the individual/community to make sense of existing social practices. In this fashion, the relation of faith refers to a sense of "ultimacy," a sense of higher order (not necessarily divine) that is not only the source of legitimization, but also the source of "sense" for things that happen both socially and individually.[3] A relation of faith is not just a relation of trust, or an epistemic position. A relation of faith presents, in this interpretation, four terms: We have the individual subject, the value/good/institution in which he has faith, the social body/companion to which he is related and this final level of ultimacy, a hidden hypostasis that acts as the guarantee for the establishment of all the previous steps. We do not establish relations of faith/belief just because we have a sense of "how things should go" but also because we have a precise idea of how the world in itself is structured. It is because the world is a certain way, because it possesses a specific ontological structure, that the things around us "make sense." The framework, then, as the connection to this given ontology, is not merely a filter that "changes" our perceptions of the world. It actually "constitutes" those experiences of the world. There is always a *Weltanschauung*, a comprehensive worldview, implied in the framework, which allows the framework of faith to make sense. In this sense, every cultural framework relies on a worldview that provides the fundamental ontological hypostasis to ground its own social/ethical claims. We are literally talking about "realms of meaning," in the sense that every relation of faith is attached to a whole sense of

---

1. And, as I will argue in the following pages, transitioning partially also in the Early Christian cultural framework.

2. Morgan, *Roman Faith and Christian Faith*, 38–46.

3. In this sense, social practices, institutions and moral claims "make sense" only insofar as they are grounded on this fundamental ontology, on these fundamental claims about the nature of the things of the world.

how existence in itself (and not just "my existence" or the "existence of the community") works. The change of a framework, therefore, represents quite literally the historical moment in which a world "dies" and a new world is "created" in its stead. Faith, therefore, represents the connection that a society and the individuals that compose it establish with such a "world."

As a last note to be made, before proceeding with the work at hand, I wish to invite the reader to consider this chapter not only an historical review of a concept, but also as the proposal of a thought-experiment derived from such analysis. While the argument I will present is certainly based on scholarly studies solidly grounded on sources, such studies are so few in numbers that they cannot constitute, yet, an established academic truth. Therefore, at the present stage I wish to propose, in the following pages, the possibility of considering "faith" as an attitude related to a *Weltanschauung*, and, for this reason, as a dynamic present in all social contexts: religious and secular alike.

FAITH OR RELIGION?

That the concept of faith did not possess a *religious overtone* is something that has been proposed by other scholars and theologians. One of the most convincing studies developed in this direction has been proposed by Ernst Feil, *Religio*. In this work, Feil investigates the history of the concept of religion, from its Greek/Roman contexts until the Reformation. His main thesis is that *religion*, in the Greek/Roman tradition, indicated something quite different from what we intend today with the term. According to Feil, religion, in the classic context, indicated a sensibility toward the careful observance of certain rules in certain given contexts, Cicero in particular seems to use the word in such a sense.[4] By these lights, *religio* was not necessarily a term referring to a super-human/divine realm, but simply the attitude of observance of certain rules in certain contexts (so that we could have a *religio civilis*, or a *religio iudicius*). According to Feil, this meaning of *religio* remains unchanged until the seventeenth century, when the Reformation gave rise to cultural processes that allowed for a different interpretation of the concept.

In the introduction of the work, Feil confirms that in the Greek language something like *pistis* is not a concept separated from *logos*, from the reason. In this sense, Philosophy and Theology represented a unity in the Greek worldview.[5] In a similar way, the Romans did not possess a "re-

---

4. Feil, *Religio*, 40–45.
5. Ibid., 9–10.

ligious" interpretation of *fides*. It was a fundamental attitude that affected the political/social congregation, more than an act of submission toward the gods.⁶ In this sense, a "correlation" surely existed between "faith" and "religion." The two concepts may have been related in certain situations, but such relations never acquired a character of "similarity," in a way that allowed using the word "faith" in the same sense as "religion." The two terms, therefore, did not indicate the same form of consciousness, but different forms of consciousness which could be related according to specific contexts; contexts that were not necessarily connected to the sphere of the divine. Such correlation and distinction, according to Feil, is preserved also in the Fathers of the Church. In Augustine's *De Vera Religione*,⁷ the terms *religio* and *fides* are used as correlative to describe the Christian *fides*. Such correlation never implies a similarity of the content expressed through the concept. *Fides* was not the same thing as *religio* and could not be used as its synonym.⁸ According to Feil, this distinction operated by Augustine is functional. It develops a connection between the two concepts of *religio* and *cultus* to develop a terminology of *religionis cultis* that could fit the Christian understanding and be opposed to paganism. Augustine, then, attempted to create a correlation between *cultus*, which meant a more significant form of conduct and observance in a context considered important and special in some way, to *religio*, that, instead, possessed a general meaning of observance.⁹ He attempts to develop a concept of *religio* as the true "observance" and good conduct of the Christian individual in a relation with the one true God, in contrast to the pagans, who adored false gods, possessed a "wrong" observance and conduct.¹⁰ The term *fides*, therefore, possessed much more importance than the term *religio*. While *religio* indicated the observance, the practical conduct of the Christian individual and community in observance to theological statements, *fides* indicated the *relation*, the connection that the Christian individual had with God.¹¹ According to Feil, this correlation and distinction between *fides* and *religio* was preserved in medieval theology as well. Feil finds a clear example of this distinction in the work of Albertus

---

6. Ibid., 43–44.
7. Augustine, *De Vera Religione*, in Feil, *Religio*, 68–69.
8. Feil, *Religio*, 68–72.
9. Ibid., 71. Confirmed also by the existence of a verbal form for *cultus*, like the expression *Deus colere*, "to praise God," while *religio* did not possess any verbal form. From this, Feil implies that for the Roman *religio* had a more practical and general meaning.
10. Ibid., 71.
11. Ibid., 69–70.

Magnus, specifically in *Liber de Natura et Origine Animae*,[12] where he traces a definition of religion as *science and cure for the divine ceremonies*.[13] Even in Albertus Magnus, then, Feil traces a meaning of *religio* that does not indicate the totality of theological statements and existential relations of the Christian with God. Instead, like in the Roman context, *religio* indicated the practical and formal observance of the ceremonies and rules of conduct in the context of ritual celebrations. Such concept of *religio*, while surely related to *fides*, was not a synonym and could not be used "in place of" faith. Feil affirms that a similar distinction could be found in Bonaventura's *Centiloquium*,[14] in which the distinction is even more evident. *Fides* was not *religio* and, although related, the two concepts indicated different situations, contexts and forms of relation.[15]

In another essay, "The Problem of Defining and Demarcating 'Religion,'" Feil affirms again that this distinction between *faith* and *religion* is preserved throughout medieval theology. The categories of reality indicated by the two concepts are, according to Feil, clearly distinct. In this way, Feil affirms that a careful study of the Christian tradition should focus not on the concept of *religio*, but on the concept of *fides*. Faith was the central concept that allowed Christianity to develop its own worldview, and it was the concept that most indicated the idea of the divine, as well as the relation that the Christian individual established with it. Therefore, Feil affirms that it was *fides* the central concept around which the Christian tradition was developed.[16] To provide further material to his argument, Feil affirms that the observation that religion identifies itself primarily as faith is of relatively recent development. It is a conceptual creation of modernity. It is a cultural product, a cultural transformation, which occurred only after the Reformation.[17] Feil aims to demonstrate that the concept of religion, as the definition of a human phenomenon, as an anthropological constant, is extremely problematic. While for a Christian understanding of the relation that human establish with God, much more helpful can be the concept of faith.[18]

While Feil dedicates great attention to the historical development of the concept of *religio* and its problematic application and definition, he

12. Albertus Magnus, *De Natura et Origine Animae*, in Feil, *Religio*, 102–4.

13. Feil, *Religio*, 102.

14. Bonaventura, *Centiloquium* 3, in *Opera Omnia*, hg., 4, bes. 217 f., in Feil, *Religio*, 104.

15. Feil, *Religio*, 104–5.

16. Feil, "Problem of Defining and Demarcating 'Religion,'" in Feil, ed., *On the Concept of Religion*, 27.

17. Ibid., 26–28.

18. Ibid., 28.

leaves unanswered the questions that arise from his analysis about the concept of "faith." Friedrich Fürstenberg, in his essay "What Do We Learn from an Analysis of Religion in Terms of the History of the Concept?,"[19] criticizes precisely this aspect of Feil's work. Feil, Fürstenberg argues, attempts to use faith both as the fundamental category for Christian theology and as a theological statement. In this way, the perspectives of the experiential sciences are suppressed.[20] Since it is impossible to mediate the phenomena of faith "empirically," the result is that theological statements become immunized from any evidence that sciences may present. In this sense, one only has to argue that "religions" include ritual modes of conduct, forms of organizations and symbolic forms of expression to be able to show that "religions" generate social forms of expression that are indispensable for the mediation of the substance of faith.[21] In this way, the strong connection between religion and faith is preserved and Feil's argument is, if not countered, at least weakened. Religion can still be considered an anthropological constant. The real problem, then, rests on this lack of description of the "substance of faith." This same argument has been presented by Hubertus Mynarek, who criticizes this lack of definition of the concept of faith in Feil's analysis.[22] To admit that the term *religio* possessed a different meaning in the Roman context, or a more varied sphere of application, does not negate that there is an anthropological constant (the belief, the abandonment to an all-encompassing idea of order) that Western culture has defined as "religion."[23] The presence of this constant is enough, for Mynarek, to question Feil's attempt to separate *fides* from *religio*, whilst giving a predominant value to faith in the Christian context.[24] Mynarek is certainly correct in affirming that Feil's dismissal of religion as an anthropological constant has been too hasty. Feil, however, is also right in affirming that the concept of religion is extremely problematic. Mynarek's criticism is simply not enough to dismiss Feil's analysis.

William T. Cavanaugh, with his work *The Myth of Religious Violence*, has offered another interesting argument against the use of religion as a synonym for faith. In this book, Cavanaugh questions the myth of religious violence, that is, the idea that:

19. Fuerstenberg, "What Do We Learn."
20. Ibid., 52–53.
21. Ibid., 54–55.
22. Mynarek, "Critique of Ernst Feil's Conception."
23. Ibid., 86–88.
24. Ibid., 90–93.

> Religion is a trans-historical and transcultural feature of human life, essentially distinct from "secular" features such as politics and economics, which has a peculiarly dangerous inclination to promote violence. Religion must therefore be tamed by restricting its access to public power. The secular nation/state then appears as natural, corresponding to a universal and timeless truth about the inherent dangers of religion.[25]

He is motivated by the desire to demonstrate how secular institutions can be as violent as religious ones. In addition, he wants to deconstruct how the concept of religious and secular have been constructed in the first place. His analysis on the genesis of the concepts of religious and secular is executed by drawing on a body of scholarly works that identify the invention of the category of religion in a specific configuration of political power in the Western and colonialist tradition. The main assumption is that there is not a transcultural and trans-historical essence of religion. The attempt to separate religious violence from secular violence is, in itself, inherently incoherent. What is religious and what is secular in any given historical context is a function of different configurations of power.[26] The contemporary function of the myth of religious violence is to legitimize the secular liberal nation-state in order to marginalize a religious other that is depicted as prone to fanaticism and intolerance.

In the introduction, Cavanaugh quotes Schmitt and affirms that he may have been right—descriptively, not normatively—in establishing the dichotomy *enemy/friend* as a constitutive foundation for the political body. Secular political forms, to legitimize themselves, needed an enemy and that enemy has become the religious other. For example, in our present context, the Muslim that does not distinguish between politics and religion. Cavanaugh questions precisely the incoherence of believing in the existence of an essence—of Christianity, Islam, Hinduism—that would be naturally inclined to violence, while secular ideologies would be free from this inherent violence. Such separation, he argues, has been an invention of the modern west. Cavanaugh also notices how secular arguments about the intrinsically violent nature of religions meet their own contradictions in the inability to separate consistently and in a convincing way a wrong religious violence from a just secular violence. Secular arguments immunize themselves from empirical evidence by deciding *a priori* their absolute correctness by

---

25. Cavanaugh, *Myth of Religious Violence*, 3.
Other works that have been helpful to understand Cavanaugh's philosophy, although not directly referred to in this work are: Cavanaugh, *Being Consumed* and *Theopolitical Imagination*.

26. Cavanaugh, *Myth of Religious Violence*, 3–4.

focusing on theological descriptions of belief and not on observations of believers' behavior. Cavanaugh concludes that, despite all the attempts, it has not been possible until now to develop a consistent theory of religious violence or an efficient concept of religion as a trans-cultural essence that could be separated easily by other cultural phenomena.[27] The problem to be considered, then, is whether the concept of religion, that originates in Western culture, is a coherent concept and if this concept can be used as an objective analytical tool to distinguish the religious from the secular. Cavanaugh answers this question negatively.[28]

Cavanaugh believes that contemporary scholarly analysis of the concept of religion has adopted two main approaches to try to define it, both of them unconvincing. He describes a substantivist approach and a functionalist approach. The substantivist approach elaborates a definition of religion, and its distinction from other social forms, based on the presence of beliefs about the nature of reality. Belief in God is, usually, the first feature to examine. However, to not exclude phenomena like Buddhism, Confucianism or Daoism, contemporary scholars use the category of transcendence to define world religions.[29] However, according to Cavanaugh, there are two main problems with this approach. First, to distinguish religion by virtue of terms like transcendence, or supranatural, opens a new debate about the correct definition of the new term. If we interpret transcendence too narrowly, then we risk being unable to define relevant social forms. However, a too vague definition makes the distinction *de facto* impossible.[30] Terms like transcendence, then, become a problem in themselves and need further scholarly analysis to define them. Second, even if we were able to come up with a correct interpretation of these terms, and establish a viable distinction, it is not certain that the new category created would provide any meaningful

---

27. Ibid., 42–56. He examines three main form of the argument through which secularity tries to reduce the sphere of influence of religion. First, religion is absolute. Second, religion is divisive. Third, religion is not rational. In all these three forms of the secular argument, Cavanaugh notices the same shortcomings. When they have to explain why these features would be exclusively religious features, secular arguments become inconsistent.

28. Ibid., 101. According to Cavanaugh, the term *religion* should be dropped entirely, and we should, instead, use the term *faith*.

29. Ibid., 102–3. In this sense, we could define Charles Taylor as a substantivist. In the sense that he is able to define as religion those social forms that possess beliefs that are tied to the transcendent.

30. Ibid., 104–5. In the immediate, this creates problems for its *transcultural* application, which does not take into account the specific differences of different traditions; also, the distinction *transcendence/immanence* or *natural/supernatural* is still problematic in the Western tradition as well.

description of the actual phenomenon. Even if we were able to create a substantial concept of religion, we still would know nothing about violence,[31] and the reason why it would be an inherent component of religion.

The functionalist approach, on the other hand, tries to define religion through the purpose it has in the social, psychological and political context. Focusing not on *what* is believed, but on *how* it is believed. Cavanaugh admits that this approach may have a better chance of developing a viable definition of the concept of religion. However, the major weakness of the functionalist approach rests in the broad expansion of the concept of religion. In a way such that there is no more need to elaborate a distinction between social forms, as everything would become religion. In this way, the category of religion becomes unable to tell us something meaningful about violence, or about any historical fact.[32]

On a methodological level, Cavanaugh believes that a functionalist approach, by addressing a wider field of analysis, is a good starting point for any future analytical attempt. However, there is a central problem that, so far, has not been solved consistently by the current analyses and that must be addressed. It has been impossible so far to individuate a trans-historical and trans-cultural essence of religion, which would work as a standard definition of different phenomena like Christianity or Hinduism. Consequently, the category of religion is currently unable to tell us anything meaningful, especially about violence. The substantivist approach is unable to analyze relevant phenomena that can create violence as effectively as religion (like ideology, nationalism, etc.). The functionalist approach, instead, is able to provide us only with tautological statements about the problem. For example, people perpetrate violence on behalf of those things they take seriously enough to do violence.[33]

The presentation of the deficiencies of the contemporary definitions of religion leads to Cavanaugh's description of the historical/cultural processes that caused the development of the concept of religion, as we understand it in secular Western societies. Cavanaugh affirms that the concept of religion in itself is part of a particular configuration of power that has been developed by modern liberal nation-states. In this context, religion is construed

---

31. Ibid., 105. In addition, Cavanaugh affirms, by ignoring the violence caused by ideologies and nationalisms, any attempted analysis in this direction would be irremediably flawed.

32. Ibid., 105–18. Cavanaugh examines, as examples of functionalist approaches, Robert H. Nelson's *Economics as Religion* and Emilio Gentile's *Politics as Religion*. In both texts, the focus is on the religious attitude of the people believing in their (economical/political) interpretation of the world.

33. Ibid., 118.

as trans-historical, transcultural, essentially interior and essentially distinct from the public-secular rationality. As both the substantivist and the functionalist approaches are unable to push the analysis in any meaningful direction, Cavanaugh examines a third distinctive way. He suggests analyzing religion as a historical concept that has been constructed in different times and different places. In this sense, then, current definitions of religion would fail because there is not an essence of religion that could be *known when we see it*.[34] As a historically constructed category, religion is not a neutral descriptor of a reality that is simply out there in the world.

Before Western modernity, it was almost impossible to separate a religious essence from other so-called institutional rival. It is not that the two fields of religion and secularism were simply jumbled together before modernity sorted them out. Cavanaugh explains how the very separation between religion as an essence that is identifiable and separable from other fields of culture and politics would have been nonsensical in the premodern era. He proposes a similar argument regarding the application of this separation in non-Western cultures.[35] To show this flaw, Cavanaugh analyzes the history of the term *religion*. He begins with the original Roman term *religio*, which indicated only a feature of an extremely complex constellation of social obligations in the roman society. This term is then traced through early Christianity, where it remained a minor concept. According to Cavanaugh, Augustine is the only one that writes an essay focused solely on *religio* (*De Vera Religione*), and the main purpose of the text was only to distinguish a fake attitude of *religio* from the true Christian one, not to define the concept itself. When Augustine again addresses the term *religio*, in *De Civitate Dei*, he finds it insufficient to express the complexities involved with the worship of the one true God. He reaches similar conclusions with the terms *cultus* and *pietas*. He will use the term only because of a lack of better words.[36] The term *religio* is even less prevalent in the medieval Christian discourse. Aquinas wrote two works in which he addresses the term *religio*, and only to refer to religious orders, not to define the concept of religion in itself.[37] While in the *Summa Theologiae*[38] he describes *religio* as a downgraded variant of justice, intended as the virtue by which mortals give God what is

---

34. Ibid., 58.

35. Ibid., 60–61.

36. Augustine, *De Vera Religione*, 1–10, in *Augustine: Earlier Writings*, 225–31. Also in Cavanaugh, *Myth of Religious Violence*, 62–64.

37. The works are *Contra Impugnantes Dei Cultum et Religionem* (1257) and *Contra Retrahentes a Religionis Ingressu* (1270). Published in Aquinas, *Apology for the Religious Orders*.

38. Aquinas, *Summa Theologiae*, II–II.80.1.

due to him (reverence and worship). *Religio* is, then, a moral virtue and not a theological concept.[39] *Religio*, therefore, in the premodern tradition, is not a universal genus of which Christianity is only a species. In addition, it is not a system of propositions or beliefs. It is described, instead, as a *habitus*. It is definitely not a purely interior impulse of the human soul nor is it an institutional force separable from other, nonreligious, secular forces. Cavanaugh, therefore, state that "any attempt to compare religion to politics or economics or some other such institutional force in medieval Christianity is unlikely to bear fruit."[40]

It is with the Renaissance that a new concept, with a much wider and different significance, came to operate under the term religion. In this new context, religion started to indicate a *universal genus* of which the particular historical religions are species. Cavanaugh traces the first use of this new understanding of *religio* in Nicola Cusa's *De Pace Fidei*,[41] where the term indicates the interior impulse of humans to worship God (even trough different rites). Together with Cusa, Cavanaugh proposes also Marsilio Ficino's *De Christiana Religione*[42] as an example of this new meaning, where religion is assimilated to something like piety.[43]

In the sixteenth and seventeenth centuries, the concept changes to focus on doctrines instead of practices. Religion indicates a system of doctrines, intellectual propositions that could be either true or false.[44] This shift solidifies during the Reformation, when the term *religio* will be used to indicate a plurality of religions, thus confirming historically the final development of the concept as a universal *genus* of the phenomenon *religio*.[45] However, the Reformation, by itself, developed neither the distinction between secular and religious nor the distinction between a public sphere and a private sphere.[46] Liberal political philosophers, like Locke, offered the firm

---

39. Cavanaugh, *Myth of Religious Violence*, 64–66. It is also an insufficient moral virtue, as it is impossible for a mortal to give to God in equal return.

40. Ibid., 64–68.

41. De Cusa, "Pace Fidei," 219.

42. Ficino, *Christiana Religione*, quoted in Cavanaugh, *Myth of Religious Violence*, 71.

43. Cavanaugh, *Myth of Religious Violence*, 70–72.

44. Ibid., 72–73. Cavanaugh uses Guillaume Postel and Thomas Becon as examples for this new understanding of religion. While Calvinism would be the clearest example in this sense, in which *religio* is a *saving knowledge*.

45. Ibid., 73–74. The peak would have been reached in the 1600, when a German jurist adopted the phrase *cuius region, eius religio*. After this it became possible to see Christianity as one *among many species* of the *genus*.

46. Ibid., 74–78. Cavanaugh presents Lord Herbert of Cherbury as a clear example of this. Although for Herbert religion is a *genus* of which exist various forms, and

division between secular state and religious churches. With political liberalism, the modern version of the spatial division of the world into religious and secular pursuits emerges.[47] When the opposition between religious clergy and secular clergy was transferred to the new concept of religion into the early modern era, it created the religion-secularism binary that we use today. In this way, the shifting of power, the change of configuration for the social authorities was put aside and guaranteed that the authority of the new secular institutions remained unquestioned.[48]

As we can see, then, the concept of *religion* possesses a complex history, so much that its contemporary use as a synonym for *faith*, or the assumption that religion is a phenomenon tied to forms of *faith*, is hardly justifiable; in this case, however, how should we try to untangle this knot? I believe that the answer is to be found in a different definition of faith, described now as an anthropological constant. I propose to use *fides*, and not *religio*, to define the anthropological constant that reproposes itself in different social contexts. Understood in this way as a fundamental connection to a worldview, it becomes an order that structures the world perceived by human communities. As I will show in the next pages, in the Greek/Roman context, faith possessed a broader field of application. It indicated a much more problematic form of consciousness than just a *religious attitude*. In the ancient context, faith already indicated a fundamental human attitude through which any social/political construct was possible. It was a fundamental connection to an interpretation of the world. Faith, then, and not religion is the anthropological constant that we should investigate. To do so, however, Feil's and Cavanaugh's analyzes simply do not exhaust all the possible arguments that can be made about the history of the concept.

PISTIS AND *FIDES*: THE ROMAN AND GREEK CONCEPTS

A historical analysis of the concept of faith in its Greek and Roman contexts is not an easy task to accomplish. The lack of historical documents and the relatively scarce attention that the concept has received in historical and philological studies represents an obstacle to any attempt to analyze the

---

although it is born from the soul of the individual, it retains a strict relation with society and authority and find in them its aims and proper channels of expression. Herbert position advocates for the state to intervene to *reduce* forms of expression of religion to five, harmless, basic forms, so that the state has a duty of *policing* toward religion, but not yet a duty of *restraint* and *confinement* in the private space.

47. Ibid., 80.
48. Ibid., 81–85.

changes the concept has undergone throughout the history of Western civilization. This applies even more for the Greek context of the term. While the Roman *fides* has received analytical attention (especially in legal studies[49]), the Greek *pistis* has received extremely scarce attention. Scholarly works that analyze the contexts of its use and meanings in Greek society are sparse and difficult to consult. It is true that recent years have seen an increase of scholarly studies that have tried to elucidate more the meanings, contexts and cultural relevance of the concept; however, much more work is to be done, as we have just scratched the surface of the complexity of the concept of faith within Roman and Greek societies. While I admit that much more work is needed, so that this study can inspire a wider cycle of scholarly analysis, I am confident in affirming that the amount of material that will be presented in the following pages will be sufficient to at least demonstrate the worthiness of pursuing future studies in this direction. Having made these preparatory statements, it is fair to open our inquiry with the following thesis:

> In the Greek and Roman tradition, the terms that indicated the concept of faith (*pistis* and *fides*) were only marginally related to the spheres of deities and religion, as we understand them today. Much more relevant were the political, existential and legal contexts to which the terms referred.

It seems appropriate to start our analysis with Homeric poems. In the *Iliad* and *Odyssey*, the term *pistis* does not appear in itself. However, we do see the appearance of the adjective *pistos*,[50] especially in the form *pistos etairos*[51] that indicates the trustworthy companion, usually the closest companions of the hero. Alternatively, we see the term appear as a vocative form in oaths.[52] Moreover, *pistos* also appears together with *xenia* in the context of ritualized friendships and hospitality, thus marking its centrality in the aristocratic ethos of ancient Greece.[53] The first appearance of the substantive *pistis*, and thus the first establishment of its etymology as "faith," can be found in Theognis. However, its context of application remains related to its

---

49. Although it could be argued that the fact that the concept is worthy of attention for jurists is already a preliminary proof supporting the argument I wish to develop. In this sense, the following studies on the concept of fides are worthy of notice: Hausmaninger, *Bona fides des Ersitzungsbesitzers*; De Wilde, "Fides Publica in Ancient Rome."

50. Seidl, "Pistis in der griechischen Literatur," 21–32.

51. Il. XV 331, 437; XVII 500, 557, 589; XVIII 235, 460; Od. XV 539.

52. Il. II 124; III 73, 94, 245, 252, 256, 269, 280, 323; IV 157; VII 351; XIX 191; XXII 262; Od. XXIV 483.

53. This is demonstrated by M. Faraguna in his short study on "Pistis and Apistia."

"social" value, which is extremely "aristocratic." Being trustworthy or faithful was the quality that allowed the *aristos* to establish reciprocal relations of hospitality and friendship. *Pistis* was one of the fundamental qualities that made them *agatos*; better than the people of lower classes, who were *apistos*, unworthy of trust and deceitful. Theognis, in fact, laments the loss of *Pistis*, which meant the loss of political importance of the aristocratic classes, making, in his eyes, any meaningful political agreement or ritual of hospitality impossible.[54]

With the change of political order of the Greek *polis* and the establishment of democratic regimes, the concept of *pistis* undergoes some etymological changes as well. As Faraguna tries to show us, the concept of *pistis* is "democratized." It started to indicate the fundamental prerequisite for the overall good functioning of society and prosperity.[55] It becomes the fundamental attitude that makes every social activity possible. Faraguna's study focuses more on the relevance of *pistis* for the economic activities of Greek cities, but, even in this narrow scope of research, we have already been presented with valuable information about the form of consciousness evoked by the term. *Pistis*, in the Greek democratic stage, becomes the "mutual trust" and "confidence" that allows the citizens to undertake agreements in good faith and preserves the social stability of the community. In the Greek classic tradition, faith was not related to a divine realm, but to the social life of the community.

We can find a more exhaustive study on the concept of *pistis* and its linguistic and philosophical value for Greek civilization, in Angelica Taglia's work *Il concetto di Pistis in Platone*. Taglia traces three fundamental meanings in the colloquial use of *pistis*: the first one, as an active action, is the trust toward another individual or a given situation. *Pistis* in this mode means the act of persuasion or the belief about something. The second meaning is *pistis* as a passive quality. It is the set of characteristics that allow other people to "give" their trust. It is the loyalty, honesty or credibility of a person, situation or concept. The third meaning is *pistis* as a passive object. It is the guarantee, or proof of trust or an argumentation on which trust can be built.[56] In addition, in the context of Greek democracies, *Pistis* was strongly related to *peitho*, persuasion, as the fundamental prepolitical quality that allowed any kind of agreement within the social body.[57] In Aeschylus' drama *The Eumenides*, the goddess *Peitho*, through *pistis*, is able to pacify the dei-

54. Ibid., 358.
55. Ibid., 363.
56. Taglia, *Concetto di Pistis in Platone*, viii–x.
57. Ibid., 1–9.

ties of light, represented by Apollo, and the Furies, marking the mythical representation of the human harmony within the *polis*.[58] It is important to notice the relational value and the connection existing between *peitho* and *pistis*. If *pistis*, born from *peitho*, is the benevolent and rational consensus obtained through an act of persuasion, *peitho*, as the act in itself, is only possible and meaningful precisely because the good Greek citizen has a natural tendency to adopt *pistis*. Without *pistis*, any kind of agreement or act of persuasion becomes impossible and we regress to a state of *bia*, a state of sheer violence. *Pistis*, therefore, not only indicated the process through which the democratic system of the polis could work properly, it also preserved its aristocratic prepolitical value. Precisely because the citizen of the polis were capable of *pistis*, the *polis* could keep itself united and could function properly. In an ideal *polis*, *pistis* was the fundamental human feature that allowed any collective action.[59]

Pistis, therefore, was the necessary foundation for any kind of social activity, independently from its moral quality. Even a morally despicable action, insofar as a group of people executes it, requires a fundamental attitude of *pistis* within the group to achieve any kind of success. As Taglia shows us, in Gorgias' *Apology*, even Palamedes, to be able to betray his Greek fellow citizens, needed a degree of *pistis* with the barbarians. Otherwise, his treachery would have been impossible. Precisely because his attempt of treachery

---

58. Ibid., 1–2.

59. Ibid., 14–27. Of course, the Greek sensibility was also aware of the negative aspects of *pistis* and *peitho*. Taglia presents us the case of Gorgias, who described the persuasion as tyrannical, since it allows the imposition of the will of an individual over others. However, the appropriate response was not to relinquish these fundamental qualities, but the move to ensure the correct orientation of them. *Pistis* was considered an unavoidable human feature that had to be correctly trained and nurtured, but never abandoned (ibid., 7–8).

According to Taglia, only Plato tried to operate a radical and dismissive criticism of *pistis*, especially the form born from argumentations that try to rely on human passions. This feature is described as a state through which the citizen abandons himself, relinquishing his own intellectual liberty to be a slave of his own passion and of the stratagems of the demagogue who uses such rhetorical instruments.

In this sense, Plato traces a similarity between *pistis* and *bia*, as a dishonest argumentation that is equivalent to an act of violence (ibid., 9–15). Still, even Plato did not want to relinquish totally the state of *pistis*. Instead, he claimed that a true relation of *pistis* should be founded on rational argumentations born from knowledge and the sharing of that knowledge. Plato, then claimed that a good foundation for the polis was still a state of *pistis*, but an informed one.

However, as Taglia notices in later pages, this allows us to see a great flaw within Platonic thought. If *the rational pistis* is a state possible between single individuals, on a collective level, it becomes much harder to achieve such informed faith. The death of Socrates, paradoxically, exhibits this impossibility to achieve a faith by sheer knowledge advocated by Plato (ibid., 20–22).

made him *apistos*, it would have been impossible for him to obtain any kind of credibility with the barbarians. In the Greek sensibility, then, every social activity had to be founded on some degree of faith between its participants; the lack of this faith marked the impossibility to undertake any form of meaningful relation with other human beings.[60]

Pistis also had a second application in the governmental-diplomatic sphere. *Pistis* represented the bond of trust between two military allies, or between an official of higher rank and the people that followed him. *Pistis*, as the one precursor that allowed friendship and stability, was a fundamental form of relation that guaranteed the proper function of any alliance between different *poleis*, or for any kind of business/army. In Thucydides, Athens was able to obtain the leadership in his alliance with the other Greek cities because it was able to obtain their faith. Later, however, Athens was unable to uphold his side of the relation of *pistis* and had to resort to sheer violence to maintain supremacy.[61] *Pistis* also was fundamental to allow a ruler's government to rule peacefully over the city. A ruler that would prove himself to be *apistos*, unworthy of trust, would have been incapacitated in his own governmental practice and would soon fall down the path of violence. Plato was not, then, the only one that advocated for an attitude of *pistis* exclusively in terms of those who were worthy of it. It was actually a sensibility rooted deeply in the whole of Greek cultural/social life. The tyrant, in fact, was the one that had showed *apistia*, a lack of faith in other people and a lack of trustworthiness from other people. In the impossibility of establishing stable and peaceful social relations, the tyrant had to resort to pure violence to keep his position of power.[62]

The third and last field of application for the concept of *pistis*, and the one I am most interested in, was the sphere of the divine. This form of relation indicated by *pistis* was very different from what we conceive today as faith. *Pistis* was not an irrational posture, enlightened by some sort of transcendental power. In the Greek sensibility, *pistis* was not expressed toward single gods, and was not interpreted as an act of entrusting oneself to those gods. *Pistis* was more similar to a form of knowledge—a form of awareness—than an act of abandonment to the will of the gods. In Plato's *Laws*, *pistis* is not anymore described in political terms, but in relation to the general laws of the *cosmos*. The act of *pistis* is described as the sensible acknowledgment, by the wise man, of the presence of a higher order in the *cosmos*, an order of which the *polis* is just a fraction. This rational acknowledgment would allow

60. Ibid., 16–19.
61. Ibid., 28–30.
62. Ibid., 31–38.

the wise man to guide his fellow citizens into the creation of a harmonious political order that would complement and emulate the higher order of the universe.[63] However, again, this act of faith is not a submission toward a specific god, or to a divinely ordered *cosmos*. It is the acknowledgment of and submission to a fundamental hypostasis that provides the existential background for everything that happens within the *cosmos*, and by consequence, would allow for the submission to the laws of the community.[64] It is a fundamental acknowledgment of the Greek *Weltanschauung*, the Greek worldview, which allows the Greek citizen to make sense and find meaning in the web of social relations and institutions in which he is embedded. The Greek citizen could submit to the laws of his city because he was aware that they represented, locally, a state of being affirmed throughout existence as whole. It was because things *were* in a certain way, that social actions *should have gone* in a certain way and hence, that things *made sense*.[65]

Even in those instances in which *pistis* indicated a connection to the divine sphere, it never indicated a relation between the faithful one and the gods, instead, it indicated a relation that started and ended on the human sphere.[66] Belief in the god was indicated with the term *nomizein*, which possessed a meaning of *common sense*. It was common sense to believe in the gods. It was a custom, more than a commitment expressed in properly ordained institutions. They possessed a formal function as guarantor for oaths and agreements, more than being the source of the loyalty that upheld those agreements.[67] For this reason, Taglia strongly disagrees with an interpretation of *pistis* as religious commitment. It is extremely rare, she affirms, to trace any use of the term *pistis* in religious/mystical contexts. Even in those cases in which the term is used in relation with a god, it never refers

---

63. Ibid., 39–44.

64. Ibid., 41–44.

65. In this sense, we see a clear example in Sophocles' *Antigone*. In the play, Antigone advocates for the burial of his brother because of the "unwritten laws" of the world. While it is true that king Creon had the legal right to order that the body of Polynices be left without burial, Antigone tries to remind him that there is a higher order of things to which the legal order of the polis should always try to refer.

66. Ibid., 67–75. In fact, Taglia rejects any interpretation of *pistis* as a term exclusively related to the *mythos*, the myths. Even in those instances, criticized by Plato, in which the myths were used to inspire *pistis* in the public, we were not in the presence of a religious faith, but something in-between the rational and the irrational. In the Greek context, in fact, the myths were always considered as something partially related to the hidden *logos* of the world. In those cases, the *pistis* was more an attitude of acceptance of the limits of certain knowledge, not a mystical posture of religious kind (ibid., 50–55).

67. Ibid., 66–67. For more information about the Greek culture and the value of the gods in their institutions see also: Yunis, *New Creed*, 19–58; also Fahr, *Problem der Anfaenge des Atheismus*, 5–8.

to the god itself, but with the higher truth about the universe that the god is presenting in that specific moment.[68] *Pistis* was always used to refer to an ontological/epistemological discourse regarding the truth of the universe, than a namely religious revealed truth. *Pistis*, therefore, had the meaning of a sensible or rational assumption that was based on the acknowledgment that the cosmos, as an ordered universe, had to rely on some kind of fundamental hypostasis to preserve the order and the balance. It was the rational acknowledgment of the existence of a fundamental law based on the proof of a perceived harmony in the *cosmos*.[69] It never had the meaning of an irrational belief without any evidence, in the sense the modern context sometimes understands the term today. Instead, it was the fundamental connection through which the Greeks upheld, and related to, their *Weltanschauung*, their worldview. It was a fundamental ontological context in which even the Gods, the political institutions, the quasi-religious rituals of the *polis* could find their sense and meaning.

If we move our examination from the Greek context to the Roman concept of *fides*, we will see that the historical analysis of the idea becomes even more complex. The Roman concept of *fides* presented an enormous variety of fields of application, which span the categories of politics, morality, divine sphere and legal principles. The amount of literature available to us also makes it extremely hard to understand what a common Roman citizen had in mind when using the word *fides*. Was it the same form of consciousness (that applied differently to the different contexts) or in different contexts did it refer to different forms of consciousness? Luigi Lombardi, in his study *Dalla Fides alla Bona Fides*, describes how it is impossible to determine one predominant meaning to ascribe to the constellation of contents referred by the concept of *fides*. A superficial study may interpret *fides* as an ethical concept and believe that, in the different contexts of applications, we may always be in the presence of the same form of consciousness. However, the unity of the word is actually in tension with a multiplicity of meanings that find expression in the different contexts in which the word is used.[70] A possible explanation, for Lombardi, may be found in the cultural tendency

---

68. Ibid., 58–61. As an example, Taglia presents Parmenides' fragment in which *pistis* is used in reference to the goddess *Peitho*. In this case, Taglia states, it is not the goddess that is worthy of *pistis*, as the goddess herself can lie according to the situation. It is not the discourse of the goddess that is *pistos*, worthy of trust. The truth that is expressed in it, as it represents this higher grade of knowledge of reality, is the thing in which we should believe.

69. Ibid., 73–75. In fact, Taglia affirms, *pistis* admitted the *limitation* of knowledge that humans had about the existence of the gods.

70. Lombardi, *Dalla Fides alla Bona Fides*, 1–7.

to use the existing linguistic instruments in the presence of new concepts and apply them analogically. In this sense, the various meaning of "fides" has been developed historically by connecting previous interpretations of the concept to new interpretations of the concepts through the same linguistic group. In this sense, then, different stages of the linguistic expression of a concept would always be historically related between each other through the historical evolution of the concept.[71]

On the specific Roman interpretation of the concept, Lombardi agrees that on a purely logical foundation, we could translate the concept of fides as referring to a sense of *guarantee*. Such a meaning would be morally neutral. However, historically, the forms of consciousness implied by the concept are much more various and applicable to different social contexts. Lombardi, analyzing Plautus' works, traces the uses and recurrences of the term fides in various contexts and is confident in affirming that, within these various contexts, various different meanings related to the same word are at play.[72] *Fides* could indicate the external quality of an individual. That is, his reputation, the trust that the other citizens had placed on a specific individual (in the case of public offices or for business agreements). This meaning of fides indicated the subjective good reputation the individual possessed among his fellows. It also indicated the subjective quality of an active subject in a relation of power; namely, the good faith of an individual.

Related to the first meaning, but on a more objective interpretation, stands the second meaning of *fides*. It could be separated by the appreciation of a third subject and refer to a perceived objective quality of the individual toward which the people had faith. The major distinction resides on the fact that this quality is not connected with a moral intention. It may have referred to the objective external features that would allow a specific subject to be worthy of fides. Thus, for example, the good results in the handling of an office might be worthy of fides. In such instances, *fides* indicates the various levels of social/political reputation an individual had in Roman society, which made him worthy of faith.[73]

Fides also indicated a disposition that was in-between a quality and a virtue. We could conceive it as the *abstract concept of the virtue* obtained from the various particular applications of the different virtues implied in the concept of faith. The specific acts of promise may have presented different moral requirements depending upon the actual position of power/social level between the two subjects undertaking it. For example, a promise or a

---

71. Ibid., 7–10.
72. Ibid., 15–19.
73. Ibid., 23–24.

vow of trust between equal partners (further consecrated by a ritualistic act of promise) required a specifically different moral disposition than in an act of promise between partners of different power of social status. In this second case, the stronger partner promised protection to a weaker partner and thus was in a much more complex relation in which the stronger partner both receives the faith from the weaker one and gives guarantee (faith) for the promises of the weaker partner. In this case, *fides* denotes the abstract concept obtained a-posteriori from the different specific moral requirements of given situations. This meaning of *fides* seems also to be the one found most commonly in international treaties.[74]

However, *fides* also indicated the fundamental, practical virtue that allowed stable social relations within Roman society. Friendships, associations (*socii*), families and the range of different Roman groups were sustained and sustainable because of the fundamental value of *fides*, which allowed the single Roman citizen to navigate through the world with stable points of civil and social reference. In this sense, then, we see a similar scenario to the Greek *pistis*. Even in the case of solemn promises taken in front of the Gods, *fides* indicated always the human dimension of the promise, while the God assumes the role of divine guarantee for the promise.[75] Again, then, we see that faith is a social virtue inherent to the human subject and always referring to him. It is only because the single individual had the capacity to have faith that it was possible to establish meaningful social relations

Fides possessed also a more objective-legal interpretation. It denoted the objective act of promise spoken in legal agreements. More than a quality, or a virtue, in this context fides indicated the single act of promise, or object that was spoken during legal proceedings. *Fides* was also the legal *act of trust*

---

74. An interesting study in this area is the one presented by Salvatore Calderone: *Pistis-Fides*. In this work, Calderone presents a comparison between the Greek *pistis* and the Roman *fides*, inspired by the international agreements between the Aetolian League and the Romans after the Macedonian war.

Calderone presents the case that *fides*, at the time, possessed more archaic features in its meanings. It indicated less a reciprocal relation and more of a one-directional disposition of the stronger toward the weaker. The stronger party, in an aristocratic relation with the weaker one, could dispose freely of the weaker party. Contrarily, the Greek *pistis* presented a bidirectional character. It was, even in the case of groups of different strength, a reciprocal relation in which both parties undertook some kind of duty toward the other.

According to Calderone, this was the reason for a long-lasting and bitter disagreement between the Romans and the Greeks after the war. However, according to Calderone, this slight difference in meaning is also reason to consider a possible enrichment of the semantic field of *fides* integrated by *pistis*, which occurred after Greek culture had been fully assimilated by the Romans.

75. Lombardi, *Dalla Fides alla Bona Fides*, 26–27.

correlative consequence of the previous spoken promise. In this sense, it represents the passive aspect of the legal proceeding. Having received reassurance of the trustworthiness of a party or a situation (by fame, or proven quality, or virtue, or legal certification) the other subject reciprocated by *giving faith*, thus entrusting his own belief and/or wealth to a given person/situation.[76]

A final meaning, that Lombardi does not take in consideration, but that we must remember, is that *Fides* was the actual goddess of the Roman pantheon. She was the goddess of trust and *bona fides* (good faith). However, we also must remember that, much like the Greek *pistis*, we see the divinization of a virtue considered as fundamental for the structure of the society as a whole and not the development of a divine/theological discourse about the Gods.

I believe we can reach, thanks to these preliminary considerations of the philological history on the concept of faith, two main conclusions. First, faith in the Greco-Roman societies did not have a specific meaning, nor a determinate context. It had various meanings according to the given context to which it was applied. However, among these different contexts, it was rare (at least as far as the present literature implies) for faith to have a religious value, in the way that we understand the concept of the *religious* today. Much more relevant was the form of consciousness referring to social, political and existential spheres of life. The concept rarely implied the actual reference to a direct divine providence in human existence or a mystical form of knowledge/relation regarding the divine sphere. Second, the concept of faith, independently from specific given contexts, seemed to imply a relational value in the strong sense. It may be between two different people, between an institution and its members, or about the individual and the world/divine sphere, but faith preserved the meaning of a relation based on a form of awareness and legitimate expectation (the degree and mix of these two aspects changing according to the context).

This opens, at this point, two different interpretative problems that must be addressed at this stage of the thesis.[77] How has it been possible for the concept of faith to change, historically, so much? How has it been possible for it to become, from a concept without given or specific context,

---

76. Ibid., 27–30. The focus of Lombardi's work is to illustrate the legal and civil relevance, in Roman society, of the concept of *bona fides*. However, Lombardi, precisely to better collocate the relevance of his study and better understand the actual meaning of *bona fides*, offers us a most important systematization of the whole concept and of all the possible uses that have been traced so far by philologists.

77. The reason being that it must be demonstrated that further analyses and scholarly works on the subject can be academically productive and socially relevant.

a concept that implies a narrow and specific social reality? How has it been possible for faith to become a *religious concept*? The second interpretative problem addresses the substance of faith. We have seen that the term, in the Greco-Roman context, referred to different forms of consciousness whose balance changed in accordance to the specific context. The focus of my interest is the persistence of these forms. In all instances examined so far, *pistis* and *fides* denoted a meaning of *trust* and *loyalty/promise*. However, these components always seemed to be given substance and legitimacy because of a hidden awareness, a *metaphysical hypostasis* that has been taken for granted, to which its implicit reference allows meaningful *relations of faith*.

I will address this second question now, at least briefly, before resuming our analysis on how faith became a religious concept; then expand the argument in successive chapters. At this stage, Jacob Taubes comes to our aid. In his *The Political Theology of Paul*, Taubes addresses Paul's epistle to the Romans and its relevance for the Christian tradition, both past and present. Taubes presents the argument that the different aspects within the society of the Roman Empire all shared a common hypostasis, a sort of hidden conspiracy.[78] For Taubes, this common hypostasis was carried through the adherence to the *Law*, the *nomos*, as a foundational structure of all the different societies under the rule of Roman authority. It could be constituted specifically to suit the needs and language of a specific group (thus, for Taubes, we had a Hellenistic, Roman or Jewish version) but all shared a foundational character through which the different groups could find a common ground of agreement. For Taubes, this is one of the most important reasons for why Judaism, despite refusing to recognize the divine figure of the emperor, was still considered as *religio licita* and allowed to exist. It shared with the Roman society the foundational acknowledgment of the *nomos* as hypostasis. Thus, it was still possible to integrate it within the social structure of the empire.[79]

In Taubes' presentation of the *nomos* as fundamental hypostasis of the Roman Empire, we are seeing the *ontological character* of the relation of faith I have introduced at the beginning of this work. According to Taubes, we should not interpret the *law* merely as a legal instrument, the acknowledgment of a legal authority. As we have presented in the previous pages, *pistis* and *fides* always implied a sort of awareness that the laws of the city/republic/empire were the representation of a greater order present in the world itself. It was because existence was organized in a certain way, that

78. I am not using the term *conspiracy* in a negative sense, but in the sense of hidden or silent agreement between the parties involved.

79. Taubes, *Political Theology of Paul*, 23–25.

the authority of the city, or of the empire, made sense. It was, then, not just a legal agreement, but also an ontological understanding of the world that Romans and Greeks shared and that Judaism, at least, was not willing to call into question. We are not talking about a specific source of value, but of a more implicit acknowledgment of a whole structure of existence. We cannot simply say, like Taylor would, that the *nomos* was the *source of good* for the Greco-Roman society. Even in those cases in which there was a talk about the ultimate nature of the law as a specific object, such discourses made sense only because they implied an entire ontological structure of existence. It is not the source of good, or value, that constitutes the framework. Rather, the source of value always implies the whole of the framework in its expression. We might say it comes with strings attached.[80] The single sources of good can make sense only because they imply a wider ontological order of the world, of which they are just the specific expression.

EMUNAH, THE JEWISH TRADITION

The *Theological Dictionary of the New Testament* presents the concept of faith in the Greek classic context in a similar way to how I have introduced it in the previous pages. *Pistis* as "trust" and "fidelity" was an existential attitude that found its main expression on a social level.[81] According to the dictionary, it is only in the Hellenistic period that *pistis* acquired an evident religious overtone.[82] However, even by affirming that the religious value of the classic concept of faith represented only a minor application of the concept, or was even totally absent, as I have presented so far, the question remains. How has "faith" become an exclusively religious concept?[83] I believe the answer to this question is provided by a historical analysis of the process of translation and intersection between the Christian tradition, born from the Jewish context, and the Greco-Roman tradition. In this sense, the philological work of Old and New Testament theology can help us. Faith, in the Jewish context, possessed, as in the Greco-Roman context, an ample variety

---

80. I will be able to give more details on this problem later, when I will be analyzing Taylor's philosophy through the anthropology of Ernesto De Martino, and his concept of *culturally conditioned nature*.

81. Friedrich, *Theological Dictionary of the New Testament*, 175–78.

82. Ibid., 78–179.

83. Again, the present study does not claim to be a philological work. We are trying to elaborate the scarce material around the concept of faith to imply that, at some point in the history of Western civilization, there has been a change in the form of consciousness that we refer to when we speak about faith. At the same time, we are also trying to demonstrate that it could be legitimate an *extension* of such a concept.

of meanings and definitions. The *Theological Dictionary of New Testament* describes faith in the Old Testament as being a "reaction" to God's primary action. The Old Testament religion was collective in structure, and it proves difficult to give expression to the inner life of the community. Thus, a wealth of usage begins to appear only when the individual breaks free from the collective bond and, based on his own experience, devotes special attention to the attitude of the man to God.[84] A consideration of faith in the OT cannot overlook the fact that there are two main groups of words to indicate the act of "faith." On the one side is fear (*yirah*), and on the other trust (*aman*). I would like to focus on this second group of words, and on a very specific concept within this group, the concept of *emunah*.[85] *Emunah* denoted the unwavering hold of the word of God against all worldly appearances.[86] It indicates a very specific form of relation, it is an innate conviction, a perception of truth that transcends, rather than evades, reason. The problem is revealed the moment we compare the terms of the word group *aman* to the members of the word group *pisteuo*. Does the attempt to translate the OT concept with the Greek word group give a true picture of the qualitative importance of the concept in the Jewish context? As we have seen, the root of the word group *pisteuo*, in the Greek context, has been conveying an existential/political message, more than a religious one. We have, then, two possibilities in front of us, either we have to consider the translation an arbitrary decision of the translator, who adopted analogically the existing linguistic tools available to him, or we can consider that, at the meeting of two different worldviews, the concept itself underwent a radical change. Teresa Morgan, in her *Roman Faith and Christian Faith*, acknowledges that the term *emunah* may be more complex and denote a greater variety of forms of consciousness than the Greek *pistis*,[87] but acknowledges that the Septuagint still translates consistently *emunah* with *pistis*. It may be, then, that more than focusing on the religious overtone of the term, we should investigate the "mentality," the form of consciousness expressed by the concept and its transformation in its contact with the Greek world. It is on this second possibility that I would like to focus.

84. Ibid., 182–83.

85. Brown, *New International Dictionary of New Testament Theology*, s.v. "faith," 596–99.

86. Because of limitations on time and broadness of the study, I do not claim to exhaust all the problems concerning the Hebrew understanding of *faith*, nor all the questions that would arise in the process of its translation in Greek and Roman language. Again, I wish to focus the attention on the possible change that the concept underwent during this phase of adaptation, hoping to inspire further future studies.

87. Morgan, *Roman Faith and Christian Faith*, 8–12.

The word group *aman*, of which *emunah* is a derivate, is of complex translation and includes a variety of meaning. The *Theological Dictionary of the Old Testament* reports that the general sense of the word group can be related to a meaning of being *secure* and *faithful*. However, it is not possible to trace an original meaning of the terms. It can only be investigated case by case and term by term.[88] The concept of *faith*, even in the language of the OT, possesses a variety of applications in both social and divine contexts.[89] The concept of *emunah*, in particular, is quite complex. It refers to the conduct of the persons, and is used almost an equal number of times to indicate the conduct of God and of man alike.[90] *Emunah*, in the LXX, is translated with *pistis*,[91] and indicates, in the OT, a way of acting which grows out of inner stability. It is not an abstract concept of reliability, but an attitude of *conscientiousness*. Whereas the other terms of the word group *aman* are always used in relation to something or someone on which it is possible to rely, *emunah* emphasize one's own inner attitude and the conduct it produces.[92] Thus, in 1 Chronicles 9:22, we read that David and Samuel appointed the gatekeepers to their offices because of their "conscientiousness." *Emunah* conveys the idea of inner stability, integrity, sobriety, which is essential for any responsible service.[93] In the OT, *emunah* is the inner attitude required for a genuine life (Ps 37:3).[94] In relation to God, the problem becomes even more complex. If God's word is *emeth*, truth, *emunah* seems to be attitude that is born out of the *emeth*, its natural practical effect. Thus, God, in Psalm 89, is constantly reminded of his deity, his conduct cannot be separated from his *emunah*. It is his very nature, which is inseparably connected with faithfulness, reliability and implies steadfast endurance.[95]

88. Botterwick and Ringgren, *Theological Dictionary of the Old Testament*, s.v. "aman," 1:292–93.

89 The verbal form of the concept, *qal*, was used to indicate the man or the woman that *takes care, care for*, usually for the education of the children (ibid., 294; also in Num 11:12; 2 Kgs 10:1; 5; Isa 49:23; Ruth 4:16).

The substantive forms of the word group are various and applied to a great variety of social/political and divine contexts. Like *niphal*, which indicated the quality of reliability of a person, or the firmness of a situation, or the quality of sureness of the word of God (ibid., 295–96; also in Prov 25:13; Isa 8:2; 49:7). Alternatively, *emeth*, which indicates the *truthfulness*, especially in the case of the word of God (ibid., 310–12; also in Josh 2:12; Deut 13:15). In the case of *emeth*, the theological dictionary also reports that the LXX translates the word with the Greek *aletheia*, truth (ibid. 310).

90. Ibid., 317.

91. Ibid., 317.

92. Ibid., 317. Also in 2 Kgs 12:16; 1 Chr 9:26.

93. Ibid., 317.

94. Ibid., 318.

95. Ibid., 319.

However, *emunah* also possesses an implication for the divine/human relation. The *Theological Wordbook of the Old Testament*[96] reports that *emunah* is used to refer to those whose lives God establishes. He expects to see faithfulness in them (Prov 12:22, 2 Chr 19:9). From this, we can see the concept as a duty, as role being entrusted to a believer, which becomes his trust and responsibility.[97] The godly man is instructed by the commandments in the will of God. He knows that he receives wisdom and knowledge from them. The act of *emunah*, therefore, is a *living act of trust in the word of God* and the dimension of human existence in a historical situation. Special stress is laid on a goal that is set in the future. The past was the starting-point but is not the goal of trust. The emphasis falls on overcoming the opposition of the ungodly ones and the realization of the divine purpose in the future.[98]

Again, in the *Theological Dictionary of the New Testament*, we see a comparison between the Jewish *aman/emunah* and the Greek *pistis*, which is the translation deployed in the Septuagint.[99] It is true that both versions share a meaning of trust, reliability and faithfulness. In the Jewish context, the person of God is the source and receiver of this faithfulness. Likewise, it can correspond to the reliability expressed in the Greek *pistis*. However, the Jewish term presents a richer understanding of the phenomenon of faithfulness. If the Greek term could also have a nuance of obedience, in the sense that it was the expected reaction to the *pistis*, the Jewish context understands this obedience born of trust in a more radical sense.[100] In the Old Testament, to have faith in God, to believe in him, is also an act. That action is the acknowledgment that *he is God*. This includes all the consequences that flow from the relation: hope, fear, trust and obedience. However, since the component of trust is radical, it represents also an overcoming of all the

---

96. Harris, *Theological Wordbook of the Old Testament*, s.v. "aman," 1:115–17.

97. Ibid., 116.

98. Brown, *New International Dictionary of New Testament Theology*, s.v. "faith," 598.

99. Friedrich, *Theological Dictionary of the New Testament*, 197–99. Also in the LXX the terms of the word group *aman* are always translated with terms of the word group *pisteuo*; this happens in Jer 25:8; Job 9:16; Exod 14:31; Deut 9:23 and other instances throughout the whole OT.

The philological consensus on the matter, if we hold true the interpretation given in the dictionary, is that this consistent translation from the word group *aman* to the word group *pisteuo* is not an accident. Although used in both divine and nondivine contexts, there was a common understanding of the phenomenon of "faithfulness" between the Jewish and the Greek contexts.

Useful studies that provide precious insights on the concept of faith in the translation of the Septuagint can be found: Dines, *Septuagint*; also Marcos, *Septuagint in Context*.

100. Friedrich, *Theological Dictionary of the New Testament*, 197.

anxieties and self-doubt of the individual.[101] In this sense, the individual who *has faith* enters a totalizing relation with God. This faith in God is not just general trust; it is both grounded in the past, a consequence of god's past actions, and is faithfulness, an expectation toward the future. The trusting man (*pisteuon*) is also the faithful man (*pistos*).[102] He has assurance that God will deliver his promise. In the OT, faith is related essentially to the history of the elected people. The individual is the subject of faith, but the consequences of the action of faith are orientated toward the future of the people and God's past action toward the people.[103] In Hellenistic Judaism, this social aspect of faith is rendered through a new emphasis on the covenant of the people with God. This covenant acquires a greater importance in particular settings. For example, it must be kept in persecution. Faith, as obedience, calls for the upholding of the covenant and of the order that God established for his people. Hence, the law and the commandments become objects of faith, because to believe in God is equivalent to obeying him.[104] In this sense, faith is not just founded on the experienced actions of God in the past, but on the overall order and law that he has established for his people.

If we recall the hypothesis I presented in the previous pages—that the Greek *pistis* did not possess a religious overtone—then we can see a radical difference of meaning between the Jewish *emunah* and the Greek equivalent. Taubes acknowledges this distinction as well, to a certain extent. In the introduction to *The Political Theology of Paul*, Taubes addresses a work from Martin Buber, *Two Types of Faith*.[105] Buber's thesis is that *emunah* is the primary, natural faith, where man finds himself in a relation of faith. The individual is a link in the community whose covenant with the unconditioned God engulfs and determines him. The second kind of faith, which Taubes identify with *pistis*, is the one that brings conversion. It is the belief in something, obedience goes hand in hand with trust.[106] I am of the opinion that Early Christianity brought these two sensibilities into conflict. We have, from one side, a kind of faith that, more than focusing on a divine substance, focuses on the unchangeable and out of time laws of the *cosmos*. Its sight is focused on a perceived harmony of the universe,

---

101. Ibid., 198.

102. Ibid., 198. Naturally, all the qualities are not equally developed in the various instances, but are given different emphasis in different texts. This is evident in Isa 7:4–9, 8:5–15.

103. Ibid., 198.

104. Ibid., 199. Examples can be found in Sir 32:24, 4 Esr 7:24. In the Greek version of Sir 33:3 the Law takes the place of God.

105. Buber, *Zwei Glaubensweisen* and *Two Types of Faith*.

106. Taubes, *Political Theology of Paul*, 6–7.

which is a source of legitimization for the order of the political community. On the other side, we have a faith focused on a divine substance, which does possesses qualities that we could define as *religious*.[107] The absolute, this time, is not the order of the universe in itself, but the divine figure that created and continually sustains that order. Both, however, aim to establish a relation of obedience based on truth, although in different degrees. In addition, both aim to develop a relation that allows the individual/community to make sense of its relation with the world in its own life-experience, from a past, perceived as the ground for the present customs, and toward a future expectation. Allow me to be clear, I am not saying that these two acts of faith involve different forms of consciousness. My point, instead, is that faith is faith independently from the context. What I want to stress is the difference of degrees, of perspectives of these two kinds of faiths. This difference is at play when Paul and the Fathers of the church were translating their works in Latin and Greek. This difference caused a process of adaptation and modification—an evolution, if we want—of the Greek *pistis* and of the Roman *fides*. This allowed the terms to better define the kind of relation that the Christian man established between himself and God, and his presence in the world.

It is at this point that we have to return to Paul. We have seen Taubes' presentation of the law as the fundamental hypostasis of the social structure of the Roman Empire. This is a structure to which, each in its own specific way, the greatest (from a Western perspective) cultural traditions of the time (Roman, Greek and Jewish) seemed to partake, more or less without questioning it. According to Taubes, Paul operates a monstrous inversion of the ancient values. A fundamental questioning of the hypostasis upon which the social stability of the empire rests.[108] The new hypostasis is Jesus, the one that, according to the laws of the old world, had to be condemned and crucified. This victim of the law is the new source of the law. Paul's critique of the law is, then, not just an accusation against the Pharisees, but also an accusation against the entire Mediterranean civilization; a criticism that strikes at the core of the balance on which the whole of the Roman institutions were founded.[109] According to Taubes, we are seeing the declaration of the end of the previous community and of the previous kinship. No more is the blood, or the law, the source of stability of the political community. Now it is the promise, the new law, the Messiah that appeared in the figure of

---

107. Although I do not love this term much, as consequence of all the material presented so far.

108. Ibid., 10–11.

109. Ibid., 24–26.

Jesus Christ.[110] I believe, beyond Taubes, that this was one of the main reasons why the Christian communities could not be integrated in the diverse, tolerant structure of the Roman Empire. The foundational ontology of the Christian faith was very different from the Roman form. For this reason, the Christians were *apistos*, unworthy of trust in the eyes of other communities. The origin of Christianity was, I believe, the ontological end of the ancient world and the establishment of a new one.

RELIGIOUS *FIDES*, THE CHRISTIAN TRADITION

Early Christian theologians had a very specific form of consciousness in mind when they translated the Hebraic *emunah* into the Greek *pistis* and the Roman *fides*. The substitution of the previous Greco-Roman ontological hypostasis with the new, Christian one had caused a restriction of application of the term faith, which stopped to refer to specific social realities. This gave birth to a different understanding of the concept. However, it is not possible to believe that the previous form of consciousness, implied in the Greek and Roman contexts, was simply substituted and swept away. It is possible to believe that the concept of *fides* had undergone changes within the new context of the Christian civilization. However, we cannot believe that the Hebraic *emunah* had simply swept away the Greek and Roman meanings. It is not possible to believe that the relation with the divine had simply erased the relation with the community and the world. In addition, it is not possible to believe that, with the gradual establishment of Christianity as the official religion of the state, the previous forms of consciousness developed by the Greek and Roman cultures to sustain their own communities simply disappeared. Concepts, and the words to express them, undergo processes of evolution, but it is hard to believe that such evolutions involve radical losses. Some categories of meaning certainly fall into disuse, and some applications of the concept/word may be forgotten in the common use of the language, but this does not imply the disappearance of the categories of meaning. It certainly does not imply that the reality to which the concept referred simply disappears.

My analysis of the concept of faith in postimperial and medieval Christianity starts precisely from this assumption. As Olga Weijers has demonstrated, in her short work on the medieval concept of *fides*,[111] the medieval concept of faith was the result of two different processes that affected the related word group. First, there is the enormous expansion of the use

---

110. Ibid., 27–28.
111. Weijers, "Some Notes on Fides."

of *fides* as it was developed within the *Christian faith*. A fact that suggests a parallel extension of the range of uses to which the word is applied in that specific context (its occurrence in combination with verbs, adjectives etc.). This idea, Weijers claims, is easily demonstrated by comparing and studying the various medieval-Latin lexica.[112] Because of the first process, Weijers assumes the existence of a second development. The same universal extension of the authorized use of *fides* as *Christian faith* had caused the gradual decline of other meanings of the word. At a time when *fides* was primarily associated with Christian faith, the word probably grew less apt to designate quite different concepts.[113] If the first process can be easily demonstrated by the study of medieval-Latin lexica, the second process is not as easily proven. For obvious reasons, since the medieval *fides* had acquired the function to indicate the Christian faith, other possible meanings were not indicated in the lexica of the period.[114] However, the absence of empirical material does not exclude, *a priori*, the possibility of the second process. The development of other words related to the same word group, to describe the non-Christian meanings of *fides* (*fidelitas, fiducia, confidentia*), is an empirical demonstration, if only a negative one, of this gradual process of exclusion of non-Christian meanings from the fundamental concept of *fides*.[115]

If we follow Weijers' assumption, *fides* did not become a religious concept per se. It became, instead, a *Christian* concept. More than indicating a religious commitment toward a Divine source, it became a very specific term of Christian theology to indicate the relation that the loyal Christian establishes with God. Like the Jewish *emunah*, which was a concept that could be structured and developed only within the Jewish tradition, *fides*, in medieval theology, was eminently a Christian concept. Still, this does not allow believing simply that the previous understandings of the concept disappeared. In developing the argument in this direction, I find useful material in Piet Fransen's study on the formula *fides et mores*.[116] In this essay, Fransen affirms that *fides*, in early Christian theology, possessed a strong relation with the lived faith of the Church. It was connected strongly with the church

112. Ibid., 77–78.
113. Ibid., 78–79.
114. Ibid., 79–80.
115. Ibid., 79–102. I refer to Weijers work for an actual philological study of the word-group developed around *fides*. As the purpose of this study is not primarily philological *per se*. The attempt of this study is to analyze (and invite further analyses on) the form of consciousness implied within the word *fides*, and its actual possible application outside the context of *religion*.
116. Fransen, "Short History."

as a social group with an actual *lived faith*. An example of this interpretation is traced in Augustine, in the *Epistola* 55,[117] in which Augustine describes the good attitude of the Christian visiting other Christian communities, as an expression of *fides et mores*. Piet Fransen will comment on this epistola:

> There is no doubt about the meaning of mores. The term has nothing to do with so-called "morals," and even less with "natural law or ethical principles" as some people may think. It simply refers to the manifold forms of Christian life, especially sacramental and liturgical, as rooted in the living tradition of the Church. . . . By "faith" Augustine meant the body of doctrines, universally accepted by the Church, that is, the living concrete life of faith of the Christian communities under the guidance of their bishops, their priests and theologians and other competent persons.[118]

By accepting Fransen's interpretation, it is possible to assume that *fides*, in its early Christian contexts, retained both the doctrinarian aspect of the Jewish *emunah*, and the social aspect of the Roman *fides* (and Greek *pistis*). It was not only an adherence of the single believer toward a corpus of doctrines and dogmas. It was a foundational structure of existence, upon which the Christian believer could organize his whole life, both individual and social.[119] Taubes' interpretation of Paul's theological language holds that Paul's criticism against the imperial order was a true trans-valuation of values in which Jesus, the victim of the law, takes the place of the *nomos*. However, it is also true that early Christianity could preserve its own apocalyptic and revolutionary charge only for a determinate period. When the Christian communities started to realize that the coming of Jesus, preached to be an event that was deemed to happen in the near future, was an event for which humanity would have to wait for an indefinite amount of time, Christian communities and theologians had to address the problem of how to achieve a stable social structure to allow for the pacific existence of the church *in the world*. Thus, Jesus, from an apocalyptic source of value, became the source of the new *nomos* of the world.

According to Stagaman, medieval theology preserved a similar interpretation of the concept of *fides*. In the Middle Ages, *fides* occupied a middle

---

117. Augustine, *Epistolae*, in Fransen, "Short History."

118. Ibid., 293–94.

119. Stagaman, in his analysis of Fransen's work ("Piet Fransen's Research") has affirmed a similar analysis: In other words, *fides et mores* denoted the living fidelity of Christians in their lives to the *depositum fidei* handed down from Christ and his apostles. In no sense did the terms allude to any kind of juridical succession. And this living fidelity was linked to the Church's indefectibility" (ibid., 72)

position between *scientia* and *opinio*, much like the Platonic understanding of *pistis*. It possessed the certitude of the first term, while retaining the lack of evidence of the second.[120] The important thing to consider, however, is that such *fides* did not indicate just the act of faith, but also the content of the act. Christian life and its concomitant practices were experienced in a concrete manner.

> They embraced the entire existence of the baptized. Thus, medievals saw their faith and customs (or articles of faith and sacraments) present in a Christian Commonwealth, which was structured and ruled by "the Lords spiritual and temporal." Heresy arose when some individual or a group obstinately refused to conform to the social and hierarchical order established in God's wisdom and mercy. This commonwealth, however, was not perfect. It was infected by sinfulness and remained in continuous need of reform. Hence, medieval men and women felt free to criticize this commonwealth, including its ecclesiastical dimension. A special target of their criticism was the clergy and monks.[121]

Faith, even in the Christian, medieval, context, was not just the trust, or the commitment, toward the divine figure of God and the authority of the Church. Faith presupposed, again, a cosmic order, an ontological structure of the world that was wholly implied whenever a particular event or structure was addressed. It was possible to have faith in the church because it represented a higher order that structured the universe itself. I do not believe it is possible to justify such structural analogy simply with the acknowledgement of the divine providence. Of course, for the Christian world to be stable and be able to function properly, the existence of God was a necessity that was not possible to question. However, for medieval theology, the question was not whether God *existed*. For the medieval church God *is* existence, existence was not just a quality that God possessed, but He was existence in its highest order. The figure of God, then, was the ontological hypostasis through which the whole of the cosmic ontology could be sustained and structured. It was a consequence of God's being that everything else was fit to partake in the order He created.

Modernity represented a decisive transformation for the interpretation of the concept of faith in the Christian context. As Charles Taylor also affirms in *A Secular Age*, with modernity we saw the disappearance of the interpretation of human beings as embedded in a social structure and

---

120. Ibid., 70–73.
121. Ibid., 73–74. See also Fransen, 302–4.

cosmos,[122] from which they are both defined and protected. This gave rise to a new interpretation of the human being as an *individual*, although still embedded in a social framework, the framework itself does not define him in a strong sense. In turn, this had to shift the attention on the act of faith not as an ontological act, or a social one, but as a form of relation in which we focus, this time, on the individual and the things in which he believes. This led to the transformation of our interpretation of the concept, which started to denote more and more the *belief* in things, than the ontological act implied in previous interpretations; thus giving rise to the development of faith as a similitude to *religion*.

An example of this shift can be found, in my opinion, in Luther, who, in his commentary to the letter to the Galatians,[123] redefines the concept of faith by separating it from any social/intellectual or existential relation. Faith becomes a *passive righteousness*,[124] belonging to the true Christian life, a righteousness that is independent from works, laws and ceremonies. Luther advocates a righteousness gifted from Christ and the Holy Spirit, abandoning all other active forms of righteousness.[125] The Christian faithful possesses faith in God not because of a cosmic order external to himself, nor as a matter for the intellect or by the observance of ceremonies. Faith becomes personal trust in the sin-forgiving grace of God. It is the product of the impression that the Divine word makes on the individual heart and conscience from their creation, not of reason. It is no longer to be understood as something that can be attained through the proper framework and through reason and acknowledgment. Now it is a mystical product of the grace of God.

After the Council of Trent, and during the enlightenment, we see a strong redefinition of the concept of faith in the Catholic tradition as well. Both Fransen and Stagaman examine Francisco Suarez as an example of this process of change. In Suarez, *fides* has become a state of the single individual, a supernatural way of discovering the truth about things, which was enlightened exclusively by God's revelation. *Fides* was set in opposition to all forms of natural knowledge, where truth was attained through the *light of reason*.[126] After the Enlightenment, Roman Catholic theologians insisted that believers could not experience the gracious presence of God in their innermost being unless they had received an infused mystical grace. As a

---

122. Taylor, *Secular Age*, 26–26
123. Luther, *Commentary on the Galatians*.
124. Ibid., 18.
125. Ibid., 18–19.
126. Ibid., 74.

result, theologians drew a sharp distinction between pure nature and the supernatural, and the latter became the action of God upon human beings without their experiencing that action. Thus, a spiritual, mystical tradition in theology, which had insisted that divine grace was and could be experienced by the recipient, was excluded from theological reflection. As a result, theologians began discussing a *fides implicita*, a faith possessed by the simple faithful, which drew its sustenance from the authority of the magisterium.[127]

This radical precipitation of the conflict between faith and reason was the result of the controversies between church and secular authorities which persisted from the low Middle Ages (for example, the investiture controversies, the rediscovery of Roman laws in the Renaissance etc.). After the Council of Trent, however, the criticism of religion by the philosophers of Enlightenment, combined with the development of the modern nation-state, led to a polarization between the vocabulary of the church and the vocabulary of the state. Thus, the transformation of the concept of *fides*, which Fransen outlines as

> We may describe it [the meaning of fides] as a shift from a more comprehensive, more complex and more concrete meaning towards a more specific, more technical and precise, even towards a more national and therefore abstract meaning.[128]

The Encyclical written by Pope John Paul II, *Fides et Ratio*, further demonstrates this change of the understanding of the term of faith.[129] Here, the Pope describes reason as a special activity of mind focused on the knowledge of immanent human things. While faith is described as the obedient response to God, the free act of submission that is born out of the acknowledgment of its divinity, guided by the Church. In *Fides et Ratio* we see the total flattening of the concept of faith. Faith as a mystical and obedient relation with God—typical of the Jewish *emunah*—and the social/existential meanings—typical of the Greco-Roman understandings—have been totally forgotten. Faith has become a technical theological term that can be used as a substitute of *religion*, both in technical and in common discourses.

There is, now, only one final problem to address in this short historical analysis. In Fransen's and Stagaman's analysis faith transitions from a term describing a form of consciousness to a technical term, more linked to authority than an actual state of mind. In the light of this transition, we encounter a viable explanation as to why the concept became an exclusively

---

127. Ibid., 74–76.
128. Fransen, "Short History," 309.
129. John Paul II, encyclical letter *Fides et Ratio*.

religious concept. However, can we assume that the modification of the concept also determined the disappearance of the form of consciousness previously indicated through the concept of faith? Has the phenomenon of faith disappeared, or, at least, confined to the realm of the individual, to his private beliefs?

A committed secularist would answer positively to this question. Taylor as well, seeing how he has structured his thought in a dichotomy between religion and secularity, as I will introduce starting from the next chapter, implies that the forms of consciousness involved in one field are different from the other. After all, religion is the realm of transcendence, while secularity is the realm of the immanent. The relation we establish between these two different existential forms *has* to be different. However, after the material I have presented so far, I disagree with this assumption. The change of the definition does not necessarily imply that the relation of faith has simply disappeared from nonreligious contexts. This is, precisely, the fundamental point that motivates my proposal to extend again the field of application of the concept of faith.

The question, then, becomes, what kind of form of consciousness was denoted with the concept of faith? I believe that the multiplicity of interpretations of the concepts of *pistis* and *fides* in the Greek and Roman contexts was motivated by the fact that the actual act of *fides* was the result of the interaction between many different forms of consciousness (hope, trust, promise, etc.). The adaptability of the concept and its different meanings were functional to the different balances of these forms registered in different situations. An act of *fides* in a legal situation required a different attitude and balance than an act of hospitality, or a promise between friends. However, all these different acts were tied to the fundamental relation that the individual/community established with their worldview, with their *Weltanschauung*. All these acts, despite the different particular contexts, were still *pistis/fides* because they possessed a fundamental common point. They were all expressions of a fundamental relation with reality that allowed them to *make sense*. The legal promise, the relation of hospitality, the promise between friends were all guaranteed by the fundamental ontological hypostasis, by their Greekness or Romanness, or via Taubes' *nomos*. They were all guaranteed by the fundamental worldview that allowed the individual/communities to make sense of those acts in the different contexts. I believe it is possible to identify three major aspects of this relation of faith. I believe these three characteristics have survived in the Christian concept of faith and are an indication of the specific attitudes that take place whenever we enter in a relation of faith.

As a first feature, we have the component of trust.[130] The technical definition of trust is the *assured reliance* of one character, ability, strength, or truth of someone or something. The act of trust, to be consistent, has to rely on a sense of consistency possessed by the person (or institution/situation) in which we place our trust. We do not trust someone or something because of a future expectation, but because of the actions/events that have already happened. These allow us to build the sense of consistency and coherence we need to enter into a relation of trust. I believe Taylor's concepts of *social imaginary* and *framework* should be understood in this sense. As in Hegel's *Sittlichkeit*, the framework is something we are born into, it is a system in which we trust because it is imbued with a sense of coherence and consistency provided by its past. It is because things have been done in a certain way in the past that we feel compelled to keep the system going on as it has always been. It is because we engage, since the moment we are born, with related sets of values and institutions that we can perceive their history and draw on that past, which is part of our *story*, to build our sense of trust in them.

A second feature is found in the reciprocal act of promise, of commitment, of loyalty.[131] A promise is a declaration that one will do or refrain from doing something specific. It is also the reason to expect something in the future. This is especially ground for expectation of success, improvement, or excellence. Unlike trust, the focus of the promise is not in the past, but in the future. The act of promise finds its own meaningfulness and coherence in an event that has yet to happen but upon which we have some degree of assurance and expectation.

The third component, however, is what ties the past and the future together. This is what allows a community/individual to have a sense of consistency and reliance on its story. This third component is a degree of existence that guarantees both the reliance on the past and the expectation toward the future. This third component is the sense of awareness of an order in things, whether divine or immanent, a sense of the whole world. I have defined is, so far, as *Weltanschauung*. It is a consistent worldview, an implicit (or explicit) ontology of the world, which allows a community to make sense of the things of the world. It is what guarantees social practices and perceptions of the world, a sense of reality. This worldview is an implicit acknowledgment that the sources of values we trust and commit make sense only because they represent some kind of order. Even those instances in

---

130. Which I believe Taylor has grasped well, as I will introduce in the following chapters.

131. This is a concept that is central in H. R. Niebuhr's analyses on the concept of faith; which I will introduce in the fourth chapter.

which this order of the world, the *Weltanschauung*, is implicit, is unrevealed in a society, are not a reason to doubt its existence. As I have proposed so far, I am strongly convinced that the relation of faith refers always to a metaphysical hypostasis, a sense of implicit order in which the things that have value find their own position and structure. A relation of faith, while focusing on a specific object, always implies the wider ontological context.

In the examples I have presented, *fides* and *pistis* presented a multiplicity of applications and meanings because they were not indicating a specific balance between the different forms of consciousness, but the various possible interactions between these three fundamental features.[132] With the advent of Christianity, the concept of faith was not understood anymore as a concept with a multiplicity of applications. Yet, the presence of the features presented above was not relinquished. The Christian individual retained a sense of trust in the institutions around him (the church, the king, etc.) because of his social/cultural framework. Of course, such frameworks were connected to the eschatological promise of the final salvation on a universal sense and, on a particular level, he was enveloped in various relations of *fidelitas* and *confidentia* that guaranteed the respect of the promises in his social context. All these relations made sense because they were connected and structured through the divine order of the universe, which was emulated, on an immanent level, by the divine authority of kings, popes and the nobility.[133] Faith, before modernity, did not represent a dogmatic stance, the acceptance and belief in some fundamental dogmas (mostly religious in kind), or the belief in a given set of doctrines. It represented the way in which the single Christian interacted with the world and society around him and their subsequent results within him. It is true that for the Romans and the Greeks this relation had many different contexts of application, while Christianity reduced its context of application to the divine structure of the world. However, this does not change, nor subtract the relational value retained by the concept of faith. Nor does it influence the analysis of

---

132. In fact, every act of trust also implies a *sense of promise* (of keeping faith to the consistency showed so far); also every promise has to concede some kind of trust (if not in the individual/institution directly, to the tradition that *guarantees* the promise—for example, the contract between parties guaranteed by a legal tradition). Both of these acts have to rely on a sense of *awareness* of the tradition, values, structures that *legitimize* the act of trust/promise.

133. In this sense, then, Giorgio Agamben's *The Kingdom and the Glory* is extremely important. There he presents his analysis on how early Christian theology developed an extremely complex theological structure to articulate the existing relations between the divine sphere and the secular sphere, God's government of the universe and the effects of this government of the human sphere. His affirmation is that part of this theological structure has been retained by modern political and economic theory.

the phenomena I have presented. I wish to close this chapter, then with a final question: when we are in the presence of a form of consciousness that helps a society establish a relation with the *world*, can we use a vocabulary of faith to define and describe it?

While it is true that the concept of faith, after modernity, underwent a further restriction of its meaning and sphere of application, this does not translate directly into the disappearance of the forms of relation that the concept of *fides* previously sought to signify. The change of meanings and languages can obscure certain processes and events, but that does not imply directly the disappearance of those events and processes. Building on this assumption, I propose a new expansion of the sphere of application of the concept of faith. The question that motivates this new expansion is: in modern ideologies/values/social structures, is it possible to find those forms of consciousness that were signified by the premodern interpretation of faith?

I will return on this topic at the end of the book; when, after having addressed Taylor's philosophy, I will have presented all the relevant concepts necessary to structure the argument through which I wish to answer this questions. I will provide examples to show that the concept of faith, as the connection to a fundamental ontological hypostasis, a *Weltanschauung*, is still present in modern contexts. Moreover, I believe that we do not possess, in our current language, a vocabulary descriptive enough to give a sense of the depth of the ongoing social processes in this relation of faith. Thus we the need to expand again the field of application of the concept of faith.

2

Secularity and Religion
The *Status Quaestionis*

HAVING INTRODUCED THE THEORETICAL background that inspired the development of this book, I will move now to discuss Taylor's philosophical work. In this chapter, I propose an analysis of Charles Taylor's interpretation of secularization theory and a successive comparison with Hans Blumenberg's and Carl Schmitt's work. The main purpose is not only to offer an introductory analysis of what I believe are the main features of Taylor's work, but also to offer some insights into what I believe is the *status quaestionis* about the secularization debate as a whole. Before proceeding with the analysis, I wish to answer a question. What kind of book is *A Secular Age*? Charles Taylor affirms that, with his book, he wants to tell us a *story*. The story of the process of secularization of Western civilization. To do this we should look at *A Secular Age* as a group of different essays presenting the same argument from different points of view, so that each one provides consistency to the others.[1] *A Secular Age* is, therefore, the attempt to develop a grand narrative of Western secularism. In developing this narrative, Taylor's argument encompass the fields of history, sociology and anthropology. A critical analysis of such a work, then, has to obey to a specific criterion to be consistent. Benedetto Croce, in his work *La Storia come Pensiero e Azione*, indicates the road I will follow with this book, by describing how we should judge a book of history.

> The judgment on a book of history can be, therefore, only expressed on its "historicity," in the same way a book of poems can

1. Taylor, *Secular Age*, 1–5.

be judged only on its poetry. Historicity can be defined as the act of comprehension and understanding induced by a need of the practical life. This need cannot be satisfied, by becoming action, unless we do not resolve first all the phantoms and doubts and shadows that stands against it, through the statement and resolution of a problem—that is—an act of thought. . . . This knowledge of "the actual situation," as it is called, refers to the process of reality as it has happened until now and, for this reason, is "historical" in itself.[2]

History, therefore, represents a connection to an actual problem of our society, and represents our attempt to increase our understanding of our present society through its connection with its past civility. Through this understanding, the chance to increase our own present civility is attained. I will analyze *A Secular Age* as book of history following this understanding. Benedetto Croce used to say that to engage seriously a philosophical/historical work is to develop a proper critique of this; therefore, I will execute my critical analysis through Croce's interpretative framework. Is *A Secular Age* a book able to present, analyze and resolve the process of secularization in our Western society? The argument I develop to answer this question will show that Taylor leaves some fundamental questions without answers. His discourse, despite attempting to remove the separation between secularity and religion ends up reinforcing their substantial difference, in the hope of a future overcoming of such difference.

This substantial difference and separation forces me to address, albeit briefly, the current debate about the process of secularization and the phenomena of secularity and religion. I believe that we can divide, even though in a rough way, the existing debate about secularization into two main categories of classification. We have, from one side, those who reject the theory of secularization and claim that modernity is a spontaneous and exceptional achievement of modern man, which has no *cultural debt* toward the previous era. The best example of this interpretation would be Hans Blumenberg. On the other side, we have those who, instead, claim secularization is a process guided by a mechanism that modernity has inherited from previous cultural forms. In this sense, secularization can be interpreted as the gradual disappearance of religion from the public space, but leaves behind a series of mechanisms of which modern institutions have taken possession. The best example of this side of the controversy would be Carl Schmitt.

Of course, I am well aware that, in between these two positions, there are various intermediate positions that could not be easily classified

---

2. Croce, *Storia come Pensiero e Azione*, 8.

according to this rigid schematization.[3] The purpose of this chapter, however, is not to offer categories of classifications for secularization theory, but, instead, to try to collocate Taylor's own theory within this complex framework of narratives and theories. The schematization between Blumenberg and Schmitt is only functional to this outcome. Moving in this direction, Taylor's work is trying to develop a "conciliatory" position in the field of secularization theories as well, not just in the debate between religion and secularity. Starting from the assumption that all theories of secularization so far have been merely negative theories (including Blumenberg's), Taylor attempts to develop a narrative that takes into account both elements of historical debt and positive spontaneous development of modern ideas. The resulting narrative is, indeed, extremely compelling. However, a further, in-depth study of Taylor's work reveals how even his conciliatory approach ends up taking a decisive and distinct side in the controversy on secularization, thus failing in its attempt at being a mediation.

TAYLOR'S NARRATIVE: THE FLAWS OF SECULARITY

Taylor's attempt is focused on reconstructing how we have reached our so-called secular age. However, a first problem that he addresses is the complexity of the concept of secularity in itself, of which he identifies three main meaning. The first meaning denotes the process through which the public spaces are emptied of God (or any reference to an ultimate reality). The second denotes the gradual falling of religious belief and practices[4]. The third, at last, is a description through which we denote a point in our civilization (Western and North Atlantic at least), in which, not only is God no longer present in public institutions and governmental organizations, but belief (or unbelief) in itself is considered one option among many others equally

---

3. Other alternative interpretations of the secularization theory, which I have found valuable for insights. In addition, a general understanding of the whole debate can be found in the following works: Casanova, *Public Religions in the Modern World*; Toulmin, *Cosmopolis*; Dupré, *Passage to Modernity*; Gregory, *Unintended Reformation*.

However, the reason for which these alternative interpretations have not been my main references for this chapter has to be found in the peculiar argument that Taylor tries to develop. As I will show in this chapter, Taylor's own position tries to mediate between a strong interpretation of the process of secularization, as a process purely determined by its Christian past, and an historical interpretation of modernity as an independent and extraordinary phenomenon. Features of both these interpretations are present in Taylor's own narrative and it is according to these features that I will analyze Taylor's work.

4. Although, as I presented in the introduction, scholarly literature about this subject is gradually questioning this interpretation.

acceptable and dignified. Taylor wishes to focus his attention on this third meaning of secularity.[5] In his analysis, he notes that any study has to take into account the change of the social framework happened with modernity.[6] With the term *framework*, he denotes the whole of our knowledge and assumptions about the world and human life, and their relation with the background in which we operate.

According to Taylor, we have moved from a framework in which the place of fullness was understood as unproblematically outside of, or beyond, human life, to a conflicted age in which this construal is challenged by others which place it (in a wide range of different ways) *within* human life. This has been the reason for many recent cultural/political struggles, against an earlier time when people fought to the death over different readings of the Christian construal.[7]

Charles Taylor believes this was possible because of the development of an exclusive humanism, which put an end to the naïve religious faith that existed before the Reformation. The conditions that allowed a naïve religious faith were determined by three principal social structures. The first was the acknowledgment, on a social level, of the presence of God and the reality of his intervention in the cosmic order, as well as in the natural events, both ordinary and extraordinary. The second was the acknowledgment of the presence of God in the social order, as the last ground upon which both the political authority and the spiritual-religious associations (parishes, guilds, etc. . .) found their legitimacy. The third was the perception of the spiritual and moral forces that directly intervened in the matters of humans as real. Taylor uses the category of *Enchanted World* to define this historical stage.[8]

In *A Secular Age*, Taylor argues that the development of our secular society was caused by the fundamental crisis of these three grand structures of premodern society; a crisis generated by the self-contradictions present within this Christian, enchanted, framework. However, he does not wish to propose just another subtraction story about secularity.[9] Instead, he argues that there must be both active and passive processes that have determined the structures of modernity.[10] If it is true that something had been lost, at the same time, he argues, something must have been gained. The positive

5. Taylor, *Secular Age*, 3–4.
6. Ibid., 13.
7. Ibid., 15.
8. Ibid., 25, Taylor here uses an expression that he himself finds partially incorrect, but is used as an antinomy in reference to Max Weber's theory of disenchantment.
9. Ibid., 26.
10. Ibid., 27–30.

development in Taylor's narrative is found in the emergence of a new humanism. A way of life that could inspire the Western civilization in finding the core of its newly established moral compass, its own *sense of fullness*, elsewhere than God. Taylor's narrative starts by analyzing the gradual but steady loss of influence of the Catholic Church between the twelfth and the fifteenth centuries. This loss of influence was determined by the spreading, among the population, of strong urges for religious renewal. In this steady process of weakening of ecclesiastical authority, Taylor identifies various processes that accelerated its crisis.[11] The first was the development of a new kind of social sensibility, which resulted in the development of a new concept of the single individual, leading to claims about the possibility to live religion more as a personal relation, without the excessive interference of the all-pervasive authority of the church.[12] The second was the weakening of the authority of the church even in its holy activity throughout the world. People began to distrust increasingly the holy magic of the church (like the relics of the saints), as this practice started to be interpreted as a form of idolatry.[13] Following these two forms of distrust towards the church, emerged a strong urge for a new kind of religious sensibility. This created good terrain for the spreading of Luther's doctrine of *salvation through faith* as an incredible strike against the authority of the church.[14] Of course, there had to be other factors. The weakening of the authority of the church is paired with the development of a new concept of the self and the beginning of a process of disenchantment that contributed to create the modern *buffered self*.[15]

11. Ibid., 45–90.

12. Ibid., 61–69. According to Taylor, those claims were caused by a diffused dissatisfaction with the hierarchical equilibrium between lay life and renunciative vocations. This hierarchical balance (or imbalance) determined that the common people had to be *carried* to heaven by the perfected ones without any possibility of personal religious gratification, or the possibility to operate outside the strict codes of priesthood.

13. Ibid., 69–73. Taylor states that in various groups, both of elites and popular pietism, there was a growing unease against the mystical causal power and properties of the artifacts. This unease began to involve any kind of artifacts, even the supposed good ones, because they were perceived as a substitution of true piety that should have been, first, an imitation of the virtues of the saints, not a worship of their relics.

14 Ibid., 73–75.

15. The concept of the *buffered self* will be properly discussed in the third chapter of this study. As an introductory note, I can say that with this concept Taylor intends to depict the process through which the world, both spiritual and physical, stopped to be perceived as a constant threat to the security of the individual human being. At the same time, the individual human being started to feel empowered in his own sense of the self, so that he could be in the world without having to fear its—once mysterious—web of spiritual and physical causalities.

Taylor identifies the Reformation as the historical crossroads at which all these crises and developments converged with each other. Rushing the claims for a new religious order and a new interpretation of the role of the church in history. The Reformation is the foundation of Taylor's narrative, as only the Reformation made it possible to abolish the concept of the enchanted cosmos and create a humanist alternative to faith.[16] How could this alternative arise? Taylor's narrative presents the case that the change in religious sensibility shifted the common interest of the believers from a dimension of faith that was fully transcendental to one that focused more and more on an independent *Nature*, an independent world that was no more under the direct influence of transcendental substances.[17] This new interest in nature was not, therefore, a step outside a religious outlook. It was, instead, a great shift within the outlook itself. However, instead of maintaining its effect just within the religious framework, this shift generated unintended consequences, that led to the new perception of nature as the centre of a new, nonreligious, humanism.[18] A change that was intended as an adjustment of the already existing framework generated, instead, a new, different framework altogether. Another important cause for this change is, in Taylor's narrative, the development of a concept of civility as a further evolution of the concept of civilization, developed during the Renaissance.[19] This generated a change in the common understanding of European societies during the sixteenth and the eighteenth centuries, giving new impulses to the arts and the sciences. This new concept of civility worked together with the new religious sensibility to create a new kind of society, more disciplined and focused on state power.[20] These changes led to the social process

16. Ibid., 77.
17. Ibid., 94.
18. Ibid., 95.
19. Ibid., 100–103.

20. Ibid., 104–12. Taylor believes that the notions of civility and reform, although related to different fields, influenced each other during the history of Western civilization. Religious reform was inhabited by a demand, felt with increasing power during the late Middle Ages and the early modern period, that not just an élite, but as far as possible all the faithful ones live up to the demands of the gospel.

It took a quantum leap with the reformations of the sixteenth century, to the point where, on the Protestant side, there was an in-principle denial of any hierarchy of vocations. Everyone was called on to live his or her faith to the full. In addition, this meant that the lives and practices of ordinary people could not just be left as they were. They had to be exhorted, commanded, and sometimes forced and bullied into giving up, e.g., the veneration of saints, the adoration of the sacrament, dancing around the maypole, and so on. There was a drive here to make certain norms universal, conceived in part as a demand of charity towards fellow human beings, but given an edge or urgency by the thought that God will punish our community for the blasphemy of its wayward

of secularization and detachment of God from worldly secular authorities. With this cultural development, we reach the end of the process of *Great Disembedding* described by Taylor. The order of Middle Age, composed by ambivalent complementarities (worldly order and churches, proper order and carnivals) is replaced by a full-pervasive order, uncompromising, coherent, all of one piece.[21]

Complementarily to this new kind of order, another important transformation took place, this time an evolution of the concept of the *self*. The process of disembedding was greatly influenced by this evolution of the concept of the self. From the medieval sense of the self, which was strictly related to its social role, we have reached a new concept of the self that led human beings to think about themselves as individuals.[22] This revolution disembeds us from the cosmic sacred; altogether, and not just partially and for certain people as in earlier post-Axial moves. It disembeds us from the social sacred; and posits a new relation to God, as designer. This new relation will in fact turn out to be dispensable, because the design underlying the moral order can be seen as directed to ordinary human flourishing. The transcendent feature of the Axial revolution is partly rolled back, and can be given a neat separation of this-worldly from other-worldly good.[23]

Taylor has addressed the development of this new concept of the self, in detail, in another work, *Sources of the Self: The Making of Modern Identity*. In this work, Taylor focuses on how the modern concept of identity has reached its actual form and what is its social function in Western civilization. In *Sources of the Self*, Taylor introduces key concepts that will be central for the development of *A Secular Age*. He affirms that the concept of self is strictly intertwined with the concept of morality.[24] Our identity is strictly connected with the social background that surrounds us, our framework. It involves the problems of our *strong evaluations*, namely, the fact that we engage in moral dilemmas in order to define our own identities. For Taylor, morality has two facets. An instinctive one, which is tied to our spontaneous

---

members. The claim of Taylor is that some of this did and had to rub off on the lay goal of imposing some of the demands of civility on the general population.

21. Ibid., 146.
22. Ibid., 150–57.
23. Ibid., 157.
24. Taylor, *Sources of The Self*, 3. In this text, Taylor tries to understand how Western modern civilization achieved its peculiar concept of the *self* and its (allegedly) unique features. He analyzes three great fundamental sources as the foundation of modern self-conscience: the first is the modern inwardness (sense of ourselves as beings with inner depths), the second is the affirmation of ordinary life, and the third is the expressivist notion of nature as an inner moral source.

feelings of right and wrong, and a second facet tied to a given *ontology of the human*. An important strand of modern consciousness has tried to diminish the ties that morality has with this second facet. Mainly because of the risks, which history presented to us, involved in discussing the characteristics of this ontology of the human.[25] Taylor aims to criticize the naturalistic and secular assumption that it is possible to create a set of moral values based only on universal assumptions. For Taylor, instead, it is impossible to create morality without a social framework.[26] In addition, our strong evaluations are deeply connected with a moral source, or constitutive good. That is, a center of value which receives the greatest importance in our framework and is considered as the ultimate source of our moral reasoning.

However, this feature of Taylor's narrative reveals some weaknesses. The first one resides in how Taylor structures the concept of strong evaluations. While I do believe that this concept is extremely important both for anthropological and ethical studies, at the same time, Taylor's assumption that strong evaluations need necessarily a moral source seems unconvincing. Instead, we can describe strong evaluations as directly existing in the world as it is experienced by humans in their relations, as embedded in the *Weltanschauung*, in the worldview. They are integral to human life, to being a person. As Ruth Abbey has explained, Charles Taylor is attempting to open up a nonanthropocentric perspective on the good, to allow us to see the *sovereignty of good* over the moral agent. In this sense, *Sources of the Self* is explicitly a retrieval of this nonanthropocentric perspective that, as he believes, philosophy since the Enlightenment has been motivated to occlude.[27] However, Taylor, to achieve this outcome, has to create a strong connection between the source of moral good and the individual identity connected to it.

Arto Laitinen offers a good critique of this problematic feature of Taylor's moral theory. He has correctly identified that Taylor's strong evaluations are too intertwined with a given concept of identity, in its modern interpretation. The process of moral reasoning, in Taylor, develops in four steps, as follows. First, the evaluative convictions of an individual directly determines what his practical identity or practical orientation is. Second, the strong evaluation of an individual guides the way in which some features are identified. Third, the actual features one identifies may play a role in the selection and specification of the orientation of an individual. Fourth, the individual judges motivations and successes in the life of an individual

---

25. Ibid., 6–7.
26. Ibid., 28–32.
27. Abbey, *Charles Taylor*, 85–86.

in the light of his strong evaluations.[28] The problem is that, as Laitinen argues, a concept of identity is constituted through various processes, not just through the field of morality. Self-evaluation, intersubjective relations, reflection on the evaluations as such play a part in the process of establishing our own identity.[29] While it is true that the problem of attaining the good life is part of the concept of identity, it is also true that an identity is formed by the personal engagement of the single individual and his evaluations to choose major values. Therefore, the concept of strong evaluation must indicate both direct and indirect moral concept, both reflective moral choices and the instinctive moral background that generates them,[30] not just a single, reflected, value that *precipitates* the framework on a society. Taylor's human agency has to be intended as both physical (following the natural law) and transcendental. However, in developing his argument in this direction, we obtain the result that *strong evaluations* determine, to a certain extent, the human interaction with the world and the other humans, both in an external and an internal way.[31] By not specifying what is meant with identity and linking it with strong evaluations, it is possible to generate misunderstandings and be exposed to methodological criticism.

In Taylor, the goods that constitute our cultural structures exist through linguistic articulations. The rather different understandings, which we see in different cultures, are the correlative of the different languages evolved in those cultures.[32] Modern philosophy has articulated, for Taylor, new kinds of languages that are unlinked with a single major good, thus generating a process of weakening of any kind of moral code.[33] However, Taylor points out, secularism has been unable to lead people towards a better society, to give them a sense of *fullness*. This happened despite secularism being, according to Taylor, an exceptional historical event. He roots the reasons for this failure in secularism's own nature. By focusing on the ideas of authenticity and self-development, we are given a sense of invulnerability; we do

---

28. Laitinen, *Strong Evaluations without Moral Sources*, 26.

29. Ibid., 20–26.

30. Ibid., 36–43. In this sense, Laitinen aims to both defend Taylor's concept of strong evaluations from possible critiques from the constructivist and subjectivist schools; while at the same time apply some "corrections" to its field of applications.

Laitinen introduces the concept of *ontological evaluative features*, that is, the claims and reflections that constitute our identity are not tied to one single moral source; the moral source itself comes embedded in a whole set of much broader considerations (ibid., 267).

31. Ibid., 76–85.

32. Taylor, *Sources of the Self*, 91.

33. Ibid., 95–98.

SECULARITY AND RELIGION 67

not perceive the world as full of dangers. At the same time, however, such experience of the self can also be lived as a limit, even a prison, making us blind or insensitive to whatever lies beyond the ordered human world and its instrumental-rational projects. According to Taylor, the absence of the transcendent in our framework is perceived also with a sense of *loss*. We can sense that we are missing something, that we are cut off from something important, and that we are living behind a screen.[34] The strength of secularism, its immanent framework, its focus on a nature unconnected to any transcendental source, but understood purely in human terms, is also its weakness. Modern human beings, therefore, would feel cross-pressured between multiple choices, both religious and materialistic in various degrees, none of which, however, is perceived as entirely satisfactory. What this new world has done is not to endorse a new materialistic concept of the world and of the life. Instead, this openness created a field of struggle where any kind of vision of the world, from the most religious to the most materialistic (going through any kind of intermediate position that lies between them) is used to try to find an ultimate sense within this social chaos. However, Taylor believes this struggle is doomed to fail. No kind of scientific theory or theological vision has been able, so far, to give human beings a concrete grasp of the world around them and at the same time a sense to their own lives.[35] In this way, Taylor implies that the so-called polemic between science and religion is, in reality, a nonissue. The real problem does not lie in science as materialism or religions as mysticism. This preconception has masked a struggle that was in reality purely ethical: which method can help us to attain a sense of fullness and find a meaning to the world? The inability to see where the real problems lie has stopped Western civilization from seeking a solution and has led to the supremacy of a strictly immanent vision of the world and the relegation of religions to a niche of society.

Today, Taylor affirms, we live in an *immanent framework*; that is, a social imaginary in which our perception of the world, of the cosmos and of the society is independent from a divine source.[36] Does this mean that the way to the transcendent has been completely closed? Taylor does not think so, as we are not utterly confined to factors that fit within our framework,

---

34. Taylor, *Secular Age*, 301–2. However, what about people that are perfectly comfortable in their secular (or nonreligious) position? Taylor does present this moral crisis as an inevitable outcome that is inherent to the secular modern self. However, this might not be case. The fact that moral crisis, in a secular framework, is not a *necessity*, is proof, in my opinion, that Taylor's analysis is unable to grasp some core features of sociality that are relevant for both secularity and religion alike.

35. Ibid., 594–98.

36. Ibid., 539.

sometimes suppressed elements of the past seem to resurface, thus Taylor wishes to question the definition of modern intended as secular.[37] Is, then, the immanent framework an act of closure against belief? That does not seem to be the case. The immanent framework is, for Taylor, bound to both openness and closeness. Both an immanent and a transcendental reading of the world involve a kind of leap of faith.[38] In the sense that we adopt an anticipatory confidence in our stance toward the world even before experiences or events of life. Even though immanentism is against any kind of theistic faith in a strict sense, such immanentism retains a kind of attitude that makes faith possible. The secularism present in Western civilization has only hidden the fact that there is a struggle taking place around the presence of faith in society.[39] As Taylor says

> The salient feature of Western societies is not so much a decline of religious faith and practice, though there has been lots of that, more in some societies than in others, but rather a mutual fragilization of different religious positions, as well as of the outlooks both of belief and unbelief. The whole culture experiences cross pressures, between the draw of the narratives of closed immanence on one side, and the sense of their inadequacy on the other, strengthened by encounter with existing milieu of religious practice, or just by some intimations of the transcendent. The cross pressures are experienced more acutely by some people and in some milieu than others, but over the whole culture, we can see them reflected in a number of middle positions, which have drawn from both sides.[40]

The struggle is not primarily between belief and unbelief; rather, the real struggle is about the best road to a sense of fullness.[41] Taylor is not trying to save the religious attitude intended as theological attitude towards reality, that is, a dogmatic position that relies on a set of institutions. What Taylor wants to focus on is the act of a spiritual search as a way to fullness that secularism could not suppress and that can still contribute to human flourishing in a great way. What Taylor seeks is, therefore, a recomposition between the religious aspiration to the transcendent and the legitimate request of respect and dignity of our human body that advanced during the modern, secular age. What kind of answer does Taylor find to solve this

37. Ibid., 546.
38. Ibid., 550.
39. Ibid., 551–53.
40. Ibid., 595.
41. Ibid., 600–601.

problem? He points out that we should interpret experience of the divine in a different way.[42] The divine should no longer be experienced as a distinct moment that is separate from observed phenomena and the observer. Instead, we should perceive the three of them as a whole that, by opening to a deeper reality, brings a life-changing fullness to our own life.[43] This means that, to have a positive attitude of faith today, we must work to change the paradigms that are the base of the secularist interpretation of human life. This can lead some religious thinkers to assume that we should reestablish a past Christian order of the society, but that is not Taylor's argument: he is firmly against theocracy.[44] Instead, he claims that a lot is lost when we transform the message of the gospel in a set of rules enforced by organizations erected for this purpose.[45] What Taylor has in mind is faith as a relation able to break the categorization of groups and the bureaucratization of human life. He seeks a form of relation that is connected with what he calls an *agape-network*. That is, a connection towards the transcendent that is reflected in morality by a personal relation between individuals that goes beyond the trivial separations of groups, religions, nations.[46]

> Modern ethics illustrates this fetishism of rules and norms. Not just law, but ethics is seen in terms of rules (Kant). The spirit of the law is important, where it is, because it too expresses some general principle. . . . In this perspective, something crucial in the Samaritan story gets lost. A world ordered by this system of rules, disciplines, organizations can only see contingency as an obstacle, even an enemy and a threat. The ideal is to master it, to extend the web of control so that contingency is reduced to a minimum. By contrast, contingency is an essential feature of the story as an answer to the question that prompted it. Who is my neighbour? The one you happen across, stumble across, who is wounded there in the road. Sheer accident also has a hand in shaping the proportionate, the appropriate response. It is telling us something, answering our deepest questions: this is your neighbour. But to hear this, we have to escape from the monomaniacal perspective in which contingency can only be an adversary requiring control.[47]

42. Ibid., 729–30.
43. Ibid., 730.
44. Ibid, 733–37.
45. Ibid., 737.
46. Ibid., 739.
47. Ibid., 742.

For this reason, Taylor affirms that today, to overcome the secularity/religion divide, to achieve a *synthesis* between the two, we need a new understanding of faith. An open faith that is not identified with a specific strict code. Because any kind of code, religious or secular, will "root in us as an answer to some of our deepest metaphysical needs, that for meaning, for instance, or that for a sense of our own goodness. The code can rapidly become the crutch for our sense of moral superiority."[48] This sense of moral superiority is what creates division, and what Taylor condemns.

> But where the firm identification with a present or past order is consolidated, faith can all too easily become defined in terms of certain codes and loyalties (or these codes and loyalties are boosted by their consecration in religion), and those who fall outside these tend to appear more easily as renegades than fellow Christians from whom one may have something to learn.[49]

More than a return to a past Christianity, Taylor wishes for a rediscovery of what Christianity, during its historical development, has lost and sidelined in the many different traditions that were crushed during the historical struggles of religions, ideologies and groups. This can lead us to retain the original meaning of the Church, as "a place in which human beings, in all their difference and disparate itineraries, come together."[50]

TAYLOR'S SECULARITY: HISTORICAL AND SOCIAL ISSUES

I believe Charles Taylor's analysis is extremely beautiful, and probably one of the best genealogical analyses of the origins of modernity and secularity. Yet, despite seeming convincing at a first reading, a careful study does reveal some critical issues, defective gears in a seemingly working machine. One of its most problematic features would be the seemingly inherent moral superiority of modernity in comparison to the previous era. Quentin Skinner already noticed this problem, in his *Modernity and Disenchantment*.[51]

---

48. Ibid., 743.
49. Ibid., 766.
50. Ibid., 772.
51. Skinner, "Modernity and Disenchantment."
   Skinner also criticizes partially Taylor's historical reconstruction. He claims that Taylor, in describing the modern era, gave too much importance to things that, nowadays, are no more considered of primary importance, such as: autonomy, labor and production, family and marriage. In this sense, he claims, Taylor's historical account can be interpreted as inconsistent (ibid., 37–42).

Skinner disagrees with Taylor's interpretation, as he believes that such interpretation considers history only as an epistemic gain, according to which the modern age created, inevitably, higher standards of morality in respect to previous eras. History, instead, is a complex combination of different events and, in addition to moral gains, it also leads to inevitable losses. For Skinner the most important of these losses, in the transition to modernity, are the roles of the figures of the *Citizen* and of the *Monk*. These two figures are the representation of a concept of active citizenship and transcendentalism that are in no way morally inferior in respect to modern standards. There have been, however, historical processes, driven by a mix of different causes[52] that determined the weakening of these specific social roles, or values, as foundational structures of society. Modernity then, even if we want to describe it as an "evolution" is still the result of a process that left its fair share of victims alongside the road.

In a similar way, Paul D. Janz, in his "Transcendence, 'Spin,' and the Jamesian Open Space,"[53] has seen the methodological limits present in Taylor's narrative. The peculiarity of Taylor's method is the ambiguity with which he deals with different philosophical positions. This does not mean that there are no clearly inferable preferences or alignments visible, but that it is hard to ascertain, in Taylor's conciliatory discourse, the lineaments of a well-defined philosophical position, or stances to which he openly commits to by constructive argumentation in support of these orientations. This ambiguity will reach its most definitive and pivotal expression in what Taylor calls the *Jamesian open space*, which is a position of quintessential ambivalence.[54] We have also seen how Taylor describes the dichotomy *transcendence/immanence* with a general sense of human flourishing more than with a specific theological sense of commitment to a reality beyond ours. This stance, however, represents a problem in itself. Taylor's definition of transcendence works merely according to its linguistically or conceptually analytical negative definition as that which is beyond the *immanent*.[55] This

---

52. Ibid., 44. For Skinner the three major causes of this development are:
   1. A social development that elbowed aside the concept of active citizenship in favour of the view of citizen as consumers of government.
   2. A political development that saw the early European states, in the modern era, to develop in such a way that the political power was concentrated in fewer and fewer hands.
   3. This evolution was greatly influenced by ruling groups, but this also means that things could have gone otherwise than the actual historical development.
53. Janz, "Transcendence, 'Spin.'"
54. Taylor, *Secular Age*, 548–56.
55. Janz, "Transcendence, 'Spin,'" 48–49.

makes transcendence not an independent ontological source, but merely the product of logical thinking, and an entirely abstract and negative one at that.[56] This brings Taylor's narrative to a result that is paradoxical, if compared with its aims. Even though, in *A Secular Age*, Taylor criticizes subtraction theories and coming of age theories about modernity, in the end he develops himself a sort of subtraction theory. It is an inverted form of subtraction, a sense of loss, which implicitly but inevitably underlies the whole development of *A Secular Age*. Developing his narrative in this direction, the subtraction becomes not a liberation from what is illusory of the previous culture. It is instead a sense of loss of something vital and fundamental, indispensable to human beings to help them understanding themselves. This only increases the sense of ambivalence in Taylor's work, ambivalence that is extreme in the concept of the *Jamesian open space*. The immanent framework, that is, the secular self-understanding, is perceived as a place of cross-pressures where two different poles conflict. Those who see immanence negating any concept of the beyond (an attitude of closure) and those who see the immanent frame as still open to a beyond. Each of these two positions constitutes what Taylor calls a possible spin in the immanent frame.[57]

Another critical feature would be the intended synthesis that has to be achieved between modernity and spirituality. Taylor is giving preference to the Christian theistic perspective, thus developing, again, a structure of inherent moral superiority to push forward his own narrative. Taylor has not been able to explain with enough consistency and historical consideration why modernity should be considered morally superior to other ideas that got lost in our historical development, and he is not explaining why a return to a Christian theistic perspective, a modified Christian understanding of transcendence, should be a solution to Modernity's problems.

Another problem in Taylor's narrative is given by the description of secularity. As presented by Casanova, in analyzing Taylor's narrative we face a fundamental question. Who are the "we" Taylor is talking about? Taylor makes clear, right at the beginning of *A Secular Age*, that he is speaking about the people "who live in the West, or perhaps Northwest, or otherwise put, the North Atlantic world."[58] Such an opening raises an important

---

56. Ibid., 49.

57. Taylor, *Secular Age*, 549–53. Also in Janz, "Transcendence, 'Spin,'" 55–59.

58. Casanova, "Secular Age," 270. In this analysis, José Casanova aims to question the *application* of the category of *Secularism* used by Charles Taylor. The main question is *who are the secular ones? Whom are the ones living in an immanent frame?* Taylor speaks simply of people of the Western civilization, while Casanova does not think that this could be a viable answer.

question for Casanova. How is one to account sociologically for the radical bifurcation in the religious situation today between the radical secularity of European societies and the still predominant condition of religious belief among the people of United States?[59]

What is at stake with this question is the very credibility of Taylor's reconstruction of the development that brought belief from naivety in the 1500s to an engaged affirmation in our contemporary society, and the category of secularization he uses to explain such affirmation.[60] Taylor uses the concept of secularism as a general category or definition, whose features are identified, mainly in Western/modern terms. However, with the global age we are indeed seeing a provincializing of Europe (primarily) and Western society as a whole (more generally), so that secularity, as characterized by Taylor, reveals itself fully only in a very specific, local, context. The phenomenon of secularism, as is described by Taylor, could be more a specific phenomenon of a specific culture than a general phenomenon that is possible to apply to all kinds of human societies, independently from the context.[61] This puts into question the validity of Taylor's definition of secularism and the social features he identifies with it.[62] Taylor's description of the third

---

59. Ibid., 271.

60. Ibid., 272. Taylor, in Part 4 of *A Secular Age*, tries to counter possible critics by describing the whole process through which the narratives of secularity were able to develop and assume their current form, but Casanova cannot help in find some faults in the overall structure of his phenomenology. As examples, Casanova indicates the following problems:

1. United States did not know a *paleo-Durkheimian* state, so that they did not have to overcome an ecclesiastical institution.
2. The very foundation of U.S. coincides with the age of mobilization, so that religious and political movement are cofoundational for the structure of the Christian secular republic itself.
3. What Taylor calls *the age of authenticity* started, in the United States, way before than the 1960 in the sphere of religion, the age of authenticity may be said to have been already present and operative during the Second Great Awakening.

61. Casanova, "Secular Age," 274. In this sense, Casanova implies, there would be a European secularism, an Indian one, a Chinese one, etc., each one with specific characteristics and conflicts.

62. Another issue that is directly linked to such rigid definition of secularism, and that will be described in detail in the second chapter of this work, is caused by Taylor's use of the Durkheimian dichotomy of sacred and profane as a classificatory scheme of all reality. It reproposes Taylor's strong distinction of an almost-perennial conflict between immanence and transcendence.

In doing so, however, it creates a categorical schematization of reality that is unable to address properly those phenomena in which immanent and transcendent intertwine with each other; such relation creates thresholds of indifference between immanence and transcendence that do not fit Taylor's rigid understanding of secularism. In the

meaning of secularity constricts our vision in such a way so that spiritual mediocrity becomes our dominant existential possibility. Taylor does not use the term spiritual mediocrity. He speaks, rather, of a declining sense of fullness. Taylor takes his notion of fullness, which is practical-existential in orientation, as cutting across belief (that is primarily Christian theistic) and naturalism construed as unbelief. However, there are versions of theism and naturalism that deny the God-nature distinction that Taylor assumes, albeit in different ways, to different degrees, and from opposing ends of the duality.[63]

The problem of Taylor's dichotomy comes from the fact that he sets up his argument in reference to *believers* and *unbelievers*. Believers denote all subjects of orthodox and traditional religion but, preeminently, to Christians. Within the category of unbelievers, he distinguishes between inclusive humanists, exclusive humanists, and neo-Nietzschean antihumanists. The bulk of Taylor's argument is directed against exclusive humanism of which much of *A Secular Age* is a long Nietzschean genealogy.[64] Taylor focuses on the extreme positions that, he argues, define the middling alternatives. By doing so, however, he fails to acknowledge intermundane, this-worldly, and naturalistic forms of transcendence.[65] This dichotomy affects the whole of Taylor's argument in important ways, weakening both his historicist reconstruction and his moral/political project. Peter Woodford, in his "Specters of the Nineteenth Century,"[66] certifies precisely this limit of Taylor's historicist account.

As Woodford writes, In *A Secular Age*, Taylor performs a historical retrieval in order to obtain some critical distance from the dominant picture

---

following pages, however, I will show how this rigid understanding affects the credibility of Taylor's historical narrative regarding secularity.

63. A very good example of this problem can be found in Hart, "Naturalizing Christian Ethics." Hart uses pantheism and pragmatic naturalism as examples for these borderline forms of belief/unbelief that do not fit well with the immanent/transcendent dichotomy (ibid., 151–52).

64. Hart, "Naturalizing Christian Ethics," 152–54. By debunking this kind of humanism, he shows how it disenchants and flattens human life, draining any element of the sublime and the tragic, while coloring everything grey.

In contrast, in Hart's interpretation, the only thing Taylor says about inclusive humanism is its vague openness to transcendence; meanwhile, neo-Nietzschean antihumanism accents the tragic, heroic, and sublime dimension of human existence that it accuses Christianity and humanism of extirpating. Oddly enough, Taylor seems to acknowledge that neo-Nietzschean antihumanism has a conception of transcendence. However, it is clearly an inferior kind insofar as it does not have a *superhuman* referent (something that is nature transcendent) of the Christian or Platonic kind.

65. Ibid., 154.

66. Woodford, "Specters of the Nineteenth Century."

of the immanent framework.[67] However, the same use that Taylor makes of human historicity to criticize presentist biases throughout his work and gain a critical foothold against the immanent frame also undermines his own normative and constructive goals. He is caught in an *aporia* between acknowledging the shifting historical backgrounds that radically condition human spiritual life and a largely implicit philosophical anthropology used to evaluate specific frameworks within which the demand for spiritual satisfaction can be met.[68] The problem of historicism, is the recognition that all concepts, ideas, norms, and ideals are subject to change and that no human self-understanding can claim universal validity or to be essential for human life or knowledge. Without the *a priori* certainties of rationalists or necessary transcendental conditions of reason, the empirical study of history seems both to confirm relativistic historicism and to threaten a corrosive cultural relativism, scepticism, and antirealism which would threaten to undermine objectivity not only in ethics, but in the *Wissenschaften* themselves, both *Geistes-* and *Naturwissenschaften*.[69] Similarly, Taylor's phenomenological notion of lived experience already precludes the possibility of justifying the validity of a *Weltanschauung*. Other older historicists accounts, like Troeltsch or Croce, continued to hold to a metaphysical notion of the *absolute* that guaranteed the validity of each historical solution[70] of the religious problematic of the enigma of life. However, Taylor lacks a convincing ground on which he can justify his own historical interpretation. The feeling is that the process in itself is also self-justificatory and pushes itself from within through the dialectic of *immanent/transcendence* or *sacred/profane*.

In *A Secular Age*, Taylor argues that the change was constituted not just by new beliefs that have been adopted or by sets of institutions that have been rearranged. What has changed has been the individual lived experience, especially with respect to the way religious beliefs and practices infuse and compose such an experience.[71] There is not a simple exchange of beliefs with better or more convenient ones. What has changed is the social imaginary, thus changing the structure of the historical world and of the living experience of people. Of course, I agree with Woodford, Taylor wishes to debunk the authority of dominant self-understandings by uncovering their specific historical conditions. His historicist geneal-

67. Ibid., 173–74.
68. Ibid., 174.
69. Ibid., 175–76.
70. For Troeltsche it was the pantheistic metaphysic that saw the religious problematic as a stage of the *enigma of life*. For Croce it was the *dialectic of the spirit* that was, primarily, a history of civility and freedom against slavery and barbarism.
71. Woodford, "Specters of the Nineteenth Century," 179.

ogy exposes that the current self-understanding is contingent, inessential, and revisable—merely one possibility among others. In doing so, however, Taylor implicitly undermines the justificatory part of his own work. The reason for this as presented by Woodford, is based on the assumption that, if self-understandings are constitutive of what human beings are, then there is little room to answer the question of which self-definition is correct. It appears that Taylor has committed himself to a kind of historicism that leaves him little with which to build a philosophical case for the superiority or appropriateness of an open interpretation of our secularity; open, that is, to theism, transcendence, and other extra-immanent conceptions.[72] Woodford also notices how Taylor's dichotomy of immanence/transcendence, by interpreting all historical developments as a road to fullness that wrestle between these two extreme, cuts out events and traditions that cannot be easily inscribed within such dichotomy[73]. The main flaw of the historicist character of Taylor's philosophy can be summed up as follows: "how can anyone's view of the good, or of human fulfillment, arising in the course of history be more adequate to humanity and its fulfillment than another?"[74]

Precisely this question is what shows us the missing pieces in Taylor's historical narrative. Because of the dichotomy of *immanence/transcendence*, Taylor's narrative is unable to provide a solid ground on which to build his proposal. Moreover, he is unable to demonstrate consistently that the secular framework is actually intrinsically defective as he claims.[75] This becomes even more evident if we compare Taylor's narrative to other historical narratives about the causes and features of modernity.

AGAINST "SECULARIZATION": TAYLOR AND BLUMENBERG

As argued so far through the support of existing literature on Charles Taylor's philosophical work, my argument is that his historical/sociological analysis possesses problematic features that undermine the validity of his narrative as a whole, or, at least, severely restrict its effective field of

---

72. Ibid., 180–84.

73. Ibid., 184–87. For example: it is unclear on what side Spinoza's pantheism, Hegel's absolute *Geist*, or the process/neoclassical metaphysics of Whitehead and Hartshorne would fall in the dichotomy between transcendence and immanence.

74. Ibid., 187.

75. It is one thing to claim that some people may feel uncomfortable or cross-pressured in a determinate framework, another thing to claim that such framework leads inevitably to this conclusion.

application. I am of the opinion that the dichotomy *transcendent/immanent* is the main reason for the weakness of his narrative. It is the central issue that undermines his narrative and is the least convincing to properly explain the historical processes that brought Western civilization to its modern, secular, stage. As I presented at the beginning of this chapter, however, I believe it is possible, at least on general terms, to identify two main poles, or general tendencies, around which every attempt to explain secularity has been built. The first pole is constituted by the attempts to establish modernity, and its secular features, as an extraordinary achievement; as a historical development brought about by human creativity that possesses no cultural debt toward the previous era. While the problems that modernity had to face may have been historical, the sources for the solution to such problems were spontaneous and brought from within the modern age. An example of such a narrative is Hans Blumenberg, with his *The Legitimacy of Modern Age*.[76] The second pole is constituted by the so-called secularization theory. This theoretical alternative develops an historical narrative in which modernity is the product of processes that are historical and traces their roots in the previous eras. Not only, then, the problems are historical, but the solutions as well are obtained through sources that are inherited from previous ages and that modernity has adapted (or refined further) into its peculiar historical/sociological forms. An example of such a narrative would be the work of authors such as Max Weber or Carl Schmitt.[77]

If we were to classify Taylor's work according to this general schematization, at a first sight he seems to look for some kind of mediation between these two major tendencies, some kind of conciliatory, middle position. While admitting that modernity is an extraordinary achievement,[78] he also claims that such an achievement could not be developed purely out of

---

76. Blumenberg, *Legitimacy of the Modern Age*. While this work from Blumenberg and the epistolary exchange he had with Schmitt have been my main sources for writing this chapter, I believe that any study on Hans Blumenberg should also include his *Work on Myth*.

For an introduction and secondary literature on Hans Blumberg, I suggest, instead, the following works: Nicholls, *Myth and the Human Sciences*; also Borsari, *Hans Blumenberg*.

77. For the sake of clarity, I am perfectly aware that such a categorization is neither complete nor precise enough to describe the whole field of studies about the theory of secularization. Nor the indications of the authors I have mentioned exhaust the academic production about the subject.

Such categorization has to be interpreted just as the attempt to describe what I believe are two major tendencies in the field of studies about secularity and to establish in which field Taylor could be collocated.

78. Taylor refers in many instances and pages of *A Secular Age* to the extraordinary features of modernity. Examples: pp. 371, 416, 498.

negative process. It had to develop positive features and had to be in some form of relation with the structures of the previous age.[79] In a few words, for Taylor, the legitimacy of the modern age comes from the transformations of the social imaginary from a transcendental/Christian one to a secularist/immanent one. Such process had to rely on both the internal changes of modernity's spontaneous developments and cultural relations with the premodern era. It is at this point that it is possible to draw an interesting comparison between Taylor's conciliatory attempt and Blumenberg's theory. The impression we receive from such comparison is that, while Taylor does mention his disagreement with Blumenberg's theory,[80] these two authors utilize similar methods, or at least they depict similar structures of historical process.

In developing his narrative, Blumenberg openly uses a language of *legitimacy* to support his theories.[81] Therefore, we are in need of a linguistic clarification before undertaking the task of making a comparison between the works of Blumenberg and Taylor. What do we mean by legitimacy? From a literal interpretation of the term, legitimacy is what exists according to laws or accepted rules and/or standards.[82] In this sense, then, although only Blumenberg openly uses the language of legitimacy to justify his theories, the concept of legitimacy is equally present in both philosophers insofar as they try to give us a history of the processes of legitimization of institutions and practices in Western cultures. By *processes of legitimization*, I mean those historical-cultural-social phenomena that determine the sense

79. Taylor, *Secular Age*, 26, 29, 90–92. According to Taylor, there had to be, to be able to obtain the extraordinary achievement of modernity, sediments of the previous era that could work as fertile ground for new cultural and social form. For example the new Aristotelian-Christian synthesis which takes its most influential form in Thomas, that brought about what one could call an autonomization of nature (ibid., 91). Alternatively, the slow, active construction of the modern self-understanding of the individual—which subtraction theory seems to take for granted (ibid., 157–59).

80. Taylor, *Secular Age*, 294.

81. For example, Blumenberg describes the theory of secularization as the application of a principle of expropriation that downsize the legitimacy of the modern age. That is, its originality and independence from the previous historical periods and concepts (*Legitimacy of Modern Age*, ch. 2, 13–25).

In this sense, Taylor does not use the vocabulary of legitimization in the same sense as Blumenberg. For example, Taylor's social imaginary is a source of legitimization in a culture, but he does not speak of legitimacy or nonlegitimacy as inherent features of determined historical period/cultures, this despite being a critic of the theory of secularization himself.

82. For this reason Schmitt would criticize Blumenberg's choice of such a vocabulary, as this would lead to the paradox of something new that seeks auto-legitimization from nothing (Schmitt, *Political Theology II*, "Postscript: On the Current Situation of the Problem: The Legitimacy of the Modern Age").

of what is right, legal, and just. These processes of legitimization have been determined: for Taylor, by the change of the social imaginary from a transcendental/Christian one to a secularist/immanent one; for Blumenberg, by the spontaneous and original attempt of the modern age to answer unsolved problems of the previous religious/Christian culture.

In *The Legitimacy of the Modern Age*, Blumenberg criticizes the concept and the narratives of *secularization*.[83] In this sense, Schmitt's interpretation of the theory is only one among many of his targets. According to Blumenberg, the essential element of the metaphorical use of the concept of secularization is the transposition of a sense of illegitimacy. Its assumption rests on the characteristics typical of the process of expropriation, characteristics that could be defined as "the identifiability of the expropriated property, the legitimacy of its initial ownership and the unilateral nature of the removal of it."[84] The category of secularization also has the purpose of rebutting the theories of discontinuity in history. The purpose of the term secularization is to make evident that the denial of historical dependence is motivated by an epochal self-interest, a simple act of *hubris* of a specific society. Secularization, then, presents the alleged break between modern rationality and its past as purely ideological while making conscious of an objective cultural debt.[85] Blumenberg identifies another tool that secular-

83. Blumenberg, *Legitimacy of the Modern Age*, 14. The origin of the concept of Secularization is traced in the historical/juridical phenomenon of expropriation of church properties established by the Peace of Westphalia. *The Final Resolution of the Reichstag's Special Commission* established the term *saecularisatio* as a concept of the usurpation of ecclesiastical rights, as a concept of the illegitimate emancipation of property from ecclesiastical care and custody. These defining elements make the attribute of illegitimacy into a characteristic mark of the concept of secularization (ibid., 17–20).

84. Ibid., 24.

85. Ibid., 24–25. Blumenberg questions precisely the existence of this cultural debt; the burden of proof of secularization, he claims, has been, most of the time, taken for granted and has remained, for the most, unclear and confuse. To demonstrate this, Blumenberg analyses the theory according to which the modern historical consciousness is derived from the secularization of the Christian idea of salvation story.

Blumenberg affirms that there is a formal, but for that reason very manifest, difference between the idea of progress and the Christian eschatology. The second speaks of an event that breaks into history, an event that transcends and is very heterogeneous to it. While the first extrapolates from a structure present in every moment to a future that is immanent in history. In such an understanding of history, a salvation that comes from outside is an obstacle to those energies and capacities that can guarantee to humans the realization of a better future.

There is also, Blumenberg says, a genetic difference between eschatology and idea of progress. In his late-medieval form, the doctrine about the final causes is an answer to something that cannot be rationally answered. That is, the sense and the correct direction of history. The idea of progress, however, in its origin does not seek to answer

ization theorists use to justify their theory. The similarities of linguistic structures between theological mechanisms and political/ideological ones. Blumenberg replies by affirming that the constancy of language is an index of a constant function for consciousness, but not of an identity of content. It is a similarity of forms, not a material identity. If the *Communist Manifesto* had an eschatological language this is not because the underlying idea of progress was eschatological in itself, but because the consciousness of the people, deluded by a disappointing present and immediate future, adopted a language familiar to their consciousness to align their hopes.[86] The language of eschatology that influenced culture for centuries and influenced even the social spectrum at that time was just a *vehicle* to transmit a different content. Blumenberg means to strike the heart of the concept of secularization intended as a continuous reduction of contemporary structures to previous cultural forms (the progress as a secularization of Christian salvation, for example).[87] This kind of continuous cultural heritage between historical periods, where ideas are imported into the future (even if in different form) is found unacceptable.

Of course, Blumenberg does not want to question the principle that "modernity would be unthinkable without Christianity."[88] What is called into question is the permanence of core ideas through the process secularization that, for the author, strip away any historical period of his proper cultural autonomy and originality.[89] Blumenberg affirms that what an epoch receives from its predecessor are the cultural precondition, the unresolved questions, the disputed human interests, which are addressed then by the society and the culture of the new historical framework with new, spontaneous, answers. For Blumenberg, speaking of secularization as the introduction and increase of worldliness into theological doctrines is an historical absurdum that negates to epochs and cultures the spiritual property of their own accomplishments.[90] If the modern age had worldliness as a

---

a general question about humanity's destiny. Instead, it limits itself to the problem of the theoretical/scientific pursuit of knowledge, perceived as a task that goes beyond the single individual and the presents.

In this way, the danger of an absolute end of history is defused. Infinite progress does make each present relative to its future but at the same time renders every absolute claim untenable; the idea of progress, in this way, becomes the only regulative principle that can make history humanly bearable, which is that all dealings must be so constituted that through them people do not become mere means (ibid., 27–35).

86. Ibid., 86–87.
87. Ibid., 26–30.
88. Ibid., 33.
89. Ibid., 32–36.
90. Ibid., 71–75.

characteristic feature, that is not the result of a process of secularization. His thesis is that Modernity represents the second overcoming of Gnosticism. The presupposition of this thesis is that the first overcoming of Gnosticism, by early Christianity, was unsuccessful.[91]

Gnosticism's systematic intention forced the church, in the interest of consolidation, to define itself in terms of dogmas. This corresponds to the thesis that the formation of the Middle Ages can only be understood as an attempt to exclude completely the Gnostic interpretation. The central effort, from Augustine to Scholasticism, was the attempt to salvage the world as creation and the dignity of the ancient cosmos for its role in the Christian order of the universe.[92] However, such system met its failure when the unresolved problems, posed by Gnosticism, became simply too much to handle for medieval theologians, thus generating a crisis that needed new

---

91. Ibid., 126. The problem of Gnosticism, left unsolved by the ancient world, regarded the question about the origin of evil. To solve this problem, Marcion, who was excommunicated in Rome in 144 AD, proposed the idea that separating the figure of the creator God from the redeemer God could constitute a positive influence for the consistency of Christian claims (ibid., 127–29). The Gnostic dogmatic principle proceeded as follows: "A theology that declares its God to be the omnipotent creator of the world and bases its trust in this God on the omnipotence thus exhibited cannot at the same time make the destruction of this world and the salvation of men from the world into the central activity of this God" (ibid., 129).

Marcion wanted to place his foreign God, free of the burden of responsibility for the world, entirely and without restriction on the side of man's salvation. The price for this was the attachment to a negative valuation to the Greek cosmic metaphysics and the destruction of the trust in the world that could have been sanctioned by the biblical conception of creation.

92. Ibid., 130. Augustine, with his rejection of Manichaean Gnosticism, created the basis for the crisis of the first Christian overcoming of Gnosticism. In his commentaries to the Genesis, he elaborated the doctrine of the creation *ex nihilo* as *concreatio*, thus preserving the dignity and the goodness of the creation. To do that, however, Augustine had to put upon humanity the responsibility for the burden of evil oppressing the world.

The balance between the condition of the world and the guilt of humankind caused Augustine to become the theologian of the original guilt of humankind and of its mythical inheritance. In Paul's epistle to the Romans, which inspired Marcion's Gnosticism, Augustine found the theological means by which to formulate the dogma of humanity's universal guilt and to conceive its justification as an absolution through an act of grace that does not remove from the world the consequences of that guilt.

Gnosticism was, therefore, exhausted as far as metaphysical world principles were concerned, but it survived in the absolute separation between the elected, the forgiven ones, and the mass of rejected. The price paid for its temporal defeat was not only the guilt that humanity was supposed to assign itself for the condition of the world, but also the resignation that its responsibility for that condition imposed upon them. The senselessness of self-assertion was the heritage of the Gnosticism, which was not overcome, but only translated (ibid., 130–43).

answers. The central role of this crisis was occupied by Nominalism, which destroyed the Platonic-Aristotelian concept of the world constructed by Scholasticism. With Nominalism, it was no longer possible to save the cosmos of Scholasticism and even the same idea that the world had been created for humanity's benefit is put in question. This disappearance of order, that caused doubt regarding the existence of a structure of reality that can be related to humans, in turn came with a new concept of human freedom. This time the responsibility given to us is for the condition of the world as a challenge relating to the future, not as an original offense in the past.[93] According to Blumenberg, Nominalism was the first symptom of the crisis that would have destroyed any kind of anthropocentric view of the world. If there is no divine principle that can rationally explain the world, then humans are left with their own self-assertion and rationality to understand the world. At the same time, this implies that nature is not developed around humanity, and that we do not have a central role in the creation. The destruction of the Christianly ordered cosmos led to a double result, the emerging of thinkers and philosophers seeking a way to articulate this rationality to understand the world (like Descartes), and philosophers who tried to reaffirm the idea of a world created by divine will for the good of humanity (like Leibniz).[94]

In this way, Blumenberg presents modernity as an independent phenomenon, unhooked by Nominalism from a heavy heritage and protected from any external conditioning. A determinate epoch, an age, is a totality freed from the need to search for points of reference outside of itself. Every truth is completely and only a product of its time. According to Blumenberg, the true interpretative error of historical events is caused by the widespread tendency to search for a beginning, a fundamentally external cause, for historical processes. In this sense, modern historicism was the victim of its own internal logic, and became the best vehicle for the category of secularization. However, this did not solve the intrinsic contradiction of the category of secularization. By proceeding from one beginning to another beginning, by always looking to previous causes for historical events, we end up looking for an *absolute beginning*, a first fundamental cause for every historical process. However, this absolute beginning is without history, is forbidden by itself to have a story.[95] In Blumenberg's narrative, historical evolutions happen through a theoretical engagement. In the case of modernity, the inherent cause was the emergence of the purely rational legitimating power of self-affirmation of reason. Self-assertion means rational autonomy, sponta-

---

93. Ibid., 137–43.
94. Ibid., 165–81.
95. Ibid., 146–47.

neity of human freedom, which reflects its unlimited power over the world. This self-affirmation of reason is a project of existence, which enables a human being to determine how he has to relate with the surrounding reality, realizing his aspirations with the help of the enormous technical potential made available by modern science. The concept of self-assertion, therefore, can be considered the core of Bumenberg's narrative and a full justification of the rationality of modernity.[96] The overcoming of Gnosticism and the subsequent success of modern reason constitute, therefore, a reassurance of reason about the legitimacy of its own claims. Such claims must be considered as having an absolute credibility. Gnosticism opened the way for the self-affirmation of reason, a reason completely resolved in technical and calculative thinking.

There are evident differences between Taylor and Blumenberg's narrative. Although both narratives are invested in preserving the extraordinary character of modernity, Taylor is willing to depict a more direct, *engaged*, historical relation between modernity and the premodern, while Blumenberg's narrative seems more focused in describing relations between ages as *indirect*. I am not using terms like *engaged* or *indirect* casually. Instead, these terms are keys that reveal how Taylor and Blumenberg's narratives, despite being different on the surface, share a common theoretical root, and are bound to face similar problems. For both Taylor and Blumenberg, modernity is fundamentally an attempt to solve some internal contradiction inherent to Western civilization. While Blumenberg traces the source of this fundamental contradiction to the problem posed by Gnosticism, Taylor traces its source in the weakening of the premodern social imaginary. Despite the difference in historical perspective, modernity retains this character of resolution. It is meant to overcome a fundamental historical question. In this theoretical struggle about modernity as a resolution, the problem of the definition of human nature plays a central role. In the arguments of both philosophers, the inherent quality of the human being as a free agent is at stake. Blumenberg's argument attempts to preserve this freedom in its most pure form, at the price of postulating history as a process of indirect influences. Taylor, instead, is willing to disempower partially the independent character of human freedom to put the human in a relation with his community, history and tradition. However, in doing so, both thinkers are actually moving in the same theoretical tradition.

Jerome Carroll[97] has presented an interesting argument in this direction. According to Carroll, we can interpret both Taylor's and Blumenberg's

---

96. Ibid., 129–41.
97. Carroll, "'Indirect' or 'Engaged.'"

theoretical efforts as a further development in the German tradition of philosophical anthropology. What separates Taylor from Blumenberg is that they emphasize different core reasons for the unavailability of an objective grasp of reality. Whereas Taylor emphasizes our embeddedness in environing backgrounds, Blumenberg lays the stress on human dignity and the open-endedness of possible human experiences and achievements.[98] Taylor focuses on an engaged view of agency. He aims to point out that we understand and interact with the world in ways that are intentional, understood not in the sense of an outcome held consciously in mind, but in the sense that our experience is predisposed by various attitudes and values. The specific parameters of this intentionality are shaped, among other things, by prior understandings, discourses, values, and our embodied nature.[99] Blumenberg shares with Taylor a sense that our world is constituted by our descriptions of it. If anything, Carroll affirms, Blumenberg states man's role in the constitution of reality more emphatically than Taylor does.[100]

In Blumenberg's view, we can interpret human life only in terms of human accomplishments. In this case, then, it makes sense that Blumenberg would establish only indirect links between historical epochs. He must resist the logical claim deriving from conceptions of secularization as process. Any epoch would not be the accomplishment of its own people, but merely an inheritance of the previous epoch. Such claim invites an unending procession toward a nonspecified beginning.[101] In Carroll's opinion, Taylor rejects precisely this overindividualized strand of philosophical anthropology[102], in which every single human being constitutes its own reality. However, in denying this specific strand, Taylor does not abandon philosophical anthropology as a whole. While Taylor is willing to preserve human historical agency (thus he keeps upholding the extraordinary character of modernity), at the same time he keeps reaffirming the embedded character

---

98. Ibid., 869.

99. Ibid., 871.

100. Ibid., 871–72.

101. In this sense, then, Taylor is right in criticizing Blumenberg as providing only another subtraction theory. If human agency is understood in Blumenberg's terms, then only the total destruction of the elements of the previous era can allow modernity to undertake its own achievement, as it would create the empty civilizational space necessary for the production of new contents.

This becomes more evident in *The Legitimacy of the Modern Age*. Blumenberg sees the turning point of the journey from ancient to modern in Francis Bacon's conception of knowledge as an application of nature, which is put in the service of man and society. The fallen world of Gnosticism, forsaken by God, leaves open a space into which humans can remake the world.

102. Carroll, "'Indirect' or 'Engaged,'" 874.

of human individuals in structures of meaning that predate these individuals. The creation of meaning, in Taylor, retains partially an individualized process; insofar the meaning goes through a subject, or a self. However, the structures of meaning we use to understand the world are not individual.[103] They are related to a source beyond the human self that must be properly considered in order to develop a historical elaboration. In this case, Carrol says, Blumenberg and Taylor may be distinguished only by their emphasis. Taylor stresses the ways in which meaning and agency are bound up with intentions and prior understandings, whereas Blumenberg celebrates man's creative and assertive nature.

However, both Taylor and Blumenberg militate against a view of reality that fixes separate subject and object sides, preferring a dialectic of human capacity for self-constitution, and environing attitudes and values. This relation may be called dialectical insofar as this background both shapes us and is shaped by us. By that token, however, both Taylor and Blumenberg ultimately rely on a critical moment, which implies that we are both engaged in discourses and understanding, and able to achieve some kind of distance from them.[104] In this sense, then, it is finally possible to see with clarity the similarity between Blumenberg's and Taylor's narrative. Both narratives rely on a moment of loss or rejection of some vital component of a previous age. This loss is necessary in order for the new age to reveal its extraordinary character. In the case of Blumenberg, premodern Christianity had to be rejected in its totality so that modernity could overcome the gnostic problem. In the case of Taylor, instead, what had to be rejected was the connection to a transcendental source of value, so that the immanent framework could develop a higher grade of moral and natural understanding of the world.

A POSITIVE NARRATIVE OF SECULARIZATION: SCHMITT'S SOCIOLOGY OF CONCEPTS

Charles Taylor, who accuses other secularization theories of being merely subtractive, in his attempt to develop a different, positive, account of modernity, still relies on a negative moment in his narrative. This negative moment may not be a *subtraction*, in the sense Taylor describes it, but is still a loss, the disappearance of a fundamental source of value from the social framework. The loss is represented by the disappearance of the transcendent, which Taylor subsequently tries to recover in terms acceptable for the modern sensibility. However, not all theories of secularization have to be

103. Ibid., 875.
104. Ibid., 878.

subtraction theories. We have been provided already the means to produce a positive theory to explain the development of modernity. A theory that, instead of relying on the loss of concepts or structures, focuses on their transposition, their change and transformation in the different historical configurations. Carl Schmitt's studies of political theology and the historical development of modern state develop in this direction. Notably, Taylor does not consider these sources at all in his own studies.

One of Schmitt's most significant works are his essays in *Political Theology*. The fundamental argument of those essays is that "Sovereign is he who decides on the exception."[105] This argument is the central statement around which Schmitt will develop his description of what sovereign power is, and how it can be understood in juristic terms. The purpose of *Political Theology* is clear, to give a proper description and, possibly, justification for the existence of sovereign power and the state of exception as *de facto* problems. The third essay begins with an interesting, and extremely important, statement.

> All significant concepts of the modern theory of the state are secularized theological concepts not only because of their historical development—in which they were transferred from theology to the theory of the state, whereby, for example, the omnipotent God became the omnipotent lawgiver—but also because of their systematic structure, the recognition of which is necessary for a sociological consideration of these concepts. The exception in jurisprudence is analogous to the miracle in theology. Only by being aware of this analogy can we appreciate the manner in which the philosophical ideas of the state developed in the last centuries.[106]

This analogy is, in my opinion, extremely important. A most relevant application of such analogy can be found in the Catholic philosophers of the counter-revolution.[107] In these works is possible to notice how, in the juridi-

---

105. Schmitt, *Political Theology*, 5. For the sake of my argument, the only works of Schmitt that will be discussed are *Political Theology*, *Political Theology II*, and the *Briefwechsel* between him and Blumenberg. However, I have found great help in understanding Schmitt's theoretical interpretation from his following works: *State, Movement, People*; *Theory of the Partisan*; *Tirannia dei Valori*.

As introduction and informative literature on Carl Schmitt, I have found the following works extremely useful: Agamben, *State of Exception* and *Homo Sacer*; Marder, *Groundless Existence*; Scheuerman, *Carl Schmitt*.

106. Schmitt, *Political Theology*, 36.

107. Ibid., 38. Also, he quotes Adolf Menzel's *Naturrecht und Soziologie* to show how sociology, in the twentieth century, exercised a role that in the seventeenth and eighteenth centuries was exercised by *natural law*, that is: to utter demands for justice and to enunciate philosophical-historical constructions or ideals.

cal texts of the seventeenth/eighteenth century, the state intervenes almost everywhere. This role of the state has been retained also in the twentieth century so that, Schmitt claims, we can talk of *omnipotence of the lawgiver*, in a way that has been derived from theology, and not only in a linguistic way.[108] In this sense, Schmitt demonstrates how in juridical structures of the time, the state is described as a metaphysical instrument. Schmitt implies that this metaphysical nature of the state is explained, historically, as an after effect of monarchical public law, in which the theistic God is identified with the king.[109] Through his analyses of juridical concepts, Schmitt presents the development of a sociology of concepts.

A sociology of concepts is different from any other kind of sociology to the degree that, although presupposing a consistent and radical ideology,[110] it cannot be merely reduced to a spiritualist philosophy of history as opposed to a materialist one.[111] This sociology of concepts proposed by Schmitt transcends juridical conceptualization oriented to immediate practical interests. Schmitt's method aims to discover the basic, radically systematic, structure of political/legal mechanisms and to compare this structure with the conceptually represented social structure of a certain epoch. The core of the problem is not represented by a discussion about the relations of causality between practical/social realities and ideal/metaphysical structures. The main purpose is to establish the proof of an existing relation between them, a substantial and spiritual identity, independently of its practical or ideal source.[112] This kind of sociology presupposes that the metaphysical image of the world forged by a distinct culture has the same structure as what that society immediately accepts as an appropriate form of political organization.[113] In the modern theory of the state, there

108. Ibid., 38.
109. Ibid., 39.
110. Ibid., 42.

111. Ibid., 42–45. In Schmitt view, both these kinds of philosophy of history present a major flaw: first, they present a contrast between two spheres, and then they resolve the contrast by reducing one of the two into the other.

112. Ibid., 45. In this sense, says Schmitt, it is not a sociology of concepts when, for example, the monarchy of seventeenth century is characterized as the real that is mirrored in the Cartesian concept of God. It is, instead, a sociology of concepts when the historical/political status of the monarchy of that epoch is shown to correspond to the general state of consciousness that was characteristic of Western Europeans and that time.

In this sense, during the various historical periods, the juristic construction of the historical-political reality is organized around concepts whose structure is in accord with the structure of the metaphysical concepts of that society. Monarchy thus becomes as self-evident in the consciousness of that period as democracy does in a later epoch.

113. Ibid., 46. *Imitate the immutable decrees of the divinity* was, for Schmitt, the

is a psychological and phenomenological identity between the sovereign and God. A continuous thread runs through the metaphysical, political and sociological conceptions that postulate the sovereign as a personal unit and primeval creator.[114]

However, this identification God/Sovereign changed when the consistency of scientific thinking permeated political ideas. The general validity of a legal prescription became identified with the lawfulness of nature, which applies without exception. The machine world, as well as the juridical machine, runs by itself.[115] However, the metaphysical/ political relation of sovereignty does not disappear. The general will of the people becomes the new sovereign, while the decisionist and personalist element in the concept of sovereign was lost. However, the necessity by which the people always will what is right, fundamental for the modern theory of the liberal state, is not identical with the rightness that emanated from the commands of the personal sovereign, whose authority was related metaphysically to the divine authority. In the struggle of opposing interests and coalitions, absolute monarchy still had to rely on a fundamental decision and thereby created the unity of the state. The conflict reached its peak after the scholars and writers of the Restoration developed a political theology, an attempt to reestablish a connection between politics and the previous divine metaphysics. The philosophers and intellectuals who opposed the existing order of the restoration directed, with heightened awareness, their ideological efforts against the belief in God altogether, fighting that belief as if it were the most fundamental expression of the belief in any authority and unity.[116] This led to only one result: the elimination of all theistic and transcendental references in politics and the formation of a new concept of legitimacy.[117] The unity that a people represents does not possess the decisionist character of the sovereign. It is an organic unity, and with national consciousness, the idea of the state originated as an organic phenomenon, not as the decision of a sovereign, but almost as a natural phenomenon. The theistic as well as the deistic concepts of God, in modernity, become unintelligible for political metaphysics.[118]

---

ideal of legal life of the state in the eighteenth century; a fact that Schmitt considers as evident already in Rousseau's essay *Political Economy*, thus marking the beginning of the appropriation, by political and juridical thought, of theological structures.

114. Ibid., 47. This line of thought will influence the whole of seventeenth- and eighteenth-century political thinking with the idea of the sole sovereign (a fact that is evident, for Schmitt, also in Hobbes).

115. Ibid., 48.

116. Ibid., 50.

117. Ibid., 51–52.

118. Ibid., 49.

However, this elimination of the divine figure of the sovereign should not be understood as a loss or a subtraction, but as a transposition of concepts. A transposition is a process of transformation and historical adaptation of the context around the concept so that it is possible for a society to create a structure befitting the new consciousness of the era. In this sense, modernity was not able to liberate itself neither from a concept of transcendence (or lose it), nor from the problem of the distinction between friend and foe. The core of these structures has been retained, in a new historical/sociological/political context, in modernity as well.

Schmitt tries to develop precisely this point in his debate with Hans Blumenberg. After Blumenberg's criticism of the concept of secularization[119] in *The Legitimacy of Modern Age*, Schmitt replies to Blumenberg in a postscript to *Political Theology II*, titled "On the Current Situation of the Problem: The Legitimacy of the Modern Age." In this postscript, Schmitt answers Blumenberg's dismissal of any political theology, claiming that such a dismissal has been motivated by a concept of science that does not accept any validity for a continuing influence of, or transposition from, the history of salvation stemming from a religion that claims to be absolute.[120] Firstly, Schmitt warns that his theory should not be confused with all sorts of misguided parallels between religious, political and eschatological ideas.[121] Schmitt's theories, after all, are not grounded in a diffuse metaphysics. Instead, they bring light to the classical case of a transposition of distinct concepts that has occurred within the systematic thoughts of the two—historically and discursively—most developed constellations of Western rationalism, the Catholic Church with its entire juridical rationality and the state of the *Ius Publicum Europaeum*, which was supposed to be Christian even in Thomas Hobbes' system.[122]

For Blumenberg, secularization is a category of social/historical injustice. He seeks to unmask it as such, and he hopes to overcome translations and transpositions of secularization theory through legitimizing the modern age. Schmitt finds this attempt problematic in itself, insofar

---

119. Blumenberg, *Legitimacy of Modern Age*, 103–5. These pages are already present in the first edition of the work, in which Schmitt will only be briefly mentioned. After the debate between the two scholars, Blumenberg will add another chapter to his work, solely dedicated to Schmitt's concept of secularization (ch. 8, "Political Theology I and II," 89–102).

120. Schmitt , *Political Theology II*, 117.

121. Blumenberg (in his letter to Schmitt on March 24, 1971) will apologize for this misunderstanding, admitting that addressing specifically Schmitt's work was not his main aim and promising a better replying regarding only Schmitt's understanding of political theology and not *secularization* as a general idea.

122. Schmitt, *Political Theology II*, 117–18.

as legitimacy rests conceptually in a justification of continuity, tradition, upbringing and heritage.[123] Legitimacy is an historical justification of the past criticized by its modern and revolutionary enemies as a *justification of the injustice of today through the justification of the injustice of yesterday*. Blumenberg's legitimacy, instead, is a justification issuing from novelty.[124] Blumenberg's position leads, then, to conclude that legitimation through genuinely rational and legal knowledge is not legitimacy, but legality. Unfortunately, Schmitt affirms, this is not possible. Law is tied conceptually in a tragic way to very old theological and metaphysical antithesis. Blumenberg's main interest, then, rests in the self-empowerment of human beings and in the human thirst for knowledge. About the second, Schmitt accuses Blumenberg's argument of being tautological and self-centered. Its immanence, directed polemically against theological transcendence, is nothing more than an act of self-empowerment.[125] Blumenberg speaks the language of a philosophy of values in which we operate not with trans-valuations but with the loss of value, with the announcement of the loss of value and even with the announcement of the invalidity of such value. Thus, the questions of legitimacy and of legality are dissolved into the universal convertibility of values. In this way, from the standpoint of a self-empowering novelty, it is logical to reject any need for justification.[126] Blumenberg affirms that the modern age is the overcoming of Gnosticism. Modernity constitutes the successful attempt to solve the problem posed by Gnosticism where the Augustinian-Christian tradition failed. Thus, detheologization implies depoliticization, in the sense that the world has ceased being *politomorph* and the distinction between friend and enemy, which Schmitt considers as the fundamental political act, is no longer a criterion of the political.[127]

123. Ibid., 118.

124. Ibid., 118. Blumenberg's legitimacy, in Schmitt's interpretation, becomes a twisted concept sprouting from the *being new* of the modern age. This would open the double dilemma of: 1) is the modern age new? In addition, 2) is the modern age better?

Of course, Schmitt would be critical of Blumenberg's position in both these issues, however, in this postscript at least, he focuses more on the first problem.

125. Ibid., 120.

126. Ibid., 120–21. How should be defined such a stance? Schmitt says that both the Latin term *curiositas* and the Greek term *hubrys* are inappropriate. Maybe the Greek term *tolma* (audacity) would be a more fitting term.

127. Ibid., 123–24. Gnostic dualism, in this sense, juxtaposes the God of love, external to the world—a God of salvation—to the just God, the Lord and Creator of this evil world. These two Gods are in a state of open war, or at least in a state of unbridgeable alienation similar to a cold war.

The reason for the persuasiveness (and contradictory difficulties) of Gnostic dualism has to be found on the fact that the almighty, benevolent, and omniscient God cannot be also the God of salvation for the created world. Augustine shifts the focus of this

However, Schmitt is willing to take into account precisely this relation between Augustine and Gnosticism. In doing so, he decides to focus on a specific problem about the criterion for the political and for a political theology, that is, about the distinction between friend and enemy.[128] It starts from Peterson's reflections upon a phrase by Gregorius of Nazianzus: "The one—*to Hen*—is always in uproar—*stasiazon*—against itself—*pros heauton*."[129] The term *stasis* is here problematic. Stasis, in Greek, has a double meaning: 1) a physical one of quiescence, tranquility, standpoint, status. 2) A political meaning of unrest, movement, uproar and civil war. At the heart of the doctrine of Trinity, we encounter a genuine politico-theological stasiology. Thus, the problem of enmity cannot be ignored.[130] Redirecting the problem towards Blumenberg's argument, Schmitt says that, looking at how modernity tried to solve the problem of the enemy and of enmity in a logically detheologized and purely human reality, we see that the problem of Gnosticism is still present in the modern world. A proof that even modernity would have failed to solve the Gnostic paradox, if we follow Blumenberg's logic. According to Schmitt, modernity is still engaged with the problem of dualism. The God of creation and the God of salvation dominate not only every religion of salvation and redemption, but also every world in need of change and renewal (even a nonreligious one). This God is both immanent and ineradicable:

> One cannot get rid of the enmity between human beings by prohibiting wars between states in the traditional sense, by advocating a world revolution and by transforming the world politics into world policing. Revolution, in contrast to reformation, reform, revision and evolution, is a hostile struggle.[131]

It is almost impossible to have friendship between the lord of a world in need of change, a misconceived world, and the liberator, the creator of a transformed world. They are by definition enemies.[132] The same happened, for Schmitt, during the Reformation. What began as a Christological-political conflict over the *ius reformandi* became a politico-theological revolution. This was the fruit of an epoch determined by the medieval idea of *ius*

---

difficulty away from the deity and onto human beings while the doctrine of the Trinity accommodates the identity of the God of creation as the God of salvation through the unity between Father and Son.

128. Ibid., 122.
129. Ibid., 123.
130. Ibid., 123.
131. Ibid., 125.
132. Ibid., 125.

reformandi on one hand, and, on the other, by the fact that the state was emerging and already claiming sovereign power. Blumenberg, according to Schmitt, has well demonstrated this paradigm shift, but has not taken into account all the transpositions that occurred during this process. Blumenberg himself gives so many examples of Christological insights that it may not be wrong to raise the problem of political theology in terms of the problem of the enemy.

Schmitt's postscript sparked two major developments in his debate with Blumenberg: the first, a long epistolary exchange, in which the two authors exchange impressions and ideas on each other's work. The second, an attempt, by Blumeneberg, to answer properly to Schmitt by adding a chapter to his work *The Legitimacy of the Modern Age*. The epistolary exchange can give us a solid grasp of the intellectual debate between the two authors. A first interesting concept is found in the first letter, from Blumenberg to Schmitt, dated 21 March 1971.[133] In this letter, Blumenberg tries to introduce the concept of reoccupation to criticize Schmitt's concept of transposition.[134] After this letter, the new edition of *The Legitimacy of the Modern Age* reads:

> What mainly occurred in the process that is interpreted as secularization, at least (so far) in all but a few recognizable and specific instances, should be described not as the transposition of authentically theological contents into secularized alienation from their origin but rather as "the reoccupation of positions that had become vacant by answers whose corresponding questions could not be eliminated."[135]

Reoccupation, as Blumenberg sees it, concerns mainly a functional system of positional values, the value of the mechanism changes alongside his position in the civilization. While for Schmitt transposition indicates the value that is inherent in the form, which is eminently a logical-juridical form, and is a purely political theological statement. The debate concerns mainly if the mechanisms, in changing the epoch, retain their previous characters and/or meaning proper of the previous epoch or if it is changed (alongside their role) in the new epoch. The debate around the concept of reoccupation will continue in the letter of the 20 October 1974.[136] In this letter, Schmitt gives a definite answer to the new chapter that Blumenberg

---

133. Schmitt and Blumenberg, *Briefwechsel*, 105.

134. The German term would be *Umbesetzung*, which should take the place of *Umsetzung* (transposition).

135. Blumenberg, *Legitimacy of Modern Age*, 65.

136. Schmitt and Blumenberg, *Briefwechsel*, 118.

added to his *Legitimacy of the Modern Age*. In this chapter, Blumenberg questions the concept of political theology as a whole, and this criticism is elaborated through the concept of reoccupation. Such concept now denotes *"the reality underlying the appearance of secularization and is driven by the neediness of a consciousness that has been overextended and then disappointed in regard to the great questions and great hopes."*[137] Blumenberg proposes a reversal of the phenomenon described by Schmitt, which is "the reverse relation of derivation by interpreting the apparent theological derivation of political concepts as a consequence of the absolute quality of political realities."[138] Schmitt's formulation, according to Blumenberg, reduces the secularization thesis to a structural analogy.[139] It makes something visible—and is consequently by no means without value—but it no longer implies any assertion about the derivation of the one structure from the other or of both from a common prototype. So that Blumenberg asks, referring directly to Schmitt: "is this already sufficient to justify talk, on the side of political theory, of a 'political theology'?"[140]

Schmitt's answer, in the letter of 20 October 1974, is direct: "Yes."[141] Schmitt also indicates to Blumenberg a short essay he had written to try to clarify his position, "Three Possibilities for a Christian Conception of History."[142] Although Schmitt himself considered the essay a failed attempt, he still had the impression of having moved forward in the debate. Schmitt also wrote another letter to Blumenberg, on the 24 November 1974, in which he will give more details on the process of transposition. In that letter Schmitt reaffirms that the process of secularization, through transposition, is a process of identity and continuity in the most juridical sense, following, inheritance, be it a testamentary one or a legitimate one.[143] Blumenberg gives a proper, and quite elaborate, answer on 7 August 1975. In that letter, he negates explicitly any possible relation between historical consciousness and theological eschatology. The process is not one of secularization, in the sense that the eschatological meaning remains and only the transcendental/divine part disappears. It is instead a total negation, a confutation of any eschatology so that modernity cannot, in any way, adopt theological mecha-

137. Blumenberg, *Legitimacy of Modern Age*, 89.
138. Ibid., 92.
139. Ibid., 94.
140. Ibid., 94.
141. Schmitt and Blumenberg, *Briefwechsel*, 120.
142. This short essay was a comment to Karl Lowith's work *Meaning in History*. The purpose was to try to pinpoint the three concepts of greatest interest in Lowith's work and the most fruitful ones both for philosophy of history and political thinking.
143. Schmitt and Blumenberg, *Briefwechsel*, 125.

nisms to put forward something that is not, neither in structure nor meaning, theological-eschatological.[144]

Through the debate between Schmitt and Blumenberg is possible to grasp the core problem of the controversy between secularism and religion, between immanent and transcendent, an understanding that allows us to tackle Taylor's philosophical proposal from a new point of view. Is it possible to combine eschatology and historical consciousness? Is a secular eschatology, a political theology possible? Of course, in the catholic tradition, a concept like political theology is not new at all. Since Augustine, the divine order of the universe has been a justification for the political order of societies, a statement that has been retained also through the modern age.[145] The key question is if a *secular political theology* is possible as well. Of course, the current state of the controversy in Western culture claims that secularism and religion move on two different planes. Secularism is immanent, rational and a-religious while religion is irrational, fideistic and moralistic. The competition between them is dictated by their diametrically different approach toward reality, by the strict delimitation of spaces that they require in society, more than a struggle for the same spaces. This state of the controversy is reflected also in Taylor's work, on which I will now return to evaluate the possible consequences of the Schmitt/Blumenberg debate. As I have described in the previous pages, Taylor, in his work, upholds the division between secularism and religion in terms that are similar to Blumenberg's narrative. While it is true that he advocates for a sort of synthesis between the phenomena of secularity and religion, such synthesis has to be achieved between a thesis and an antithesis. In Taylor's narrative, there is no space for a possible transposition of concepts between theology and politics. Taylor argues, "Western modernity, including its secularity, is the fruit of new inventions, newly constructed self-understandings and related practices, and can't be explained in terms of perennial features of human life."[146] According to Taylor, the change has been brought by the shift in our understanding of the sources that lead to our sense to fullness.[147] From a condition in which our highest spiritual and moral aspirations point us inescapably to God, to one in which they can be related to a host of different sources, and frequently are referred to sources which deny God. In Taylor's narrative, although related in problematic and ambiguous ways, secularism

---

144. Ibid., 130–35.

145. Schmitt's studies on Donoso Cortes, in the fourth chapter of *Political Theology*, are a proof in this sense.

146. Taylor, *Secular Age*, 22.

147. Ibid., 26.

and religion, theology and politics are specific and separate fields. Each of them has its own field of action and they can struggle when these fields, in moment of crisis or social change, overlap. Taylor conceives the whole structure of Western society as a construct integrated with many pieces. Some pieces can conflict, some other can be taken away (transcendence for example) but each one of them retains its own specific features.

However, now a question arises. If Taylor is correct that Blumenberg's theory is a subtraction story, then how should Schmitt's theory be evaluated? Is it possible to consider Schmitt's work just another subtraction story? I do not think this is the case. The continuity that Schmitt established between theology and modern politics was precisely what Blumenberg attacked the most. We cannot consider Schmitt's theory a subtraction story. Transcendence does not disappear in Schmitt's theory. Rather, he believes in a possible bridge between eschatology and history. It is a specific *figure of God*, as a symbol of power, which loses authority, not transcendence as such. We reach the stage of an immanent transcendence, so to speak. A transcendence that is tied to worldly things (the state, the ideology, the party, the race) but that retains an eschatological character. Holding this true, we can consider Schmitt's theory of secularization as a different account of the modern age. A positive account in which transcendence itself has not disappeared but has been transposed, to not say misplaced. Could it be possible that Schmitt was right and we are looking at a crisis that is much deeper than the loss of transcendence? A crisis that creates fractures in the framework as a whole while its single pieces are all falling in the same threshold of ambiguity.

SOCIOLOGY OF CONCEPTS TODAY

The purpose of this chapter is to argue that Charles Taylor's understanding of secularization presents flaws that undermine his narrative in *A Secular Age*. In doing so, however, I have also been able to touch, albeit briefly at this stage, the core argument I wish to develop in this work. Through the analyses of the work of Blumenberg, Schmitt and Taylor, I have identified a fundamental question for philosophy of history (as well as political philosophy and ethics). A question that Taylor, in his strict separation between religion and secularity, has overlooked. Is it possible to have an eschatological view combined with an historical consciousness? Is it possible to have a secular eschatology? What language should we use to analyze such possibility? This question also involves a redefinition of the concept of faith. Because, if a secular eschatology is possible, then what is faith? Evidently, it cannot be considered merely as a religious attitude toward reality, as Taylor's narrative implies.

However, this leads to the problem of the language required and available to us in discussing such possibility. Schmitt, while convinced that modern *secular* social forms were imbued with eschatological charges, was, at the same time, pessimist regarding the possibility of critically analyzing these forms through a consistent theory. As it is possible to read in the letters he exchanged with Blumenberg, Schmitt confessed to lack a proper historical narrative through which develop his analyses consistently. I am of the opinion that Taylor's analysis is equally insufficient to present properly the complexity of the problem, as it does not address in depth problems that I believe are central not only for our comprehension of modernity, but also to understand our contemporary political and social framework.

However, I am confident that Schmitt also provided us with indications regarding the theoretical direction in which we should develop a sociology of concepts as he intended it. As Schmitt revealed to Blumenberg in one letter, he appreciated Löwith's attempt in *Meaning in History*,[148] believing that this work was a move in the right direction. Yet, Löwith's attempt is considered, ultimately, unsuccessful. This, I believe, is the problem that should be investigated in the conclusion of this chapter, as a final criticism of Taylor regarding the concept of *secularization*. Why was Löwith's attempt judged insufficient to provide the technical tools for a sociology of concepts? The answer to this question and the development of an answer will allow me to get closer to the language I believe we should develop to discuss the problem of faith, and secular faiths, today.

In *Meaning in History*, Löwith provides a narrative that affirms the dependence of *Philosophy of History* to *Theology of History*.[149] The term *philosophy of history*, according to Löwith, was invented by Voltaire to distinguish it from a theological interpretation of history. Löwith uses the term *theology of history* to mean a systematic interpretation of universal history in accordance with a principle by which historical events and successions are unified and directed toward an ultimate sense. Against this interpretation, modern philosophers decided to reject any prescientific treatment of history altogether and accepted Voltaire's empirical method. However, Löwith's aim is to demonstrate that the concept of *history*, in itself, finds

---

148. Schmitt dedicated a commentary essay to this work, appreciating the theoretical problems that this work could inspire for the fields of political philosophy and philosophy of history as a whole. The essay original title was *Drei Möglichkeiten eines christlichen Geschichtsbildes*, published in English with the title "Three Possibilities for a Christian Conception of History."

149. Löwith, *Meaning in History*, 1.

its origins in the Hebrew and Christian faith in a final fulfillment, and ends with the secularization of this eschatological pattern.[150] To develop this argument, Löwith decides to proceed backward from Burckhardt until Augustine, from a modern author to a classic one. His aim was to find a principle of continuity in Western tradition. The ancients, Löwith says, were more moderate in their speculations. They did not presume to make sense of the world or to discover its meaning. In the classic tradition, especially Greek, everything moved in a recurrence. This interpretation satisfied them because it was a rational and natural understanding of the universe, combining a recognition of temporal changes with periodic regularity. In this intellectual climate, there was no room for the universal significance of a unique, incomparable historical event. To the Jews and the Christian, however, history was (is) a matter of salvation, a *history of salvation* and, as such, the proper concern of prophets, preachers and teachers. The very existence of a philosophy of history and its quest for meaning is connected to the existence of these histories of salvation. History can be meaningful only by indicating some transcendent purpose beyond worldly facts.[151] Ultimate meaning and a transcendent purpose are focused toward an expected future. This expectation was most common among the Hebrew prophets, while it was totally absent in the Greco-Roman worldview.[152]

In the Greco-Roman mythologies, in fact, the past is represented as an ever-lasting foundation. In the Jewish/Christian tradition, instead, it is a promise to the future.[153] Greek philosophers were convinced that whatever is to happen would retain the same pattern and character of past and present events. To substantiate this claim, Löwith examines rapidly the cases of Herodotus, Thucydides and Polybius. All three of them had no interest in the future as such and had no interest in judging the historical course of events from the viewpoint of future, which is distinct from the past by having an open horizon and an ultimate goal. This was also a way to explain and accept events such as the mutability of fortune and fate. It also made possible for the ancients to foresee and speculate on the future, as it would have been an event happening according to rules that were already known and accepted. The fact that the ancients felt no difficulty in prognosticating fu-

---

150. Ibid., 2.

151. Ibid., 5.

152. In addressing this concept, we return to the fundamental ontological hypostasis that I have introduced in the previous chapter. The fundamental ontology of the Greeks and Romans was not, in fact, historical. Intended as a consistent path toward an expected future. The expectations of the Greeks and Romans were resolved in their social context and the harmony between this social context and the rules of the universe.

153. Ibid., 6–7.

ture developments indicates the fundamental difference between the classic and the Christian outlook, and in their attitude concerning the future. To the ancients, it was an easy matter to foretell the future by inference of the past. To the Old Testament writers, only God, through his prophets, could reveal future, which is independent of all that has happened in the past and that cannot be inferred from it as a natural consequence.[154] For Löwith this new interpretation of the future as an historical paradigm is born from the Jewish/Christian tradition, which has been claimed and made its own by modern philosophy of history. The future has become the focus of speculation and our study of history is functional to a promised future. In Löwith's interpretation, then, Burckhardt had to retain a concept of continuity in history, a history that is launched toward future. Even those scholars and philosophers that tried to give theoretical prognostication of the future[155] had to collocate the final stage in an indefinite future. In the end, they had to struggle within the inner contradiction of having to keep the future open, and yet still constrained by a definite outcome.

The ancients were concerned about their own present world, modern historian are concerned about our own future world. This change in paradigm has been a perversion of the classic meaning of *historien* and, at the same time, invalidated the classical view of the future as something that can be investigated and known as a fact. This new paradigm can also be interpreted through the teleological, or rather eschatological, structure of the historical process that makes history universal. God is not the necessary factor for establishing this universality. What is necessary, instead, is to give a sense of unity to the history of humanity through the future glory of a final purpose. For Löwith, therefore, the problem of history as a whole is *de facto* unanswerable. Historical processes as such do not bear any evidence of a comprehensive and ultimate meaning. The farther back we go from the modern era, the less we find an elaborate plan of progressive history. This because history as such, was never the focus or main interest of scholars and philosophers, and always did find its meaning outside of itself, beyond itself. The modern overemphasis on secular history as the *scene of humanity's destiny* is a product of our alienation from the natural theology of antiquity and from the supernatural theology of Christianity. The importance of secular history decreases in direct proportion to the intensity of humanity's concern with God, and the opposed process is also true. According to Löwith, modernity is the product of a process of secularization that is both Christian and un-Christian at the same time. It is un-Christian in its rejection of any

154. Ibid., 9.
155. Ibid., 10–16.

transcendental meaning, Christian in the continuous emphasis toward a destiny and a fulfillment for humanity.

We should not be surprised that Blumenberg criticized heavily Löwith's position. While Schmitt, despite appreciating the attempt, declared his failure. Despite being very evocative, Löwith's narrative possesses great limitations. It is evident that, whenever we are dealing with an historical narrative, an element of arbitrariness is inescapable. This because the mere choice of the events analyzed presupposes that our sight is fixed on determined facts instead of others. Moreover, in our analyses we are always looking at events with a bias given by our own conceptual framework. Despite all the claims for objectivity, the mere fact that our analysis works through a determinate choice of concepts is in itself a bias. This is, then, the first step that must be solved if we want to proceed further in our analysis. In this sense, then, Löwith's attempt to trace the Christian roots of modernity is in itself antihistorical. He has utilized the modern concepts of religion and secularity as analytical instruments to evaluate events that precede the origins of those concepts themselves. We can see, in Löwith, the reaffirmation of the great prejudice that sees religion and secularity as two distinct and easily discernible phenomena. The two concepts become suprahistorical *genera*, used to define single historical events. However, precisely this approach is the one that Schmitt, together with Blumenberg, wanted to avoid. We cannot discuss, then, modernity according to prefixed understanding of the concepts of secularity and religion. Instead, modernity represents a stage of great ambiguity. The great ambiguity of modern political/social forms lies in a threshold of indifference between what is religious and what is secular. Our inability to define clearly this threshold is our greatest challenge today. This because the threshold, the border that would allegedly define the two concept, is constantly on the move together with the historical procession of events. In this way, it develops accordingly to the metaphysical/political structures of a determinate society

This clarification of the problem helps me introduce a critical point concerning the contemporary controversy on secularization and highly relevant for my presentation of the problem of faith. As I already argued, I am deeply dissatisfied with how the current controversy split in a definitive and definite manner what is religious from what is not. Taylor as well repeats the same paradigm, thus reapplying the concepts of religion and secularity as overencompassing *genera*, which can be applied to single historical events from the outside. Schmitt was dissatisfied with this separation as well, and that was his first reason to undertake a work like *Political Theology*. Schmitt understood the process of secularization as a process of inheritance, of continuity. The modern concept of the state is simply intertwined too much with theological mechanisms to deny the existence of a relation of identity between some concepts. How should we understand this identity?

I believe that theoretical proposals like the one proposed by Cavanaugh, which I introduced in the first chapter, are moving in the right direction. Both Schmitt and Cavanaugh may be right in establishing the dichotomy *enemy/friend* as a constitutive foundation for the political body. Secular political forms, to legitimize themselves, needed an enemy and that enemy has become the religious other, an enemy that is perceived almost as an *ontological* threat. This point, I believe, can be a striking critique to the core of Taylor's narrative. Taylor's narrative relies precisely on a structural distinction between what is religious and what is secular. Taylor's philosophical work intends to overcome this distinction, through a moral attitude of open faith, which should avoid the attitude of moral superiority. However, to question the reliability of the distinction would question the very foundation on which Taylor establishes his proposal. This also calls for an examination of Taylor's narrative. By affirming that the contemporary concept of religion is not a viable tool to understand the contemporary controversy with secularity, Taylor's position is equivalent to Löwith's fundamental analytical error, to have used a concept that has been elaborated in the modern context as a general historical category. A fundamental criticism of the category of religion, by consequence, has effects also on the interpretation of the concepts that are connected to it. If the concept of religion is a creation of modern understanding to legitimize the secular state, then in what relation does faith stand with social/political structures? Can we still consider it just a religious concept? Is it possible to extend its field of application?

I am of the opinion that Cavanaugh's proposal reveals the sensibility that a sociology of concepts, à la Schmitt, should possess. Beyond using the concepts as analytical tools in themselves, a serious analytical approach should examine their historical modification/creation. It should also ask how such concepts satisfy specific contextual problem in any given society. Namely, how the *Weltanschauung*, the worldview, influences the meaning and the applications of the concepts themselves. In Cavanaugh's example, the concept of religion is a tool to legitimize the authority of the secular state; it is meant to sustain the new, modern, worldview, and to confirm the secular understanding of the world. A sociology of concepts should not only investigate the meaning expressed by the concept, but also should locate such meaning historically. In a way similar to Schmitt, who believed exception and sovereignty were categories whose meanings changed according to the balances of power in any given historical context, the category of religion, in Cavanaugh, possesses different meanings according to the specific historical needs of the society. The modern concept of religion is only another mechanism through which political authorities constructed their own political theologies.

Through Cavanaugh's insights, then, it is revealed that the historical process of construction of concepts is influenced by historical and cultural developments. By connecting Cavanaugh's history of the concept of religion with Schmitt's political theology, the link between the concepts through which a society structures itself and its interpretation of reality as a whole is revealed. If there is always a link between metaphysical and political self-understanding of a society, then, the process of construction of the concepts of religion and secularity through the modern age were functional to the expression of a new perceived reality, both metaphysical and immanent. Following this approach, then, we obtain a divergent history than the one Taylor, or Blumenberg, develop. Their historical narratives conceive only one story and one reality, in which we obtain a progressively more perfect epistemic understanding of reality and of human beings, a history of improvement and progress. Schmitt's and Cavanaugh's historical narratives, instead, admits a multiplicity of realities throughout human history. It is only because any given epoch and society relies on its own *Weltanschauung*, which is different than the ones of other cultural contexts, that is possible to describe the change, transformation and evolution of concepts and institutions as historical facts, not tied to one, all-encompassing, idea of progress. By comparing Schmitt's insights with Taylor's historical narrative and interpretation of secularism, we see that a positive theory of secularization does not rely on negative aspects, nor does it rely on a narrow interpretations of the concepts of religion and secularism. Sociology of concepts investigates historical facts in their own historical conditions. It abandons predetermined categories and abandons the expectation to understand different stories through one, consistent, fundamental narrative.

3

Hegelian and Post-Hegelian Approaches

IN THE PREVIOUS CHAPTER, I argued that Taylor's understanding of the concepts of religion and secularity was too rigid and ineffective to provide a fully convincing historical analysis. I have presented the argument that the narrative provided by Taylor' in *A Secular Age* possesses a fundamental flaw. Such flaw has been found in his schematic understanding of the concepts of religion and secularity. Taylor applies these concepts as general categories of history, as *genera*, that describe specific social phenomena from the outside. However, in doing so, Taylor is unable to provide a convincing account of how the concepts of religion and secularity have been produced in the first place. Secularity and religion, as historical and social phenomena, are described in a way that conveniently fits the definitions of the concepts and, vice-versa, the definitions of the concepts conveniently fit the features of the social and historical events of modernity. It is true that Taylor uses the concepts of *sources of good* and *highest values* to describe both religious and immanent frameworks.[1] However, the use of the category of *sources* is, in itself, extremely problematic. It generates a sense of fracture between different frameworks, thus extending further the sense of separation between secularity and religion and making even harder to achieve the synthesis he wishes to achieve between them.

If one framework uses a specific source, for example a secular source of good, then, by consequence, other, nonsecular or alternative secular, sources have to be discarded. A secular source of good, which has been established as being the highest value in a given society, cannot be questioned

---

1. Taylor, *Secular Age*, 544–46.

by alternative sources. The same thing happens in the case of a religious source of good. In Taylor's theoretical structure, then, the source defines all the underlying features of the framework; a religious source generates religious structures of society, oriented toward the transcendent, while a secular source generates secular structures, oriented toward the immanent. In this way, in the end, the human group embedded in a given framework understands the world through social, spiritual and cognitive tools that are very different from groups embedded in different frameworks.

The consequence of Taylor's rigid approach is, for example, that the secular individual would always conceive his concept of the good within a naturalist understanding of the world that remains purely mechanical and immanent. While the religious individual would always understand his concept of the good in transcendental terms, using the tools of faith (no matter how enlightened or naïve) and spirituality. For Taylor, the fact that the secular/naturalist argument claim to reject any transcendental reference (mainly God) is enough to describe it as immanentist *tout-court*. Thus forbidding any uses of the categories of transcendence or faith or spirituality in discussing these frameworks. By consequence, a similar exclusion, in the opposite direction, is executed for religious frameworks.

There are many consequences to this kind of theoretical approach, which I will illustrate in this chapter, the main one being the transformation of secularity into a fixed category for historical analysis. Already José Casanova, in his essay "A Secular Age: Dawn or Twilight?," argues that Taylor, has overlooked the fact that even secularism in itself is not a homogeneous social category, and that there are different forms of it according to the different cultural environments.[2] In the previous chapter, I have also presented Carroll's interpretation of Taylor's approach as a further attempt to develop a philosophical anthropological narrative, which would put him in the same theoretical path used by Hans Blumenberg. Despite Taylor's best attempt to develop a different theory than a subtraction theory, he has to rely, like Blumenberg, on a moment of loss or rejection of some vital component of the premodern age. In Taylor's case, modernity had to reject God as a source of good and transcendence as a framework, so that the immanent framework could develop a higher level of moral and scientific understanding of the world.

I am of the opinion that Taylor's approach has not only been influenced by the German tradition in philosophical anthropology. I believe there is a more fundamental influence that has determined the structure of Taylor's narrative. Such influence has to be found in his studies on Hegel, studies

---

2. Casanova, "Secular Age," 265.

that inspired Taylor in adopting a dialectic understanding of historical and social events, thus determining the rigid logical structure of his narrative. Therefore, in this chapter I will focus the attention on the theoretical relation that Taylor establishes between historical categories. I argue that Taylor's application of an implicit triadic structure of history is strongly tied to his studies on Hegel and that such influence undermines the descriptive power of his historical narrative. By analyzing Taylor's Hegelianism with respect to its historical, sociological and anthropological value, I will also show how his use of Hegelian concepts represents also the biggest obstacle to achieve the synthesis he aims to achieve. Specifically, I will focus my attention on three fundamental features that will reveal the importance of Hegel for Taylor's own philosophy: the dialectic between *immanence/transcendence*, the presentation of secularity as a *loss of transcendence*, and the concept of the *buffered self*.

However, precisely through a different interpretation of Hegel's philosophy, I will show a way to complete and correct Taylor's historical understanding and make it more sensible to the problem of the *Weltanschauung* and the faith it inspires in the social body. Such different interpretation of Hegel will be provided through Croce's criticism of the Hegelian dialectic and will show how, within the Hegelian tradition, is possible to find resources that improve the historical narrative of secularization, and provide us with a more precise description of the processes involved in the development of Western modernity. Particularly, I will discuss how Benedetto Croce's *Absolute Historicism* and Ernesto De Martino's anthropology, inspired by Croce's work, provide us the tools to identify a theoretical and existential framework of reference for the phenomenon of faith, a phenomenon that Taylor has not addressed deeply enough in his narrative.

TAYLOR'S HEGELIAN DIALECTIC

Charles Taylor has already been, in many occasions, defined as a *Hegelian*[3] philosopher. An interesting contribution that addresses such interpretation

---

3. An example can also be found in the review that Michael L. Morgan wrote about *A Secular Age* (in *Notre Dame Philosophical Reviews*), in which is said that Taylor's work has been inspired, among many, primarily by Hegel and Foucault. Moreover, Morgan affirms that Taylor's aim to demonstrate that the ultimate ground of our moral demands is our aspiration to wholeness and that this claim is central to a Christianity, whose principal affirmation is the Incarnation of the divine in the human, is a very Hegelian commitment.

Another example is the review by Craig Calhoun, in which is said that Taylor's argument about how we can work through the various obstacles to having a sense of living

of Taylor's thought is Vincent Descombes' essay "Is There an Objective Spirit?" In this essay, Descombes analyzes Taylor's interpretation of the Hegelian concept of objective spirit. According to Descombes Taylor retains a sort of positivist Hegelianism, a baggage of Hegelian concepts freed from their theological/ontological value and used now as sociological instruments.[4] The fundamental assumption behind Taylor's Hegelian interpretation of social events is that social life is not reducible to the necessities of common life, but that it has a meaning. The individuals that partake in any social life derive a fundamental something, a meaningfulness, from it.[5] The problem, then, would be to understand properly the effective social reality of this meaningfulness, defined by Descombes as the objective spirit of a society, in a Hegelian sense. He affirms that, to understand Taylor's philosophical proposal correctly, we should interpret this concept of objective spirit as "a sharable state of mind or a rule to follow." That is, a condition for the social exercise of intelligent activity, a condition to which individuals would be subjects in a manner not requiring their expressed consent.[6] According to Descombes, Taylor's strategy is twofold. He shows how any social practice presupposes common (as opposed to merely shared) meanings. In addition, he argues that institutions express the mentioned ideas and meanings, which resemble the Hegelian objective spirit. The functions of institutions, therefore, can be compared, to those of a language,[7] I agree with Descombes that this peculiarity is what makes Taylor's narrative extremely compelling. At the same time, however, precisely the use of Hegelian concepts as sociological tools is the main cause of its most remarkable flaws. Through the adoption of such Hegelian dialectics, Taylor wishes to achieve a synthesis between the immanence of secularity and the transcendence of religion. The use of such categories, however, ends up reinforcing further the sense of difference between secular and religious framework. As a result, it ignores those areas of uncertainty and indeterminacy that exist between secular and religious interpretations of the world. Ultimately, this process negates the very synthesis that Taylor tries to achieve.

---

amid transcendence to experience it in richer ways, is loosely Hegelian (not surprisingly, adds Calhoun, since he is one of the greatest interpreters and analysts of Hegel).

Also, Ruth Abbey, in her work *Charles Taylor*, affirms that Taylor's hope that seeming antithesis might be reconciled is one reflection of the influence of Hegel on his thinking.

4. Descombes, "Is There an Objective Spirit?"
5. Ibid., 97–98.
6. Ibid., 97–100.
7. Ibid., 106.

It is possible to find a first example of the rigid structures that Taylor has inherited from Hegel by examining how the two philosophers share the same understanding of religion. Which is described as an important and necessary form of human cultural expression. In the introduction to *A Secular Age*, in fact, we can read

> The big obvious contrast here is that for believers, the account of the place of fullness requires reference to God, that is, to something beyond human life and/or nature; where for unbelievers this is not the case; they rather will leave any account open, or understand fullness in terms of a potentiality of human beings understood naturalistically. But so far this description of the contrast seems to be still a belief description. What we need to do is to get a sense of the difference of lived experience. Of course, this is incredibly various. But perhaps some recurring themes can be identified. For believers, often or typically, the sense is that fullness comes to them, that it is something they receive; moreover, receive in something like a personal relation, from another being capable of love and giving; approaching fullness involves among other things, practices of devotion and prayer (as well as charity, giving); and they are aware of being very far from the condition of full devotion and giving; they are aware of being self-enclosed, bound to lesser things and goals, not able to open themselves and receive/give as they would at the place of fullness. So there is the notion of receiving power or fullness in a relation; but the receiver isn't simply empowered in his/her present condition; he/she needs to be opened, transformed, brought out of self. This is a very Christian formulation.[8]

Religion is the social form that locates the source of the sense of fullness externally, from something beyond our historical/natural world. It is opposed to secularity, presented as unbelief, which, instead, finds the source of fullness in an inner potentiality, or inherent value, within human nature. Charles Taylor understands religion in the context of a decisive distinction between transcendent and immanent.[9] In this sense, then, religion is the

---

8. Taylor, *Secular Age*, 8.

9. Ibid., 15–16. It is useful to quote here the paragraph in which this thought is expressed:

> In other words, a reading of religion in terms of the distinction transcendent/ immanent is going to serve our purposes here. This is the beauty of the prudent (or cowardly) move I am proposing here. It is far from being the case that religion in general can be defined in terms of this distinction. One could even argue that marking our particular hard-and-fast distinction here is something which we (Westerners, Latin Christians)

HEGELIAN AND POST-HEGELIAN APPROACHES 107

social form that puts the origin of the *sense of fullness* in a supernatural source. To achieve his intended outcome, that is, a stage of open faith in our social context, Taylor describes the problem of achieving a *synthesis* between religion and secularity as

> How to define our highest spiritual or moral aspirations for human beings, while showing a path to the transformation involved which doesn't crush, mutilate or deny what is essential to our humanity? Let us call this the "maximal demand."[10]

As I already presented in the previous chapter, Taylor seeks a new composition between the religious aspiration towards the transcendent and the legitimate demands for respect and dignity of our human body and rationality[11] that advanced particularly during the modern, secular, age. However, Taylor's most Hegelian features are revealed precisely through this strict separation between the two terms of the dichotomy and the attempt to create a recomposition between them. An interesting first example of these Hegelian features can be found in how Taylor interprets religion as the only form of expression of what we call faith. According to Taylor, faith is something that belongs only to the field of religious sensibility. It is a form

---

alone have done, be it to our intellectual glory or stultification (some of each, I will argue later) . . .

This notion of the immanent involved denying—or at least isolating and problematizing—any form of interpenetration between the things of Nature, on one hand, and the supernatural on the other, be this understood in terms of the one transcendent God, or of Gods or spirits, or magic forces, or whatever. So defining religion in terms of the distinction immanent/transcendent is a move tailor-made for our culture. This may be seen as parochial, incestuous, navel-gazing, but I would argue that this is a wise move, since we are trying to understand changes in a culture for which this distinction has become foundational. So instead of asking whether the source of fullness is seen/lived as within or without, as we did in the above discussion, we could ask whether people recognize something beyond or transcendent to their lives.

Taylor, in describing his distinction, tries also to defend himself precisely from criticism like the one I am proposing in this study. His affirmation rests on the fact that it is not important, for the sake of his analysis, the effective disappearance of transcendence from the secular context, just to certify and analyze how a cultural form in which the transcendent is not considered foundational can be born and be developed historically.

At first, Taylor analysis seems to make sense and be perfectly viable; however, as this chapter will try to demonstrate, the dichotomy transcendence/immanence make use of a very restricted field of meaning of the two terms, so that Taylor, in the end, is unable to properly defend the outcome of his work.

10. Ibid., 640.
11. Ibid., 640–41.

of relation with one or more sources of good that takes into account only their being transcendental—as opposed to being immanent—and can be articulated only through those social phenomena that we call religion.[12] Despite acknowledging that the controversy about moral sources cannot be simply polarized in a conflict between religious and nonreligious ways of life, Taylor cannot help but qualify the religious attitude as faith in strict sense, contrarily to the various examples of secular unbelief to which the term faith cannot be applied.[13] There is, then, a strong identification of the concept of religion with the concept of faith.

The identification between religion and faith is a constant topic in Taylor's work. If we examine Taylor's work on Hegel's philosophy, we can see how he embraces the Hegelian concept of *Glaube* (faith) and reaffirms its deep and exclusive connection with the dimension of religion. Although rejecting the ontological claims of Hegelian metaphysics, Taylor is interested in defining the category of religion as the only form in which faith can be expressed, and as an inescapable stage of human communities. We can read:

> Religion has two dimensions: a representation of God and a powerful sense of separation from him which the believer longs to overcome. But there is also a third dimension: the cult. Religion is not just the locus of this consciousness and longing, but it also englobes the way that man strives to overcome this separateness. This is the essence of the cult.[14]

---

12. Ibid., 550–51. In these pages, there is a clear example of such an exclusive relation between faith and religion. Charles Taylor, in fact, says that:

> The term faith has a different meaning when we speak of theistic religion. Here it refers to a crucial feature of our over-all sense of things, namely the personal relation of trust and confidence in God, rather than to our motives for taking this stance. It describes the content of our position, not the reasons for it. Of course, experience can bring an increase in our confidence in our stance. But we never move to a point beyond all anticipation, beyond all hunches, to the kind of certainty that we can enjoy in certain narrower questions, say, in natural science or ordinary life. (ibid., 551).

So, a secular nonreligious humanist, although related with his sources of good, is not described by Taylor as *having faith*. In the same way, communities ruled by a strong belief that is not religious/spiritual in the proper sense (ideologies, extreme nationalisms) do not fall in any sense under the category of faith for Taylor.

13. Ibid., 602–7. Of course, under the qualification of unbelief fall also those examples of church chauvinism that Taylor rejects completely, as well as any kind of secular understanding of life, either social or political. As we have seen with Cavanaugh, however, a strict interpretation of the term *religion* is at risk of being antihistorical and insufficient to achieve a proper cultural analysis.

14. Taylor, *Hegel*, 482.

Later, he continues:

> We can see why religion has a continuing role if we remember that it has three dimensions, not only knowledge of God, not only cult, but also devotion, feeling. Religion unites man to the absolute in heart and sensibility.[15]

In this sense, Taylor's work is also an attempt to describe how religion, as a social form, is, essentially, inescapable.[16] Again, in *A Secular Age*, we read:

> ... all the above shows that the religious dimension is inescapable. Perhaps there is only the choice between good and bad religion... But an analogous point to the one just made about humanism can be made about these religious positions. Just adopting some religion, even an in principle "good" one, doesn't do the trick... Where does this leave us in our search for a third kind of measure in our programme?[17]

Taylor's project to achieve this third kind of measure is the affirmation of a new kind of Western/modern sensibility that is able to go beyond the mere categorization of groups while at the same time retaining the religious sensibility toward the transcendence. In either case, this theoretical development transforms religion in a historical category of human culture. Religion becomes, in this way, a necessary function, a persistent anthropological constant, that defines any sense of attachment towards *transcendental* sources of values.[18] The description of religion provided by Taylor is extremely similar to the one provided by Hegel. For Hegel, religions are forms of expression of the consciousness of the *Absolute Spirit*.[19] Its content is in the form of pure thought, although it is not self-consciousness of the Spirit,

---

15. Ibid., 486. According to Hegel the last, and perfect, conclusion of the dialectical process would have been the *philosophy* as a perfect *self-consciousness* of the spirit through *reason*. Taylor clearly rejects this ontological aspect of the Hegelian philosophy. However, the concept of religion as the *connection* to the absolute is, in my opinion, a recurrent theme in Taylor's philosophy and a clear reference to Hegelian categories.

16 Ibid., 708–10.

17 Ibid., 708.

18. Consequently, religion becomes precisely what Cavanaugh criticized, a *genus*, a sociological instrument that tries to define almost mathematically what is *religious* and what is not.

Consequently, the concepts and languages tied to religion (faith, theology, eschatology, etc.) become restricted in their field of application so that it is not possible to talk about a political theology or about the sense of the sacred in secular structure and in nonreligious groups.

19. Hegel, *Phenomenology of Spirit*, 321.

but merely our incomplete consciousness of it.[20] This concept of limited consciousness is important because, for Hegel, such is the nature of faith in the cultural world. For this reason, faith, as limited consciousness, can only be expressed through the religious phenomenon, which is not a fully rational stage of human existence.[21] Hegel, then, placed the Enlightenment (as an ideology of reason) in symmetrical opposition to faith (as religion of the absolute). In Hegel's dialectics both religion and the Enlightenment represent the same phenomenon, which is the process of self-consciousness of the *Absolute Spirit*, but from two antithetical poles.[22] However, precisely because of the dialectical movement, they are able to attain only a partial self-consciousness of the spirit, a fact that contributes to their antithetical opposition.[23] In this dialectical process, for both Taylor and Hegel, religious consciousness is a necessary and inescapable category of human culture, a constant that *has to* happen. The reason being that religion grasps specific

---

20. In the *Absolute Spirit*, every form represents a dialectical moment in the relation between finite and infinite: in art, the infinite is declined in the finite; in *religion*, there is opposition between the two and, in the end, in philosophy we obtain the fusion between finite and infinite. Religion is, for Hegel, a *relation with the infinite* in an incomplete form; it can be described as *devotion* (*Andacht*). It is a longing for the infinite beyond us that is realized through feelings and images, without the complete realization through reason.

The *Andacht* is not a precise and determinate act; it is a *situation of the conscience*, and its limit is that the *Absolute Spirit* remains only an *image*, something that still retain a naïve character. However, nonetheless, it is a *necessary* and *extremely important* state of the conscience. The *Andacht*, whose primary source is the *Glaube*, the faith, create a relation with the absolute in a unique and special way, although still perceiving our separation from the Absolute Substance (God), we long to overcome this separation.

For an introduction about the dialectic relation between the different form of self-consciousness search in: Adorno, *Hegel*.

21. Hegel, *Phenomenology of Spirit*, 322.

22. Ibid., 322–55. The phenomenon is the historical dialectical movement of the Geist. The Enlightenment understood, rightly, the important role of subjective self-consciousness but limited this rationality only to the human level (completely disregarding the universal rationality of the Geist); Faith (*Glaube*) instead is a form of religious consciousness that projects the true reconciliation of spirit and reality, but this happens in another world. The error of faith is that it is unconscious of the nature of the spirit as an object of thought and understand it only through metaphor and images.

23. For Hegel, there is a cultural and dialectical relation between Christianity and Enlightenment. Christianity had the perception and the longing for the infinite, the Absolute Substance, but it sacrificed the individual reason for an enforced affirmation of the *Andacht*. The Enlightenment had the merit of reaffirming the dignity of the individual reason, but in doing so, sacrificed the infinite and postulated its nonexistence, thus forbidding the dialectical resolution of the individual in the Absolute Spirit through reason. Charles Taylor dedicates extremely detailed explanations about Hegel's criticism of the Enlightenment in his work *Hegel*, in the chapter "Reason and History" (389–27).

features of human life and appeal to specific forms of consciousness. In the Hegelian dialectic, religion is a necessary stage in which the *Geist* is revealed in itself, but is still represented through images and representations of an infinite transcendent.[24] Faith is, in the Hegelian philosophy, a state of incomplete knowledge of Geist, a state in which the process of consciousness of the Geist is still insubstantial. It still represents an inferior stage of self-consciousness in respect to the one attained through reason.[25]

Taylor articulates this fundamental difference between religion and nonreligion through the concept of social imaginary, a vital concept in his philosophical work. Taylor gives the reaffirmation of this genetic difference between secularity and religion by explaining how our social imaginary changed in the modern era. As he explains in *Modern Social Imaginaries*, we can understand a social imaginary as:

> Something much broader and deeper that the intellectual schemes people may entertain when they think about social reality in a disengaged mode. I am thinking, rather, of the ways people imagine their social existence, how they fit together with others, how things go on between them and their fellows, the expectations that are normally met, and the deeper normative notions and images that underlie these expectations.[26]

The social imaginary is not a social theory. It is an epistemic structure through which human beings interpret their relations with, and within, their society. It is not only a simple scheme of relation, a collection of beliefs about the common life. It incorporates some sense of how we all fit together, both on a social and a normative plane. Through our social imaginary, we have a sense of how social things go and how should they go. This generates in us the perception of what steps are acceptable, and which ones, instead, are against the social practice, both in a factual and normative way.[27] At the same time, however, the social imaginary is not described as a *Weltanschauung*, as a worldview. I believe the definition of the social imaginary as an

---

24. Hegel, *Phenomenology of Spirit*, 416.

25. Ibid., 322–24. This may seem a contradiction to what said before on the conflict between Christianity and the Enlightenment. We have to keep in mind the difference between *Religion* as a dialectical stage of the self-consciousness of the Geist, and its *particular* realization in the field of History. In this sense, the conflict between Christianity and Enlightenment can be interpreted as a failed resolution of the category of *religion* in the category of *philosophy of the Spirit*. For an introduction to the problem of the relation between Hegel's philosophy and Christianity, search in: Caird, *Hegel*; also Stepelevich, "Hegel and Roman Catholicism."

26. Taylor, *Modern Social Imaginaries*, 23.

27. Ibid., 25–26.

epistemic structure is most appropriate. Taylor is not interested in describing the social imaginary as connected to an ontology of the world. He describes the social imaginary as a filter through which we understand our web of social relations in a given neutral world and in a specific cultural context. It identifies the fundamental social structure that allow social relations to make sense, but Taylor does not describe it as connected with an ontology as such. In *A Secular Age*, the social imaginary provides a sense of *how things should go*, not of *how things are*. For this reason, Taylor inscribes the social imaginary in the progressivist dialectic of thesis and antithesis. Since the social imaginary is just an epistemic structure, it obeys to the fundamental law of progression of Hegelian dialectics and German philosophical anthropology. Every epoch represents an epistemic gain in comparison to the previous ones; it understands a neutral world better. Like Hegel, Taylor retains an understanding of religion as an incomplete epistemic structure, although he removes any reference to a cosmic spirit.

According to Taylor, the processes involved in the transformation of social imaginary are not necessarily linear and do not need, at least at the moment of their origin, institutional support. A social imaginary can start as a set of claims belonging to a restricted group niche and then expand to embrace the whole community. This is what happened in the modern age, through the theories of Locke and Grotius.[28] Thanks to Locke's philosophy of nature and Grotius' view of normative order, modern society acquired, slowly but steadily, the sensibility that society exists for the mutual benefit of the individuals and to protect their rights.[29] A new picture of society was, thus, developed, one in which individuals come together to form a political entity against certain preexisting moral backgrounds and with certain ends in view. In modernity, the moral background, or source, was one of natural rights, where the people already have certain moral obligations toward each other, while the ends sought were certain common benefits, of which security was the most important.[30] In the specific case of modernity, the new social structure—with its underlying concept of moral order—influenced the development of modern society along three axes. First, in extension—starting from a restricted niche of thinkers and philosophers, it has influenced the social discourse in other niches until it has encompassed the whole of Western communities. Second, in intensity—the demands we make on society became more complex and ramified. In addition, lastly, in the demands society itself makes on us—while making our demands, it is

---

28. Ibid., 24.
29. Ibid., 4.
30. Ibid., 4–8.

incumbent on us to take some kind of action or attitude as a counterpart, as a duty.³¹ These three axes of modification also involved a separation of the modern moral order from any kind of connection to a transcendent source of good. The premodern understandings of moral order (egalitarian, like the law of the people, or hierarchical, inspired from the platonic/Aristotelian philosophy) were connected to a transcendent order of the cosmos, such that a breach of the law was equivalent to a breach of the order of the cosmos itself. According to Taylor, the modern moral order had no such ontic or cosmic reference, it was an order made for the here and now.³²

It is within this enormous transformation of social imaginary that Taylor identifies three, very specific, forms of social self-understanding as social imaginaries born from Locke's and Grotius' theories of moral order. The first one has been *Economy*, which came to be considered as an objectified reality. Taylor finds the greatest example of this new development in Adam Smith's theory of the *invisible hand*. Where economy becomes the fundamental model of society,³³ not only as a metaphor, but also as the dominant end of human activity.³⁴ The second social imaginary was the public sphere. This concept indicates not only the official sphere of government, but communication in society as a whole. The public sphere is a common space in which members of society have to meet through a variety of media. In addition, communication is not only present between members of society, but also between media themselves.³⁵ The public sphere is

31. Ibid., 6–7.

32. Ibid., 10–11. The difference is a great one, while the previous concept of moral order stated that the individual is complementary to the whole, so that the first task of the single is to work to preserve the community, with the modern concept of people and moral order the relation is reversed, it is now the individual that should be preserved, and the purpose of the society is to guarantee his safety.

33. Ibid., 69–71. Economy was obviously linked with the self-understanding of polite civilizations as grounded in a commercial society. However, in the eighteenth century is added an appreciation of the way human life is designed to produce mutual benefit. Emphasis is put on the *invisible hand* factor. With this, Taylor means the theory in which we are supposed to be *programmed* to commit to specific actions and attitudes that have, systematically, beneficent results for the general happiness. Adam Smith, in the *Wealth of Nations*, provides us with the better example of this mechanism.

This new understanding of providence is already evident in Locke's formulation of natural law theory in the *Second Treatise*; we can see how much importance the economic dimension is taking on in the new notion of order. The two main goals of an organized society become, therefore, security and economic prosperity. This lead to a study of economy as an objectified reality with its law and mechanism, as object of *science*; but this also determine the complete independence of economy from the political plane.

34. Ibid., 72.

35. Ibid., 83.

so important that, even in conditions were it is controlled or abolished, its existence is still faked[36] to attain control on the population. We have come to consider this space as distinct from the political space, and, at the same time, a benchmark of legitimacy for the political authority.[37] The final social imaginary has been popular sovereignty. The two great revolutions of the eighteenth century (French and American) created the conditions for the interplay of social imaginaries, new and traditional, which helped determine their respective courses and culminated with the affirmation of popular sovereignty. According to Taylor, revolutionary brutality made it possible for ideologies, that found support only in minor circles (like the republican theory of Rousseau), to spread among people. This generated the development of the new social imaginary in which the legitimization of the power resides in the population.[38] From a vertical society, so, we shifted to a horizontal society.[39]

---

36. Ibid., 83–85.

37. Ibid., 86–99. Taylor describe the public sphere as a *metatopical common space*; a topical common space is a space where people come together in a common act of focus for whatever purpose (a ritual, a conversation, the celebration of a major event, etc...). A metatopical common space transcends such topical spaces; it knits together a plurality of such spaces into one larger space of nonassembly.

38. Ibid., 109–41. Taylor considers the American Revolution as the result of a shift in a traditional social imaginary. The reigning notions of legitimacy in Britain and America, the ones that fired the English Civil War as well as the beginning of the colonies' rebellion, were backward looking. They turned around the idea of an ancient constitution, an order based on law holding since time out of mind, in which Parliament had its rightful place beside the king. This older idea emerges from the American Revolution transformed into a full-fledged foundation in popular sovereignty.

Quite different was the case in the French Revolution. The French case was a range of theories influenced by Rousseau. These had two features that were fateful for the course of the Revolution: the conception of *la volonté générale* and the concept of *le moi commun*. The fact that these theories, although diffused in a circle of nobles and bourgeois, could not become a common social imaginary is a cause of the failure of French Revolution. The other cause has to be found in the inherent problems present in Rousseau's conceptions.

39. Ibid., 154–61. Essentially, Taylor examines the shift that led to a society in which the order was guaranteed by a transcendental order, to a society in which the order is achieved by common action, as in the secular age. Taylor calls this new form of society, created in the contemporary age, a *direct-access society*. With this term, he means to indicate a society where everyone sees himself as part of the worldwide audience of media.

Taylor affirms that the new concept of moral order started from a niche and became the criterion for the political action of the elites, at some point it became the common rule followed by the whole of society, thus not needing any more a strict normative enforcement. This is affirmed by Taylor both in *Modern Social Imaginaries* and in *A Secular Age*.

Taylor's historical analysis is a very refined form of sociological Hegelianism. In addition to the similar interpretation of religion, the two philosophers share another fundamental similarity, which is found through a comparison between the concept of social imaginary and the Hegelian concept of *Sittlichkeit*. The concept of *Sittlichkeit* is difficult to translate in other languages,[40] it indicates the moral obligations we possess toward an ongoing community of which we are members. The *Sittlichkeit* refers to a common life that already exists. It also contributes to the constitution of the *sittlich*[41] of an individual. It is by virtue of this ethical order being an ongoing affair that the individual possesses these obligations. The fulfillment of these obligations is what sustains the ethical order and maintains its existence. This ethical order is, therefore, different from *Moralität*,[42] in which the individual has an obligation to realize something which does not exist, that may even be in contrast with the existing moral order. The obligations provided by *moralität* bind the individual not by virtue of being part of a larger community, but as an individual and rational will.[43] For Hegel *Sittlichkeit*, the world of common customs or shared life, is extremely important for the development of an ethic of the duty, a philosophical trait that Taylor has inherited. The *Ethos* of the individual has its source in the customs.[44] For this reason, the customs are described by Hegel as a *zweite*

---

40. It could be translated as *objective ethics*, *ethical life*, or *concrete ethics*; but none of these translations would be adequate. In Italian, we render this concept simply with *morality*, knowing fully that this is a limitation of the Hegelian concept. Perhaps the best translation would be *rectitude*, intended with its most strong sense from the Latin term *rectitudo*.

41. With the term *Sittlich*, we mean the ethicality of the single individual, whose source Hegel collocates in the *Sittlichkeit*, the common customs. In a few words, the source to develop the ethics of the single individual has to be found in the common customs of his cultural background.

For a discussion of the Hegelian *Sittlichkeit* search in Ferrarin, *Hegel and Aristotle*, 325–72. Also Singer, *Hegel*, 24–44. Particularly interesting is Singer's criticism against the principles of neoliberal economy using Hegelian categories.

42. Hegel uses the term *Moralität* in its Kantian sense, and it is precisely the Kantian interpretation of morality that Hegel desires to criticize. For Hegel, Kant made the error to consider human will (in this, following the Enlightenment tradition) as a rational will that can be separated completely by its surrounding cultural background, perpetuating the concept of *absolute freedom* that led the French Revolution to failure and that is intrinsically impossible to realize in actual practice.

43. Hegel, *Elements of the Philosophy of Right*, 193

44. This because the *ethos*, the ethical consciousness, can be realized only in the social life and find its highest objective in the state system.

Hegel is polemic against the Kantian concept of individual morality, as it considers only the *moral intention*, not the actual reality, creating a conflict between *being* and *having-to-be*, making morality like a duel in front of a mirror, rationally without solution.

Natur, a second nature that permeates the purely natural will and creates the substance of the ethical mind.[45]

In his work *Hegel and Modern Society*, Taylor describes how, for Hegel, the fulfillment of morality is reached when society reaches a superior state of *Sittlichkeit*.[46] Taylor focuses on the fact that, when we discuss human identity, we always discuss a culturally situated phenomenon. We can think about a single individual in abstraction from his community only as an organism, but when we develop thoughts about a human being, we also think about related sets of ways to experience the world, which are culturally produced and that form his identity. "What we are as human beings," Taylor says, "we are only in a cultural community."[47] Taylor's historical analysis shares with Hegel's method the structural deficiency of using abstract categories (that are historically developed) as objective and neutral definition of reality; in Taylor's case secularity and religion, or transcendence and immanence. The use of such categories, in Taylor's system, aims to develop a triadic movement in history that aims to the recovery of the transcendent in the final synthesis between secularity and religion. Taylor, in his work *Hegel*, gives substantial evidence to support the dialectic movement as a valid sociological argument. If we remove any theological/ontological claim from it, he affirms that the dialectic movement preserves its usefulness for historical/sociological analysis. In the chapter dedicated to the *dialectic of consciousness*, in fact, we can read:

> We shall see a parallel with Hegel's dialectical arguments, both historical and ontological, which always operate with three terms, the true purpose or standard, an inadequate conception of it, and the reality where they meet and separate. We can thus see how a Hegelian dialectic can get started without our having to accept at the outset Hegel's entire vision. We only need to find

---

Hegel denies that there is a natural law, a law that is preexisting in respect to the laws set forth by the state. According to Hegel, morality is not a personal matter; it is not a relationship with an absolute law nor a relationship with a Destiny. Humans can achieve an ethical consciousness only through the dialectical process that starts in the category of the *family*, find its antithesis in the *civil society* and is fully realized in the *state as synthesis*. According to Hegel, we reach ethical achievements only through social phenomena.

45. Hegel, *Elements of the Philosophy of Right*, 108–9.

46. Taylor, *Hegel and Modern Society*, 82–84. In putting the *Sittlichkeit* as the highest level of morality, Taylor affirms that Hegel is clearly following an Aristotelian concept of politics (as also Aristotle believed that society is the minimum self-sufficient human reality).

47. Ibid., 87.

a starting point whereby some finite reality is to be seen as the (attempted) realization of a goal or fulfilment of a standard.[48]

Of course, Taylor does not use the dialectic movement in his historical/sociological constructions in the same straightforward way Hegel did. Taylor does acknowledge that every epoch and transition between epochs represents a complex constellation of relations and mutual influences.[49] Nonetheless, the general triadic structure is preserved in his rigid understanding of concepts used to explain social reality, for example religion as transcendence and secularity as immanence. An understanding that preserves the dialectic of thesis/antithesis aimed to a synthesis. Taylor's narrative is still a dialectic movement of history, a complex dialectic, but still a dialectic nonetheless. It is by virtue of this dialectic that Taylor affirms that "modernity was an epoch without precedent,"[50] and not just because of his connections with the German tradition of philosophical anthropology. Like the antithesis, that finds its own origin from an internal contradiction of the thesis, the internal contradictions of the previous Christian/religious era, pressed to their extremes, unleashed the chaos of religious wars in Europe, thus causing the elites to search a new source of legitimization outside religious authority.[51] Secularity represented both the general

48. Taylor, *Hegel*, 134.

49. An example of this can be found in *A Secular Age*, in the chapter "The Spectre of Idealism" (212–19). In this chapter Charles Taylor objects to the critics about being an *idealist* philosopher. He claims that it is impossible to determinate the causes of the historical events as only *material* or *ideal*. In this, then, both *Marxist* and *idealistic* philosophers were wrong. Historical events are determined by a *nexus of both material and ideal causes* that is event by event different.

In this sense, then, history is determined both by *material* (economic/structural) causes and *ideal* (philosophies, ideologies, religions) causes that are mixed in a different degree in every historical moment. In this sense, then, even if we can depict Taylor's history as a *dialectical movement*, we cannot assume the same direct connectivity that exists in the *Hegelian dialectic*; in this, Taylor declines the dialectic in a more complex way than Hegel does.

50. Ibid., 218.

51. Taylor, *Secular Age*. Taylor focuses in the first chapter of his book ("The Bulwark of Belief," 25–89) on the phenomenon of the disenchanting that began to detach the humans from their enchanted world.

In the second chapter ("The Rise of Disciplinary Society," 90–145) Taylor focuses on the shift from the common interest of the believers in a dimension of faith that was fully transcendental to one that focuses more and more on an independent nature; on the social side this corresponded to the increased importance of the notion of civility. In the third chapter ("The Great Disembedding," 146–58), Taylor describes the process of disembedding that led society to replace the order of the Middle Ages, composed by ambivalent complementarities (worldly order and churches, proper order and carnivals) with a fully pervasive order, uncompromising and coherent.

antithesis of religion and the synthesis of the contradictions existing within the previous social framework. However, secularity itself is haunted both by its own internal contradictions and by its ongoing conflict with the religious framework. From this dialectic interpretation of our past and present, Taylor finds the only answer in a final synthesis, which would represent both an overcoming of the internal contradictions of secularity and of the overarching contradiction between secularity and religion. The Hegelian triadic movement is still present in all its strength and rigidity.

In Taylor's narrative, there is the premodern, Christian, era as the thesis. A coherent phenomenon, a consistent social imaginary that has preserved the social balance and integrity around the transcendent sources of good, like God or the cosmic order. Such phenomenon develops its own institutions and languages to represent itself and excludes certain other phenomena, perceived as rival, to present itself as a static entity. However, the internal contradiction of the thesis produced its antithesis. The second moment is the reversal of Christianity into its opposite. A stage in which religious legitimization and the religious interpretation of the world is rejected in favor of a naturalistic and secular view of the world. This is proved further by Taylor's inability, despite his best attempt, to provide a convincing description of secularity as an additive and positive phenomenon. The presentation of secularity as a loss of transcendence, a negation of religious transcendence toward the immanent further reinforces its interpretation as an antithesis. The third moment is the unification of opposites, the synthesis. Which is Taylor's proposal of a rediscovery of spiritual search as a way to fullness in a way that goes in accordance with the secular framework. Secularism could not suppress the *quest for transcendence*, however, at the same time, could not simply accept religious faith in its naïve nature. The solution is to free transcendence from a strict theological interpretation of the world, typical of the premodern era, and combine the religious aspiration to the transcendent with the legitimate request of the immanent advanced through modernity. I see, in Taylor's historical interpretation a proposal that focuses on the dialectical process of thesis, antithesis and synthesis, a strong Hegelian structure. Of course, I would like to remind that Taylor rejects all of the Hegelian theology/ontology. He does not believe in the social imaginary or the framework as possessing an ontological charge, nor does he believe in the existence of a cosmic *Geist*. However, although not connected with any kind of theory of the *Geist*, Taylor's idea of society develops through a dialectical movement of continuous crises and overcoming of those crises.

At the same time, however, I would not describe Taylor as a Marxist philosopher. Of course, Marxist philosophers are, inevitably, also Hegelian philosophers; nonetheless, Taylor does not fit such category. He explicitly criticizes any kind of Marxist understanding of history that reduces historical events only to their material causes. It is true that, as well as Marxist philosophers, Taylor reject all of Hegel's ontology, but there is, in my opinion, a strong difference between Taylor's account history and a Marxist one. In assigning only to material causes the causal power in history, Marxist philosopher do not take only a position in philosophy of history, but also in ontology. The negation that there are no ideal or ontological causes is an ontological assumption in itself. Taylor's assumption is radically different; he rejects Hegel's ontology but not ontology altogether. In Taylor's work, there is not any reference to a cosmic Spirit, but there is for sure a reference to what humans are in their cultural life and social interactions, and there is also reference to the history-shaping power of ideas. For these reason I would not describe Taylor as a Marxist philosopher, his kind of Hegelianism is more complex than that. However, with this being said, it is undeniable that Hegelianism plays an important role in Taylor's philosophy. The historical change is caused by the overall negation of the previous *Sittlichkeit* that is no longer able to convey meaning. The crises are still symptoms of a major dialectical conflict.

TAYLOR'S TRIADIC STRUCTURE AND ITS CRITICISM THROUGH CROCE'S DIALECTIC OF DISTINCTS

Holding true that Hegel's philosophy is a strong influence on Taylor's historical narrative, then, the criticism that can be applied against Hegel's system retains its validity against Taylor's philosophy as well. In Taylor's specific case, it is possible to present two major critiques to his dialectical structures. The first is that Taylor, in his attempt to develop a consistent narrative of secularity, ends up submitting the hermeneutics to the dialectic. That is, the identification of an ideal sequence of events becomes in itself an all-encompassing explanation of the phenomenon of secularity so that we submit human contingencies to logical categories of explanation. The second criticism is a consequence of the first; Taylor proposes a Hegelian triadic structure of reality that reinforces the phenomenon of negation and the sense of substantial difference between the social phenomena of religion and secularity.[52] In this way, the intended synthesis between the two becomes an inconsistent result; it does not follow logically from the premises.

---

52. Secularity becomes an expression of the category *immanence*, religion an expression of *transcendence*. Secularity then, as the solution developed through the inner contradiction of Christianity can be understood only as the *negation* of Christianity.

Taylor, in his work on Hegel, has correctly interpreted that the Hegelian system has to be understood not only as a further development of Kantian idealism, but also as a development of the metacritique of Kant carried out by Hamann and Herder.[53] While Kant and his successors were concerned with the activity of the thinking subject in his own internal categories of consciousness, Hamann and Herder were concerned with the external modifications made by humanity through art and language. They correctly understood that there could not be thought—and therefore, no thinking subject—outside these spheres. The knowledge we have of ourselves is strictly related to the knowledge we have about the world, precisely because both are expressed through language. In this sense, Hegel—and consequently, Taylor—correctly understood that the phenomenon called human is always a *culturally situated phenomenon*.[54] This is a point that I consider self-evident as well. In Hegel's phenomenology, human thought and subjectivity evolve only through cultural production, which involves a series of interactions between a subject and the world around him, and between a subject and other human beings.[55] In this sense, Taylor, by admitting the different mixture of material and ideal causes in determining social phenomena, is maintaining a Hegelian paradigm.

However, this paradigm presents a major flaw, which is a direct consequence of its dialectical structure. I believe that John Milbank, in his *Theology and Social Theory*, discerns correctly the nature of this major flaw: Hegelian logic is unable to conceive difference as the consequence of an alternative analysis, or the unfolding of a series of events. It must imply, instead, a contradiction or denial of an ultimate, given, identity:[56]

> In consequence, difference cannot here result (as for neo-Platonism, stoicism and Leibniz) from analysis, or the unfolding of a series, but must imply contradiction, or denial of the ultimate identity. This could only have been avoided if Hegel had stepped out of panlogicism and simply admitted 'other' identities: but this he was not prepared to do. As a result, difference cannot, for Hegel, result either from analysis or from simple 'positive' assertion: instead, the initiative lies with negation. And this coalesces nicely with the fiction of a polarity between subject and object; these are not, for Hegel, commensurable, but nor are they merely two different things to which one might add a third: on the contrary, they are comprehensive, totalizing genera. One

---

53. Taylor, *Hegel*, 107–33.
54. Taylor, *Hegel and Modern Society*, 85–90.
55. Hegel, *Phenomenology of Spirit*, 73–76.
56. Milbank, *Theology and Social Theory*, 153–58.

can only relate them in terms of opposition, and only derive a separate object from an all-sufficient subject by means of a denial.[57]

As a result, reality becomes a game of polarities. There are not structures of difference in which we can simply add another term. Difference, instead, always imply the distinction of two contradicting terms and the exclusion of one of them. The categories of identity and contradiction encompass the various social phenomena, generating an interpretation of history and society that can see only a relation of conflict between historical/social events. The consequences on Taylor's narrative—in which he tries to apply Hegelian concepts to an historical/sociological narrative—are that events become understandable only in terms of opposition. One can derive a separate object only as a term of denial of a previous all-sufficient subject. Because of its stronger initiative, negation has always to be determinate negation, in the sense that it always negates a specific subject. In doing so, the crisis leads itself to a new positive upshot. Through this structure, history assumes a characteristic of inevitability and necessity that leads from one moment to another by virtue of the contradiction between them. Milbank is right in criticizing Taylor in his attempt to use this feature of Hegelian logic as a viable instrument for historical/sociological analysis, without adequately attending to the problems involved.[58] The risk implied in all Hegelian philosophical systems is to assume a situated cultural value as the rational foundation of historical events—for example freedom, or the good. Events are then understood only as the unraveling of such value through the dialectic of thesis/antithesis. In this way, Hegelian systems become the affirmation of a situated historical/cultural identity, or concept, as the universal foundation of human history. The assumption that history finds its ultimate end in the realization of a universal value leads the dialectic structure to assume more importance than the hermeneutic moment. The interpretation of the historical/sociological facts becomes merely the support to further the deployment of a historical preunderstanding.

This problematic feature of Hegelian narrations is evident in Taylor's narrative as well. In fact, at the end of both *Hegel and Modern Society* and *Hegel*, Taylor discusses the relevance of Hegel's system for contemporary philosophical, historical and sociological analyses. Taylor focuses his attention especially on the concept of situated freedom. That is, a concept of freedom that escapes the contradictions of the Kantian absolute and

57. Ibid., 156.
58. Ibid., 157–58.

self-dependent will[59] by accepting its own defining situation.[60] Hegel's philosophy, for Taylor, is still relevant to us because of its concept of the human being as a situated phenomenon in culture, language and society. Through these spheres of life, humanity tries to achieve a higher degree of freedom. In pursuing a philosophical analysis of this phenomenon, as Taylor affirms,[61] Hegel gives us the best attempts to work out a vision of embodied subjectivity. This concept of situated freedom is connected, in my opinion, to what Taylor describes, in *A Secular Age*, as the never-ending human research for a sense of fullness. We can read, in fact:

> We all see our lives, and/or the space wherein we live our lives, as having a certain moral/spiritual shape. Somewhere, in some activity, or condition, lies a fullness, a richness; that is, in that place (activity or condition), life is fuller, richer, deeper, more worthwhile, more admirable, more what it should be. This is perhaps a place of power: we often experience this as deeply moving, as inspiring. Perhaps this sense of fullness is something we just catch glimpses of from afar off; we have the powerful intuition of what fullness would be, were we to be in that condition, e.g., of peace or wholeness; or able to act on that level, of integrity or generosity or abandonment or self-forgetfulness.[62]

The sense of fullness that Taylor describes in *A Secular Age* is clearly not something abstract. While being a state of being of a higher degree, it is, at the same time, always rooted in our living condition. As Taylor describes it, the moment in which our sense of fullness is fully attained is a moment in which our embodied subjectivity is able to reach, through the experiencing of our given social/historical situation, a better understanding of our own nature and to further elevate it. The importance that Taylor gives to the social imaginary and the processes through which it changes are finalized to the improvement of this embodied understanding of our own lives.[63] However this also represents the affirmation of the existence of a rational superstructure underlying historical and social developments. Taylor admits that the self-dependent absolute will does not exist as pure freedom, but is always embodied subject. However, at the same time even

---

59. Taylor, *Hegel*, 561–64. The first being *emptiness*, in the sense that the maximum amount of freedom would be the demolition of *every situation* that could represent a restraint to human will, therefore, generating a void space of being.

60. Ibid., 563.

61. Taylor, *Hegel and Modern Society*, 168.

62. Taylor, *Secular Age*, 5.

63. Ibid., 175.

this embodied subject is described as possessing a defining nature, freedom, or a natural tendency to achieve a sense of fullness. Because of this defining nature, it will always try to achieve a more perfect and superior expression of it. Taylor, in inheriting Hegel's theory of the situated subject, is also inheriting its main flaw, that is, the presumption of having a rational principle underlying social/historical developments.[64]

Milbank's criticism reveals a problematic aspect of Hegel's logic—and, by consequence, of Taylor's. However, there is more to be said about Hegel's philosophical system. Hegel's thought possesses important features that even Milbank, in his criticism, has missed. Moreover, even though through different means, Milbank does retain a sense of deep incommunicability between religion and secularity.[65] Hegel's, and Taylor's, philosophical structures are aimed to achieve a sense of unity in their ontological and/or historical narrative. The dialectic of thesis/antithesis is functional to this achievement. Milbank has criticized correctly the importance of the negative moment in the dialectic structure. However, he has not dedicated enough attention to a proper criticism to the concept of synthesis, and the role it plays as the purpose of the dialectical movement. A consistent criticism of dialectic can be achieved only by analyzing the possibility itself of a synthesis as an intended historical result, or unintended production of the hetero-genesis of ends. Milbank has not considered enough this part of the dialectic movement, simply because he deems such synthesis impossible in the first place. Contrarily to Milbank, I believe that the Hegelian system, despite its imperfections, is able to provide us with useful tools to understand our cultural development. However, against Taylor, I also believe that

---

64. In the same way, for example, Milbank, in *The World Made Strange*, 125, criticizes the Hegelian concept of heterogenesis of ends, in which human historical formations, despite escaping their original intended purpose, yet answer to some unintelligible superior purpose. In proposing his account of social imaginary as a way to achieve a better sense of fullness, Taylor is dangerously approaching this interpretation of the heterogenesis of ends.

A better account (and Milbank would probably agree) would be the one given by Vico: the heterogenesis is described as a poetic moment in which we are, at the same time, responsible and not responsible of our action. A moment in which we open ourselves both to the possibility of civility and its corruption, or, in Milbank's words, to the possibility of grace and sinful corruption, without having to imply a preexistent tendency or invisible hand or fall into a radical determinism.

65. In a sense, I believe it would be possible to affirm that Milbank as well, while claiming the contingency of secularism and the fact that it is culturally produced like other social phenomena (thus rejecting its inevitability and necessity), still retains the dualistic interpretation immanence/transcendence like Taylor does. In this way, Milbank is unable to escape the great prejudice that sees religion and secularity as appealing to different resources of the human mind.

Hegelian dialectic needs a further refinement, and not just the removal of its theological/ontological claims, to become a useful philosophical instrument. To seek this further refinement of Hegel's philosophy, I turn to Benedetto Croce's work *What Is Living and What Is Dead of the Philosophy of Hegel*.

Croce affirms that to *think dialectically*, and to think the *logical theory of dialectic*, are two distinct mental acts.[66] According to Benedetto Croce, it is true that Hegel, in his philosophical structure, gives primary importance to the negative moment. However, it is also true that his system contributed to reveal the abstract nature of some dualistic structures born from empirical sciences, perception and phenomenological sciences.[67] If the concepts developed in these dualistic structures were really distinct objects, we would face the problem of the connection of distinct features in a concrete concept. If they were really opposed, we would have the problem of the synthesis of oppositions as an impossible result. Through Hegel's system, we understand that such distinctions are not real oppositions, they become such only in the moment of abstract knowledge of the subject. Their critique, that has to be negative, moves along a different principle of a positive dialectic.[68] The abstract distinctions of categories are, in fact, not conceivable as reality. Every attempt to solve dialectical dualities through the predominance of one term over the other ends up recreating the other term through different means.[69]

---

66. Croce, *What Is Living*, 37.

67. Ibid., 37. These sciences, just because they are immersed in phenomena, whenever they attempt to rise to the universal are compelled to break up reality into: appearance and essence, external and internal, accident and substance, manifestation and force, finite and infinite, many and one, sensible and supersensible, matter and spirit, and such like terms. If these terms are considered as truly distinct (or if they truly designated distinct objects), they would give rise to philosophical problems.

68. Ibid., 38.

69. Ibid., 38. Quoting Croce:

> Materialism preserves the phenomenon, matter, the finite, the sensible, the external, etc.; but, since that term is naturally so constituted as to require its other, the infinite appears again in that finite, assuming the form of a quantitative infinite, of a finite from which another finite is born, then another finite, then another, to infinity. This is what Hegel called the false or bad infinite. Supernaturalism preserves the other term as sole reality; but essence without appearance, the internal without the external, and the infinite without the finite, become something inscrutable and unknowable. Here appears the thing-in-itself, which would better be called vacuity in itself: the great mystery, which {Hegel says} is a very easy thing to know; because not only is the thing-in-itself not outside thought, but on the contrary is a product of thought, of thought which has been pushed on to pure abstraction, and which takes as its object empty identity with itself. The thing-in-itself, from its very inanity,

Applied to historical/sociological studies, this principle confirms that only the careful consideration of both material and ideal causes can give a proper account of the events.[70] Moreover, Croce admits that a dialectic process, to be functional, necessarily needs a process of *opposition between terms*.[71] The reason being that it is only through opposition that reality can unfold. However, we have to understand this concept of *reality through opposition* on a very specific level. We have to understand this process as a construction of *cultural categories*.[72] If we understand the problem in these terms, it is possible, according to Croce, to grasp the real meaning of the Hegelian statement "what is real is also rational, what is rational is also real." This process of creation of culture is a process through which we establish categories of reality by confronting such categories with their negation. For example, an irrational thought is not thought but the negation of thought. A horrible work of art is not art, but the negation of art. This is not to say that such negation is not real, it finds its material reality as negation of a category and not by becoming a category by itself.[73] In this sense, from an historical point of view, it becomes harder to qualify Hegelianism as a form of optimism or teleology. It is, instead, a philosophical system that tries to explain how we achieve the categories through which we evaluate our own environment,

---

leads back to the phenomenon, to the finite, to the external, as alone real and thinkable; and precisely in as much as it is phenomenon, it is finite and external.

70. In fact, a purely materialistic interpretation of history, like the Marxist one, while trying to be very materialistic, ends up relying on ideal concepts like *class conscience* and *bad conscience* (or concepts like *market* in the capitalist interpretation). A purely spiritual account of history, as the one Löwith tried to develop, has to rely on a rational abstraction of an omnipresent Christian eschatological mechanism, which becomes the sole force able to push forward history.

71. Ibid., 39–40.

72. Ibid., 39. As Croce says:

The negative is the spring of development; opposition is the very soul of the real. The lack of all contact with error is not thought and is not truth; but is the absence of thought, and therefore of truth. Innocence is a characteristic, not of action, but of inaction: he who acts, errs; he who acts is at grips with evil. A true felicity, a felicity that is truly human or manly, is not a beatitude that knows no suffering. Such a beatitude would be possible only to fatuity and imbecility; and the conditions of it find no place in the history of a world which, where strife is wanting (says Hegel), "shows its pages blank."

Croce means that, on the moment of thought and moral discernment, we operate a distinction between being and nonbeing (being thought, nonbeing moral, etc.). This distinction can operate only through a process of opposition, and is an inescapable moment in every process of culture creation.

73. Ibid., 40.

how we create cultural categories to interact with our world.[74] It explains the instruments through which we develop our own sense of rationality.[75] On this interpretation and appreciation of Hegelian philosophy, Croce would totally agree with Charles Taylor.

However, Croce admits that the predominance of the negative moment as the source of reality still represents a problem in Hegel's system. Because of this, we would struggle in obtaining a good interpretation of the introduction of difference in history and society.[76] A historical narrative that would justify the change only through opposition and conflict would be unacceptable and antihistorical. As we have seen, a concept of truth that is given by a different postulation, or interpretation, of reality is, in the Hegelian triadic system, *de facto* impossible. Croce, in his attempt to solve the problem of the predominance of negation in Hegel's system, after discussing what he believes is still valid, *alive*, in Hegel's philosophy, turns to what he believes is *dead* in his system.[77] Croce affirms that the first important thing that we should take notice, in examining Hegel's philosophy, is that we do not face just a problem of application.[78] We face also a fundamental philosophical error that threatens all the Hegelian and post-Hegelian

---

74. In this sense, for example, Milbank is wrong in accusing Hegel of justifying the existence of evil. Hegel, instead, justifies the function of evil in the moral process that allows us to actually conceive what is evil and what is good.

75. Ibid., 43–45. In fact, Hegel rejects the Kantian *Sollen*, a virtuous duty that is always disconnected from reality. At the same time, any political ideology is always involved in constructing its own sense of rationality, through which can call irrational its adversaries. In this sense, for Croce, there is much more similarity than difference between Vico and Hegel.

In the same way, for Vico, history is the identification of truth with fact, a truth that is always historical truth (in the sense of contingent) and a fact that is always historical fact (that is related with its contingent truth). As full knowledge is possible only on the things of which we are actually responsible during the process of creation, Vico can establish that history is the only science fully understandable and knowable by humankind.

76. In fact, William E. Connolly, in his work *Identity/Difference*, notices precisely this impossibility in Taylor's narrative. In developing his theory of the self as embedded in a set of prejudgments, Taylor always also uses a rhetoric style that implies the acknowledgment of truth that the self ascribes to these prejudgments.

Taylor's self, essentially, is unable to autonomously self-criticize its own prejudgments without the presence of a very different other that aims to destroy those prejudgments. Again, we fall into attributing historical reality to a principle of rationality that is, instead, always contextual and we conceive difference only as a conflict.

77. Ibid., 51–52.

78. Ibid., 51–52. So we could not say that Hegel's philosophical structures could be applied, as they are, just to specific branches of knowledge (like history, science, politics, etc.) and not in others.

systems. Having established that a dialectical process is necessary to create meaningful categories of reality, Croce affirms that the main flaw of Hegel's philosophical system is to be found in its process of classification, or, to use Croce's definition, in the relation between *distinct concepts*.

Hegelian systems are unable to provide a "meaningful distinction between concepts,"[79] in the sense that they are unable to distinguish a general spiritual (or historical) category from the sub-categories that compose it. Such sub-categories retain and preserve their own distinct reality that cannot be strictly identified with the general category with which they participate. Hegel's systems is, in a few words, unable to distinguish between different *degrees of reality*. In this way, Croce affirms that Hegel's system does not need a theory of universal classification, but a theory of degrees.

In Hegel's dialectic, we are presented with three terms: *A*, which is the thesis, *B*, which is the antithesis, and *C*, which represents the overcoming, or synthesis. In the dialectical relation, *B* defines its own conceptual nature only in its opposition to *A*. While *A* and *B* gain reality only in their own overcoming in *C*. We are establishing a relation of exclusion between abstract concepts. A relation between *genera* that exclude each other through opposition and long for a form of further fulfillment. However, precisely because of this relation, they can never exist as distinct concepts; they can only be thought and understood in their relation of opposition.[80] So far, we are not going further than Milbank's criticism. However, Croce identifies another risk in the dialectic movement. If reality would unfold purely through contradiction, it would reveal, within history, the presence of a suprahistorical principle that leads to a necessary progress. However, such acknowledgment implies that having attained to the state of *B*, every return to the previous state of *A* would be a regression to an inferior state of reality.[81] This would establish the inherent superiority of an epoch in respect to the previous ones, an attitude that can lead to historiographic arrogance.

---

79. Ibid., 53–54.

80. Ibid., 55–58.

81. Ibid., 57–59. Again, Croce refers here, primarily, to pure categories of the Spirit. In fact, how would it be possible to consider art, for example, as inferior to philosophy? While art may be of a lesser degree, in no way, for Croce, it would imply that art is inferior to philosophy. It would just mean, for him, that philosophy, in its own unfolding, has to imply also an artistic component.

Same relation between morality and economy; it is not that an action that seeks what is useful is necessarily inferior to a moral action; instead, a moral action also implies a degree of usefulness, because, for Croce, what is good is also useful.

Hegelian dialectic, instead, would always imply that the successive moment would be intrinsically superior to the previous one, and it would not be possible to go back to that specific moment. For example, once attained the philosophical moment it would

Applied to historical studies, this analytical structure does not provide acceptable interpretations. In Taylor's narrative, in fact, there is a relation of necessary contradiction between religion and secularity.[82] In addition, because secularity is the resolution to the inner contradictions of Christianity, there is the affirmation of secularity as a superior epistemic state, higher than religion. As modern secularity presents fewer contradictions, every attempt to revitalize religion is interpreted as an attempt to regress to a lesser state of civility.[83] I believe this becomes most clear if we examine Taylor's essay "What Does Secularism Mean?," Taylor does admit that the term secular can be extremely problematic. However, when he goes to analyze the origin of its meaning, he still describes it through the distinction between secularity and religion as the basic dyad through which the premodern society was organized. If religion referred to the transcendental level of existence, secularity referred to the immanent level of existence.[84] This dyad was internal during the premodern era,[85] and then became external with modernity.[86] Moreover, Taylor associates secularity with the concept of democracy as a necessary historical connection.[87] Democratic governments have to be secular in the sense that they must not operate preferences toward specific positions as a way to preserve and protect diversity. This, however, refers very strongly to certain political principles, like human rights, equality, rule of law and democracy.[88] In describing the question in these terms, however, Taylor is developing a very specific understanding of the relation between secularity and religion. While he admits that secular context are, indeed, at risk of fetishizing their own contexts and fixating

---

be impossible to produce pure art, a process that, for Croce, is a deep contradiction.

82. In which religion and secularity are considered as totalizing *genera* that are *equal to themselves in every part* (religion as the locus of transcendence, secularity as the locus of immanence), which is unrealistic in itself.

83. Which, paradoxically, would bring to a result opposite to the one Taylor aims to. However, his description of premodern Christianity as naïve faith could be interpreted as an unwilling support to this position.

84. Taylor, *Dilemmas and Connections*, 304.

85. In the sense that the two terms could not be conceived without each other.

86. In the sense that the two terms began to be seen as opposites. Ibid., 306–7.

87. Ibid., 309–11.

88. Ibid., 310. Taylor, for example, quotes Casanova's account of American Catholicism as a story of a group that, chastised as inassimilable in a liberal context, underwent evolution to adapt itself to the new context and improve. A similar thing could, and should, happen for Muslim communities. However, it could be said that this is just a reproposition of the dialectical structure of reality: where A is opposed by B and can undergo improvement only through the opposition constituted by B.

on religions as a privileged target,[89] he still believes that secular regimes have not born just to antagonize religion. Secularism is the *correct* answer to the issue of diversity and represents the attempt to maximize the basic goals of liberty and equality between basic beliefs.[90] It is simply a superior and more civilized way to understand and structure social life. If we refer these statements to the expanded history of secularity that Taylor proposes in *A Secular Age*, becomes evident how he ends up reproposing the totalizing triadic structure of history that Croce so much chastised in Hegel. In Taylor's narrative, modern secularity represents a superior state of civility from which we cannot go back, as every attempt to return to a premodern religious context would be a return to an inferior epistemic/social structure.

Croce's *theory of degrees* is vital for my argument precisely in this context. Because it would allow us to develop, within a post-Hegelian tradition, an alternative narrative that, while keeping some of Hegel's philosophical structures, would allow for a different interpretation of the history of Western cultures. In this sense, I believe Croce's theory of degrees offers valuable insights to historical/sociological studies as well. In the same way Taylor considers Hegelianism as a useful source of instruments for historical/sociological studies, I want to make a similar move with Croce's work and demonstrate how it can be a useful historical tool. Croce introduces his theory of degrees with an important statement, "The philosophical concept, the concrete universal or the Idea, is the synthesis of distinctives, just as it is the synthesis of opposites."[91] For example, we can speak about a spiritual activity or of a philosophical concept in a general way. However, we also can make a further distinction between all the different particular forms that are part of the specific activity/concept we are discussing. In addition, we must be careful to not confuse between particular forms and be able to distinguish them from each other.[92] Croce states that such a logic of *distinctives* cannot operate through a relation of opposition. Instead, it will work through a relation of implication. One distinctive will be related to the other not as something different, but as something united although separable on a conceptual level. To make Croce's proposal clearer, let us examine a logical example. We have the concept *A* that is inferior in degree in respect to the concept *B*. At the same time, because of their relation of implication, *A* is united to *B* yet distinct from it. Now we can assume that if we can examine

89. Ibid., 312–15.
90. Ibid., 311, 316–17.
91. Croce, *What Is Living*, 53.
92. Ibid., 53–54. As a preliminary example: we divide social activities in economics, sciences, arts, and ethics. In the same way, we divide academic subjects further into specific fields.

A without *B*, at the same time, we cannot examine *B* without *A*, as the superior term has to *imply* the inferior one. For every *B*, then, *A* is implied. As a practical example to show the application of this logical/philosophical structure to theoretical categories, Benedetto Croce offers us the example of the relation between *law* and *morality*. Every time we think about the concept of *law*, intended as a legal structure, we do not necessarily have to think about a concept of morality, but we cannot think about morality without also a concept of law.[93]

Before I present more examples, to show how such logical structure is relevant for historical studies, I want to note two things. First, we have to understand that Croce's *theory of degrees* is, primarily, a theory that was meant to be applied to the *categories of the Spirit*.[94] While Croce was critical of Hegel's concept of *Geist* as a pure transcendental principle, at the same time this criticism did not proceed so far to reject the concept of *Spirit* as a whole. For Croce, the *Spirit* unfolds itself through history and is understood *only in history*, not as a cosmic principle but as an historical one. The categories of the spirit, then, are *historical* categories, principles that can be discovered in their historical unfolding and that are understood in the way that is proper to the specific historical epoch. Second, Croce might have been surprised at the way I am applying his theory of degrees. An application that is separated from the concept of *Spirit* and applied to the categories of culture and framework. Croce would be particularly dissatisfied by the use of these terms, particularly of the latter. This because Croce was firmly against any kind of history that would reduce the fundamental freedom of the human being. For Croce, the history of the *Spirit* was primarily the history of freedom, and he would define any attempt to tell a story in which the

---

93. Ibid., 55–56. In the sense that moral reasoning always implies also a *legislative moment*. That is, the moral reasoning always claim a universal legitimacy for its own claims. To be able to understand this statement, we must understand that Croce has always been extremely critical of the *reason of state*.

In this sense, for Croce, morality is always also the process (either of an individual or of a group) to question and change the state from within as well. Croce abhorred a concept of politics independent from morality and negated the assumption that politics could only be the product of relations between states/political bodies. Thus, if the legal structure is certainly a reality that does not necessarily implies morality, morality, as a superior reality, always has to imply also a higher grade of political/legal life.

94. Ibid., 56. In fact the example Croce presents in this work regards the categories of art and philosophy as pure categories of the Spirit. Philosophy implies art, in the sense that every philosophy also possesses an artistic sense.

In this way, while we can have art that is not philosophy, we cannot possess a philosophy that is not artistic; the category of philosophy contains and resolves the category of art. In their historical development, they are unfolding of the *Spirit*.

culture or the framework play a causal role as *psychological historiography*, with a negative meaning.[95]

Croce's theory of degrees also had an influence on his historiographic method. Croce, in fact, possessed a historical sensibility that allowed him to distinguish between general concepts of definition and specific human cultural features that, although implied in those general concepts, were not fully identifiable with them. A first proof for such sensibility in Benedetto Croce's work is given, I believe, by the extreme liberality with which he used the term religion.[96] In *La Storia come Pensiero e Azione* Croce dedicates a paragraph to *religious historiography*.[97] In this paragraph, Croce makes a bold claim: every moral action that transcends the individual physiological-economic interest is *religious* in itself.[98] For the purpose of historiographic research, we can identify a *technical* application of the term religion. Application that indicates an attitude of faith that is not born out of pure thought.

---

95. Croce strongly believed in culture and believed that the cultural background of a society does play an effect in the choices and events of that society. However, such effects and events never perform a causality in the scientific or theological sense, which outshines the individual creativity; *historiographic necessity* is something different from scientific causality. This because, for Croce, history is always contemporary history, in the sense that the historian, in studying the historical documentation, is attempting to solve problems that he also perceives in his own present.

In *La Storia come Pensiero e Azione* (translated in English as *History as the Story of Liberty*) Croce dedicates a few pages in describing psychological historiography. He rejects interpretations that describe human historical actions as driven from the external factors (family, social environment, cultural dispositions, foreign influences, etc.). The reasons of historical actions are always internal, that is, driven by the rational elaboration of the individual (or social group). Cultural frameworks may provide the tools, or the means for historical actions, but are never the cause. For Croce, history is *thought* (*Pensiero*) and *action* (*Azione*), always-rational thought and rational action that finds its origin in its contemporary relations and not in previous relations. For example, again in *La Storia come Pensiero e Azione*, he expressed harsh criticism of Weber's historical analysis on Protestant ethics and its connection to capitalism.

I have to say, I have to commit a partial parricide in developing my own historical narrative. While I do agree with Croce that historical events do not relate with scientific causality in the unfolding of events, at the same time, I believe he underestimated the amount of influence that cultural frameworks can play on the individual/social group. The last paragraph of this chapter, in which I will discuss Ernesto De Martino's work, will offer more details about this argument.

96. As an example, in his *Storia dell'età Barocca in Italia*, Croce defines the new rationalist movements born after the Counter-Reformation as the *Catholic Churches of reason* and even depicts a paragon between the Company of Jesus, found by Loyola, to the Masonry.

97. Croce, *Storia come Pensiero e Azione*, 200–203.

98. Ibid., 200.

It works, according to Croce, through images and shadows.[99] It is a process of mind, in-between imagination and thought, which relies on myths, symbols and allegories, not on a pure act of reasoning.[100] In this process, human action is not the product of human consciousness, but an act that comes from a power or presence outside the human being. The interesting point is that this phantasmal religious activity is not an exclusive activity of institutional religions. While it is true that positive religions may show the most characteristics of this impure process of thought, such activity takes place in philosophical or civilizational narratives as well. The function of the process, independently from the context, is always directed to the development of rational and moral truths. Namely, to a process of education of the human being that is always related to its historical context of activity and always depends on a sort of *religious sentiment*.[101] Croce still developed a hierarchy between religious and nonreligious thought. Nonreligious thought was the one that had an easier and more rational access to those moral truths. While religious thought had to access to these truths through imagination and myths. However, institutional religion is simply the last, historical, result of general processes, anthropological phenomena that are not exclusive to institutional religious forms. In a few words, we can say that institutional religions imply these impure processes of thought, this religious sentiment, but we could have those processes without institutional religions. Croce's theory of degrees allowed him to understand that the concept of *religious* cannot be understood in a narrow way, as Taylor does. This is further demonstrated in another paragraph of *La Storia come Pensiero e Azione*, dedicated to *religiosity and religion*.[102] In this paragraph, Croce affirms that, if we consider religion as a way of life with its correspondent ethical claims, then secular liberalism itself has to be defined as a religion, it cannot be defined differently.[103] Croce affirms that, precisely like any other religion, liberalism has inspired faith and martyrs; it demands a comprehensive presence within the social sphere that rejects alternative ways of life. Liberalism, like any other religion, claims to express a fundamental truth and uses its own myths and symbols to inspire the people.[104] For this reason, according to Croce,

---

99. Ibid., 201.

100 Ibid., 200–201. For Croce only pure philosophy was actual thought. Thus, in every historiographical/philosophical attempt, he always tried to identify a pure form of reasoning that was located at the peak of human activity. Whether this can be considered a valid attempt or not, I leave to the reader's decision.

101. Ibid., 201–2.

102. Ibid., 228–33.

103. Ibid., 228–29.

104. Ibid., 228–29.

liberalism has to acknowledge its own right to fight against other religions and interpretations of the world with its own instruments, or at least create an environment in which the other interpretations are forced to adapt and abandon their own myths and symbols.[105]

However, besides technical application of the concept of the religious, the term, for Croce, indicated also a *general moral activity* that pertained to human action as such, independently from the technically religious or rational context. We find evidences of this general religiosity of human activity in Croce's political writings. As Walter L. Adamson shows us, in his article "Benedetto Croce and the Death of Ideology,"[106] Benedetto Croce, in the period in which he was writing articles for the journal *La Critica*, wrote an article titled "Fede e Programmi" (Faith and Programs).[107] In this article, Benedetto Croce analyzes the failure of the great political parties of his time, particularly the socialist one. Croce finds the main reason for such failure in the mistaken confusion created by politicians between faith and programs in their political activity.[108] Croce describes faith as the moral activity that has to be the foundation of the program, while the program is just the technical application in the social context, its pragmatic expression.[109] He found the cause of the decadence of political parties of his time in the attempt to transform the programs themselves into faith. In this way, faith disappears from the social context. It becomes impossible for the individual to recognize his own moral activity inscribed in a general moral framework and every individual/group becomes focused only in its immediate gain.[110] It is extremely interesting how Croce uses the concept of faith in this article, as well as, in general, his use of the concept of religion in his political writings. He uses the concept of faith to refer to a general human activity, an activity that is fundamentally moral and that takes place in the moment in which the individual enters into a relation with the social framework around him. Croce is able to operate such a distinction, without being constrained by a narrow understanding of the term religion, precisely because, through the sensibility acquired through his theory of degrees, he is able to distinguish between particular and general historical categories, and is able to still maintain a theoretical distinction between them.

---

105. Ibid., 229–30.
106. Adamson, "Benedetto Croce and the Death of Ideology."
107. Croce, "Fede e Programmi."
108. Adamson, "Benedetto Croce and the Death of Ideology," 211.
109. Ibid., 212.
110. Ibid., 211–13.

The material obtained through Croce's work allows for the development of new considerations on Taylor's narrative. His description of premodern society as working through the dyad of secularity/religion is not a very precise one. Primarily because, as we have seen in the first chapter, the concept of religion itself is not a neutral definition. It is the product of a specific historical sensibility typical of the modern era. The premodern dyad, described by Taylor as a real conceptual distinction, was simply a configuration of authority through which the premodern, Christian, *Weltanschauung* could be organized and structured. Both religious and secular authorities, in fact, still possessed a reference to the divine realm, although through different means. The dyadic structure between transcendence and immanence is hardly applicable to the premodern era. The ontological structure of the premodern universe did not simply separate and then connect a transcendent reality and an immanent reality. Instead, they penetrated each other. The influence of God's providence in the world was perceived as real and immanent, as it was the influence of evil spirits. In the same way, the political authority was the actual representation of a divine authority. We cannot understand the conflict between papacy and empire, in the Middle Ages, if we do not understand that both sides were claiming to be invested with divine transcendental authority.

In addition, modern secularity, precisely because it connects itself with concepts as democracy, human rights and rule of law, as Taylor affirms, is hardly immanent in itself. The concepts through which modern secular regimes legitimize their own authority are still forms of abstraction of general categories. These abstract categories are expressed and realized immanently in the social context by political authorities. In modern secular governments is still present the attitude of faith that Croce describes as indispensable for the actuation of political programs. Despite Taylor criticizes the secular obsession over religion, he still accepts the modern secular narrative about the modern secular state being the only possible resolution to the postulated inherent violence of religions. In this narrative, secular regimes are born to improve the previous, religious, social order that was not guaranteeing equal rights and freedom to different groups of people. A proof for this interpretation is found in Taylor rejection of the concept of secularity as a religious form.[111] Taylor tries to demonstrate how the term secularity has been used in opposition to the term religion, as a different form of social order whose function was precisely to restrain some groups for the common good. This is exactly what Cavanaugh has described as the main narrative of secularity. It also reaffirms the Hegelian dyadic structure

---

111. Taylor, *Dilemmas and Connections*, 311–13.

of opposition. Taylor, despite his best attempts to tell us a positive story about secularity, still gives us another negative story in the form of the *loss of transcendence*. This is a necessary step dictated by the Hegelian structure that he is using, unified with the secular narrative he embraces. If Taylor conceives the relation between religion and secularity as a basic dyadic structure of Western modern civilization, and if the purpose of secularity is precisely to further the basic claims of liberty in human societies, this could happen only by negating the main feature of the religious thesis, that is transcendence.

Taylor hardly escapes the Hegelian paradox of considering a rational principle, which is historical and contingent, as the basic attribute of human life. He tries to use the concept of sense of fullness to provide a more versatile concept of analysis, but he fails to support his argument consistently. The sense of fullness becomes just another way to describe the allegedly inherent human tendency to reach superior states of freedom and civility. A proof for this is provided, again, by how Taylor describes the loss of transcendence as a negative experience. The secular person, he claims, should feel dissatisfied and unable to achieve the sense of fullness and wholeness for which religious people strive. At the same time, religious people can no longer keep a naïve faith in their religions, as secularity represents an unmasking and resolution to the inner contradiction of the premodern era. There are, however, various counter-arguments that weaken Taylor's proposal. First, secular people may not feel dissatisfied with their own account of reality. Precisely because Hegel's system is a good explanation of how we do create our own sense of rationality, secular people can be—and many of them are—perfectly happy with the sense of reality they possess and evaluate it as the most rational one. Second, because we are not dealing with material categories of reality, but with abstract generalization, it is impossible to achieve a historical/practical synthesis between religion and secularity. Cavanaugh and Schmitt have showed how both concepts are historically contingent interpretations that have the purpose to reinforce and sustain a very specific sense of rationality, which is the modern secular one. In this sense, we do not have a dialectical struggle between two different historical terms. As Croce has said, the same cultural framework produces its own rational and irrational and develops them dialectically to further sustain itself. When Taylor uses the dichotomies religion/secularity or transcendence/immanence, he uses categories that have been produced in the modern, secular, cultural framework as a criticism of the previous one. He is trying to achieve a synthesis only through tools that have been produced by the antithesis.

The question, at this point, is: How can Croce's theory of degrees help us to improve Taylor's historical narrative? First, through his critique to the concept of synthesis, we can be free from the relation of necessity and opposition applied to historical/sociological analysis. As Croce says: "But if this (the Hegelian) principle affirms the synthesis of being and not-being, it does not, therefore, possess the virtue of changing not-being into being."[112] The Hegelian structure, as it is, becomes a game of polarities and transformations that is, ultimately, deemed to fail. In the same way, Taylor's narrative is a process in which a religious sensibility transformed in its opposite, secularity, while the purpose of this transformation is to achieve a further transformation into a superior state of free religiosity, an open faith. Croce's correction to Hegel's logic, instead, allows us to recognize, firstly, that terms like immanence and transcendence are false opposites (like religion and secularity). They are a product of our system of rationalization, of our historical narrative and, therefore, their value is linguistic and expressive, but not historically factual. These terms, when applied as historical categories, become *genera* that encompasses all phenomena, making it impossible to analyze eventual areas of blurriness or confusion.

In addition, the theory of degrees, applied to historical analysis, allows us to distinguish between necessary facts without implying an exclusion between them, and, more importantly, without having to subsume them into universal categories. Through Croce's theory of degrees we develop an alternative narrative regarding secularity in which we can focus on more fundamental phenomena that are present, without need for an opposition or an exclusion, both in religion and secularity. As they are anthropological constants that take place precisely by virtue of human beings being historical creatures. As we have seen, Croce is able to distinguish between general activities of human moral/historical action and technical categories, like religion. If religion, to take its historical form, has to imply some fundamental religiosity—a faith—this faith is not necessarily an exclusive feature of historical religions. On practical terms and addressing the problem at hand, a relation of implication between social/historical phenomena allow us to develop a theory of secularity that not only is positive, in Schmitt's sense, but also allows us to understand historical relations in a different form than opposition between secularity and religion.[113]

---

112. Croce, *What Is Living*, 64.

113. In addition, it would help us solve Schmitt's problem about the relation between metaphysical structures and political/legal structures of a given society.

TAYLOR'S PROGRESSIVISM: THE BUFFERED SELF

Croce's criticism of Hegelian dialectics offers useful tools to improve the sociological/historical use of Hegel's system, together with developing a useful criticism of Taylor's historical narrative. However, there is also another feature of Taylor's proposal I would like to address, providing, in this way, more details on why I believe that his progressivism represents an unsolved philosophical problem. It will also help me to demonstrate further the importance of an anthropological interpretation of faith, this religious sentiment that takes place in religious and secular contexts alike. The problem I would like to present now would be the final confirmation of Taylor's Hegelian progressivism and its impossibility to achieve a true synthesis between secularity and religion, at least in the form it has been presented in *A Secular Age*. I refer here to the concept of the *buffered self*, which is a clear proof of the oppositional difference between religion and secularity in Taylor's narrative.

Taylor affirms that one of the most important changes that allowed the modern era to take place was the shift from a self that is "open, porous and vulnerable to a world of spirits and powers to a buffered one."[114] This premodern *weak self* was immersed in an enchanted world; the world of spirits, demons, moral forces that our predecessors acknowledged as existent.[115] The process of disenchantment meant the disappearance of this world, and its substitution with the world in which we live today. A world in which the only locus of thoughts, feelings, spiritual élan is the individual mind. Since the only minds recognized as existent in the cosmos are those of humans, these minds are bounded, so that these thoughts, feelings, etc., are situated within them. According to Taylor, the relation with the world that premodern people possessed was naïve. We have moved from a naïve acceptance of the reality of spiritual beings, to a sensibility that considers a disputed and problematic terrain to either affirm or deny such realities. There are no more naïve theists, just as there are no naïve atheists.[116] This change is connected to the change in our sense of the world, from one in which these spirits existed just unproblematically, impinging on us, to one in which they can no longer be taken seriously. Indeed, many of the ways in which they were believed to exist and affect us have become inconceivable. The central difference between the premodern and modern era is the locus in which they find their *center of meaning*. In modernity, we found this

---

114. Taylor, *Secular Age*, 27.
115. Ibid., 29.
116. Ibid., 31.

center in the human mind, in the sense that things only have the meaning they do in that they awaken a certain response in us. This process has to do with our nature as creatures who are thus capable of such responses, which means creatures with feelings, with desires, aversions, etc. The situation of the enchanted world was, according to Taylor, quite different:

> But in the enchanted world, meanings are not in the mind in this sense, certainly not in the human mind. If we look at the lives of ordinary people—and even to a large degree of élites—500 years ago, we can see in a myriad ways how this was so. First, they lived in a world of spirits, both good and bad. The bad ones include Satan, of course, but beside him, the world was full of a host of demons, threatening from all sides: demons and spirits of the forest, and wilderness, but also those which can threaten us in our everyday lives. Spirit agents were also numerous on the good side. Not just God, but also his saints, to whom one prayed, and whose shrines one visited in certain cases, in hopes of a cure, or in thanks for a cure already prayed for and granted, or for rescue from extreme danger, e.g., at sea.[117]

Not only the world was filled with these spiritual beings, also the things in themselves possessed a mysterious (benevolent or malevolent) power, for example relics and curses. These objects were *loci* of spiritual power, which is why they had to be handled with care, and if abused could wreak terrible damage. This is the point that Taylor wants to stress, in the enchanted world, the line between personal agency and impersonal force was not at all clearly drawn. In the enchanted world, there is a whole gamut of forces, positive and negative, that exercise an influence outside our capacity of agency. For Taylor, the enchanted world, in contrast to our universe of buffered selves and minds, shows a perplexing absence of certain boundaries which seem to us essential.[118] This becomes evident if we look at two major properties that these things/spiritual subjects possessed. The first is the power to impose a certain meaning on us. In our modern world, things acquire meaning after our response. They acquire meaning after we have elaborated an answer to the relation we establish with them, after our *encounter* with them, they do not possess meaning in themselves. In the enchanted world, the meaning exists already outside of us, prior to contact. It can take us over; we can fall into its field of force. It comes on us from the outside.[119] The second great difference is that, in the enchanted world, the meaning in things also

117. Ibid, 32.
118. Ibid., 33.
119. Ibid., 33–34.

includes another power. These *charged* objects can affect not only us but also other things in the world. They can affect cures, save ships from wreck, end hail and lightning, and so on. They have what we usually call magic powers. In the enchanted world, charged things have a causal power, which matches their incorporated meaning.[120] This way of thinking is very different from our post-Galilean, mind-centered disenchantment. If thoughts and meanings are only in minds, then there can be no charged objects, and the causal relations between things cannot be in any way dependent on their meanings, which must be projected on them from our minds. In other words, the physical world, outside the mind, must proceed by causal laws, which in no way depends on the moral meanings we apply to things. In the enchanted world, instead, charged things can impose meanings, and bring about physical outcomes proportionate to their meanings. They have influence and causal power.[121]

The enchanted world represents, therefore, a very different existential condition from the modern world. For the modern, buffered self, in fact, exists the possibility of taking a distance from everything outside the mind, disengaging from our framework. The ultimate purposes are those that arise within ourselves, the crucial meanings of things are those defined in our responses to them.[122] For the premodern porous self, instead, the source of its most powerful and important emotions are outside the mind. To be clearer, for the weak, porous self the very notion that there is a clear boundary, allowing us to define an inner base area, grounded, in which we can disengage from the rest, makes no sense. As a strong self, instead, we can see the boundary that separates us from the things outside us as a buffer, such that the things beyond are not able to harm us in any way. Having exposed his presentation of the problem, we should be able to understand better Taylor's use of the term *buffered*. He affirms that "this self can see itself as invulnerable, as master of the meanings of the things around him."[123] The porous self is vulnerable to spirits, demons, and cosmic forces, along with these sources of fear there are contextual fears that can grip the individual and shake his own sense of security, like natural disasters for example. The buffered self, instead, has removed these two kinds of fear from his world, we do not fear anymore spirits or cosmic forces and we do not inscribe any more a mysterious, dangerous, meaning to circumstantial events.[124]

120. Ibid., 34–36.
121. Ibid., 35–38.
122. Ibid., 38.
123. Ibid., 38.
124. Ibid., 38–39. It is interesting that, while presenting this new way of being into the world, Taylor also take into account the permanence of old attitudes. For example,

Because of this polarity between porous self and buffered self, Taylor develops a narrative in which belief is an anthropological necessity in premodern era, while is unneeded in modernity.

> Disbelief is hard in the enchanted world. This is not so much because spirits are part of the undeniable furniture of things and God is a spirit, ergo undeniable. Much more important, God figures in this world as the dominant spirit, and moreover, as the only thing that guarantees that in this awe-inspiring and frightening field of forces, good will triumph. Of course, just this will mean that our relations with, feelings about God will probably be tinged with ambiguity, as they always are. But it will also mean that the prospect of rejecting God does not involve retiring to the safe redoubt of the buffered self, but rather chancing ourselves in the field of forces without him. Practically our only recourse can be to seek another protector.[125]

Taylor does admit that the use of terms like *porous* and *buffered* may be misleading. According to him, the concept of *buffered self* denotes a state in which the individual self is aware of the possibility of disengagement. Disengagement that is carried out in relation to one's whole surroundings, natural and social.[126] The porous self of premodern era, instead, lived his experience of the world eminently as a social action. To question common rites and customs, in the enchanted world, represented a danger to the whole community as a whole, not just individuals. This perception remained even in the Enlightenment, in a semi-rationalized form that believed that oaths of allegiance would have to be invalid for atheists, who by definition fear no retribution in the afterlife.[127] The social bond at all these levels was intertwined in the sacred, and indeed, it was unimaginable otherwise. However, while Taylor admits that, for the premodern self, the presence of God and spirits was real and had a physical influence on their life, he still analyzes the issue through the polarity transcendence/immanence. Yet, for the pre-

---

the reaction of some people to the AIDS epidemic or the way people with cancer are often told that they are stricken because of their bad life style.

Taylor still connects these attitudes to the religious use of sacred objects, an attitude that has lingered into modernity and that still is described as *going against the grain* of the modern identity in a fundamental way, a weird belief. Taylor does not give any chance to the possibility that, instead, it could be some other, basic human feature that is trying to express itself through modernity in its own terms, in the same way it would express itself in a premodern context.

125. Ibid., 42.
126. Ibid., 42.
127. Ibid., 42–43.

modern sensibility, such distinction was pointless. Not only the threat of spirits was, for them, real, but it was also an immanent issue, the boundary between transcendent and immanent did not exist for the premodern individual; in the same way, it did not exist a boundary that separated him from the world.

In addition, Taylor's interpretation about the disappearance of the premodern web of causalities and influences can be quite problematic, especially when he compares it to secular societies. For example, even if the common individual, in a secular society, does not see any more spirits and relics as *loci* of meaning, it is also true that his social life is organized around objects that preserve their meaningfulness independently from the interpretation of the individual. The modern individual is still embedded in a *Weltanschauung* that provides him with fundamental meanings that are considered objective and independent from any possible response of the single individual.[128] Of course, Taylor finds the element of novelty in the ability of the modern self to disengage itself from its context, thus, being buffered. However, Taylor himself is wary of this pure individual, totally disengaged from his own context. Instead, *A Secular Age* is a work that advances the claim that we are always tied, in some way, to our social context. After all, Taylor agrees with Hegel on the claim that human beings are always culturally situated phenomena. By proposing the concept of buffered self, Charles Taylor claims that modernity gave to humanity a stronger and better interpretation of the world. The modern framework is, epistemically, a superior stage for Western culture. It provides a better ontology. The human being is necessarily safer and more secure than its predecessors were in the previous stage. In doing this, however, he transforms secularity in an epistemic/ontological category that provides an improved version of humanity in comparison to the previous era. In this way, the Hegelian triadic movement is still preserved and Taylor enforces further the sense of division between secular and religious contexts. After all, why should the secular context concede anything to religion, when it does offer a better version of humanity, a buffered one?

This happens because Taylor, influenced by his strong interpretation of Hegelian structures, connects morality with identity and sources in a

128. We could look at the political public discourse or at the media forms of communication. We see reference to *loci of meaning* quite frequently (the state, democracy, human rights, etc.) that are considered as *possessing meaningfulness* in themselves, regarding from the *interaction* with the single individual. For example: the whole discourse about *human rights* relies precisely on their being *meaningful* and *self-evident* regarding the relation with single individuals; a similar case could be argued for *freedom*. Precisely their being *abstract*, that is, *not tied to specific individual condition*, but *always* self-evident and independent, is the core of the argument in their support.

strong sense. It is worth here to go back, briefly, to Arto Laitinen's criticism against Taylor. In *Strong Evaluation without Moral Sources*, Laitinen presents us, against Taylor, with the argument that the lifeworld is infiltrated with values. Contrarily to Taylor's narrative, we do not live in a neutral space of value-free facts, in which then we identify a moral source.[129] We live in an evaluative and normative space of requirements, demands, and claims, which supervene on facts. Things we encounter are already good or bad, and provide us reasons to act, feel, and think in some ways rather than some other ways. Ideas of goods are cultural and are already provided by our own cultural context even before we can execute our activity of disengagement, instead, they may even represent an obstacle to such disengagement.[130] In this context, Laitinen presents the concept of *ontological evaluative features*,[131] instead of moral sources. These features provide the basic ontological understanding of life to individuals. Instead of theorize a singular source that is separate from the moral framework, Laitinen theorizes a plurality of sources articulated in the framework itself. If my life is meaningful, thanks to the features around me, the reflective question of its general meaning does not necessarily arise.

From Laitinen's presentation of the problem, we understand that the single source of good does not constitutes the goodness of all the goods involved in the framework. A deeper web of ontological connections is involved in the establishment of what is good and acceptable in the social context. In addition, the connection of the individual to such web is not necessarily a self-reflective operation, even in the modern secular framework. The different goods possess different features, both immanent and transcendent and are interconnected between each other. In this way, they connect the individual with the *Weltanschauung* through which he can navigate the world. The ontological features of the bearer of value can be of help in making intelligible why it is good, inscribe it in a wider order, but do not necessarily constitute the concept of good in itself. A good example offered by Laitinen pertains the case of animal suffering. The reason why we think animals ought not to be tortured derives from our belief that they are sentient (an ontological background feature), and is independent of whether we think that morality is in the end a matter of human will, divine will, or ontic logos (the constitutive reality).[132] Both help the individual navigate the

---

129. God, the self, democracy, etc.
130. Laitinen, *Strong Evaluation without Moral Sources*, 185–216.
131. Ibid., 267.
132. Ibid., 287–89.

world around him, are part of his *Weltanschauung*, and it is not possible to identify one as the fundamental source of good.

In the transition from premodernity to modernity, then, what happened has been a redefinition of the categories of reality, of the ontological evaluative features. The pure" individual self, as a constitutive good of modernity, is one of the concepts through which the modern framework constructed its own sense of *rationality* against the *supposed irrationality* of religions and other cultures. In this case, however, the modern individual would not be necessarily buffered just because he does not fear any more devils and spirits, considered non-real. If devils and spirit were not anymore immanent and real, in a way that they have a real influence on the ontological security of the modern man, the process of projection that identified new threats to the security of the individuals did not stop. A new process of identification of new threats and new mechanisms of security designed to counter them took place. The whole process of creation of the enemy, of the nation-state, or modern propaganda is exemplary in this sense.

To develop my argument in this direction, I wish to refer to the work of an Italian anthropologist, Ernesto De Martino. Student of Benedetto Croce and an expert of Southern Italian traditions, Ernesto De Martino dedicated much of his work to understanding the historical dramas of humanity and the relation they established with their own world. His most interesting work is the book *Il Mondo Magico: Prolegomeni a una Storia del Magismo*. In this work, De Martino proposed an interesting interpretative option. The reason why De Martino wrote such a book was very straightforward:

> As soon as the scholar turns his sight on the magical world, with the intention of understanding its secret, he faces a problem of prejudice that influence substantially the orientation and purpose of the research: the problem of magical powers. Usually such a problem is eluded with extreme easiness, as it is immediately assumed as obvious the fact that all magical pretentions are non-real and that magical practices are deemed to failure. . . . So that it is believed more fruitful to try to establish how magic in itself could arise and exist despite its non-reality and its failures. However, precisely in this "obvious" assumption, not worthy of verification, lies a set of extremely severe problems, hidden and side lined by a scholarly laziness so strong that is, in itself, a problem.[133]

---

133. De Martino, *Mondo Magico*, 9.

144   FIDES AND SECULARITY

For De Martino it is worthy, then, to investigate properly the problem of the *reality of magical powers*.[134] In addressing this problem, he soon realizes that a scholarly study about this matter has to address not only the magical powers, but also the concept of reality to which magical powers are tied. It is not only a problem about the subject (magical powers) but also about the categories of judgment over it (the concept of reality).[135] According to De Martino, we have only two possible way to address the problem at hand, either we rely on paranormal psychology and other occult subjects that claim to be able to penetrate the mystery (an outcome he firmly rejects), or we have to admit that the reality of magical powers is tied to a different concept of reality.[136] It is not only a problem about perceptions and the relation that human beings have and establish with the world around them. The world itself acquires certain ontological categories in certain cultural context. It is not just an epistemic structure of individuals or communities; the world itself obtains certain ontological properties that influence *a priori* the epistemic structure of a society. Our experiences of the world can, then, be constituted a priori by our cultural interpretations, that can lead to empirical evidence that are firmly denied in a different cultural context. We face, according to De Martino, a problem of *culturally conditioned nature*.[137] Modernity as well is not able to escape this problem. The ontology of modernity has been established as a contradictory polemic against the reality of magical powers, a struggle that becomes particularly evident when we address naturalistic sciences and their reactions in front of claims of alleged magical powers or paranormal realities. To address the problem of magical/religious powers from a posture different from total rejection would put again into question the historical and cultural presupposition that guarantee the modern cultural stability.[138] It can easily become a case of cultural pride, even arrogance. However, precisely this strong rejection reveals how the problem of the culturally conditioned nature is, *de facto*, inescapable. Not only the reality of magical powers has to be referred to their culture of origin, but also the modern rejection of such powers and the establishment of a different nature, a different *Weltanschauung*, has to be related to the same historical/cultural process. From De Martino, then, we obtain the insight that there is a fundamental anthropological constant at work in the

---

134. Of course, his aim is not to *prove* that the sorcerer or the priest *actually possess* some *causal effect* over matter, people, or nature.
135. Ibid., 10.
136. Ibid., 10–11.
137. Ibid., 51–54.
138. Ibid., 53.

history of human societies, in such a way that the problem of culturally conditioned nature is always present in all epochs and societies.

The phenomenon of the culturally conditioned nature is, for De Martino, a historical drama that is nourished and reinforced by a fundamental social phenomenon.

> If we analyze the "olon" state, we find, as its core characteristic, a presence that surrenders without conditions. Everything happens as if a weak, un-guaranteed, unstable presence would be unable to resist the "shock" caused by a particular emotional content. Unable to find sufficient energy to keep itself "present" in front of the event, recognizing, re-appropriating and controlling it in a web of definite relations. In this way, the content is lost as "content of a present conscience." The presence tends to remain absorbed in a determinate content, unable to go "beyond" it, and, therefore, disappears and surrenders as "presence." The distinction between presence and world disappears.[139]

Taylor is able to depict this aspect of premodern societies with precision; he correctly grasps the problem of the absence of boundaries between the individual and the world around him.[140] However, there is a major difference between his historical perspective and De Martino's. For Taylor the phenomenon of the buffered self is an epistemic evolution that is there to stay. At its foundation, we find the Kantian absolute subject as guaranteed presence in the world. This subject is the agent of a progressive history in which the aim is to attain a *sense of fullness*. Taylor describes a fascinating game of oppositions and polarities between premodernity and modernity to develop his narrative of this struggle. In Taylor's narrative, we are still embedded in a Hegelian dynamic of progress toward an absolute subject that is inherently free. De Martino's perspective, in this regard, is quite different. Modernity is still haunted by the same historical drama. Such drama is created by the will to exist, as *presence*, in front of the risk of nonexistence. The condition of the *presence* has always to be related to the *concrete historical drama* it lives in.[141]

139. Ibid., 72–73.

140. Although I am also confident that a detailed comparison between Taylor's narrative and De Martino's anthropological analyses will reveal the limits of Taylor's description of medieval magic.

141. Ibid., 154–55. Therefore, it is useless to make comparison between conditions of different epochs. The state of altered mind of the schizophrenic, in the modern Western context, is a different matter from the state of altered mind of the shaman in a primitive context. What has to be researched, in both cases, is the concrete historical drama with which the presence is trying to cope.

At the same time, precisely the analysis of the concrete historical drama of Western civilization reveals, according to De Martino, a conflict unresolved that persists in the modern age. For De Martino, the principle of the autonomy of the individual is a core feature of Western civilization and is what identifies and distinguishes our civilization from all others. However, he traces the origin of this feature in the Greek ethics, particularly in Plato. With Christianity, it began that slow historical process that would lead us to the discovery of this autonomy that finds its culmination in the Kantian transcendental unity of the conscience.[142] However, this absolute subject still is an historical product of a specific form of civility, which is not isolated from the general existential problem of the presence. For De Martino, now that we have posed an autonomous individual in relation with an autonomous world, we have also reached the maximum amount of risk for the presence.[143] Precisely because the individual form is the result of a

---

142. Ibid., 156–58. It is interesting, then, that for De Martino Christianity already represents its own concrete historical context, separated from other ones. In Taylor's narrative, instead, the premodern era is assimilated, by analogy, to any other magical civilization, a position that De Martino would criticize as antihistorical and disrespectful for both Christianity and other civilizations. The reason being that, according to De Martino, with Greek philosophy, followed by Christian philosophy, we already see the first attempts to establish some boundaries between the self and the world. In the sense that the world starts to lose its autonomy of action in its processes of influences and interactions with the human self (ibid., 157–59).

As an example, De Martino describes the magic world as a state in which the world is really and very autonomous in its possibility to influence the individual self, or a community. The magical tragedy may happen in a totally spontaneous way; it does not require a reason to happen. The individual presence does not exist as a constituted reality, because it is constantly threatened by the risk of nonexistence. The magical practices, the establishment of taboos, the creation of magical items are interpreted, by De Martino, as an attempt to constitute the autonomy of the presence in front of the constant risk of a threatening world.

Greek/Roman philosophy, and then Christianity, represent already a different stage in this interaction of risk/security. In the Greek/Roman tradition and in the Christian one the world already does not possess a total autonomy in its possibility of representing a risk—something that Taylor himself admits, unknowingly. In his statement that "to breach the social rules is to breach the rules of the cosmos" lies the difference between the premodern Western traditions and other ones. If there is the need for a *breach of the rules* to be the victim of the consequences, then we are already in a stage in which the cultural context has created a *de jure* situation for the individual/communitarian presence. Any attempt to breach the *de jure* situation represents the creation of a risk, but it also means that without the breach, there can be no risks. Therefore, we already see a state of security that, for De Martino, did not exist in the magical world. In this sense, modernity can be interpreted as the attempt to further reinforce the *de jure* condition of security of the individual, to the point that there cannot be any kind of breaches that can threaten it.

143. Ibid., 158.

self-production, it includes within itself the possibility of failure, hence the maximum amount of risk of nonexistence. The supreme risk, for the modern man, becomes the supreme abandonment of its autonomy whenever he faces contents and events that he is unable to assimilate and control[144]. This acknowledgment leads De Martino to two main conclusions. First, that even the autonomy of the person, the individual self, as historical product, "does not represent any factual reality."[145] It is, as other cultural productions, a process of abstraction and categorization. Even the procedures through which we claim to be able to find this unified autonomous conscience, by investigating its capabilities, categories, fields of operation, already imply the individual conscience in its totality.[146] Second, precisely because the individual guaranteed presence, with its ontological security, is a historical product, and not a neutral fact, the possibility of its weakening and disappearance is always implied in the historical process. De Martino affirms that events like mental illness or death of a loved one can be as destructive for the presence of a single individual as wars and great tragedies are for the presence of whole civilizations.[147] The modern man can still lose himself, as well as its entire civilization.

The important thing on which I wish to focus is that even the autonomous conscience, this *buffered self*, is not buffered at all in its own historical factuality. The buffer is only a cultural product. The process of empowerment that makes it buffered relies on the same ontological fear that threatens all human societies, premodern and modern, at least in our Western history. For this reason, De Martino states, Western civilization is unable to conceive the human conscience in terms different from its own. That is the supreme individual self, able to disengage itself from the world. Any admission of difference would allow an increasing amount of risk that our ontological security is not able to sustain. Pushing further this reasoning, all those categories through which the modern conscience is structured (the state, the nation, freedom, democracy, human rights, etc...) are instruments and tools through which the modern framework creates its own culturally conditioned nature, a way through which the modern man reinforces its own sense of being. The modern *Weltanschauung* is deeply at work and has to rely on a nonrational, *a priori* acceptance of its own, fundamental, ontological statements to be able to sustain itself.

144. Ibid., 158–61.
145. Ibid., 161.
146. Ibid., 161–62.
147. Ibid., 162.

We have found the main contrast between Taylor and De Martino. By positing the concept of buffered self, Taylor assumes that the ontological security acquired through modernity is a result that cannot be lost, we have reached an epistemic level from which we cannot go back, the modern human being is inherently better than its ancestors are. Following De Martino, instead, we are able to develop a different analysis of the social/historical phenomena that have determined and will determine in the future our own cultural condition. A war, situations of deaths of loved ones, or mental illness prove that the sources of danger and the center of securities, and of power, of our sense of the selfhood, our individuality, have not disappeared. Modernity, the new worldview, has simply transposed them toward different centers and relations (the family, the state, the ideology, the mind, etc...). The process of formation, sustainment and enforcement of a given *Weltanschauung* has not stopped, nor have disappeared the anthropological processes involved.

Crises in these sources of security and value have proven to be as socially/culturally damaging as the fear of spirits and devils in a premodern era. The phenomena of totalitarian states, in which a single person or a party becomes the guarantor for the security of the whole nation is, in this sense, a good example that Taylor has not considered sufficiently. Even though the focus of attention has been moved from God and his ordained universe, this has not meant a disappearance of transcendence *tout-court*, mainly because the ontological process of *creation/reinforcement/dissipation* of categories of reality has not stopped and has continued throughout the whole of modern era. What has happened has been a transposition of God, as a central figure of security and authority, towards a plurality of figures. Now, if this does confirm Taylor's narrative of plurality,[148] at the same time, however, it invalidates his historical narrative on the nature of secularity as immanence and its process of generation. A fundamental question, then, arises at this point. If we want to describe a history of continuity between premodernity and modernity that relies on the perception of this ongoing ontological process, this continuous establishment and negotiation of *ontological evaluative features* or *culturally conditioned nature*, or *Weltanschauung*, where should we focus our attention?

I believe that the answer lies in the analysis of the phenomenon of faith in human existence, a phenomenon to which Taylor has not given enough consideration or attention. This universal religious sentiment, this attitude of faith that seems to establish categories of reality and of society may be

---

148. The first question of *A Secular Age*: How was it possible to believe in God in the Middle Ages, and not believe in him in modern age?

the correct answer to develop a new philosophical narrative that is able to make sense of the historical events which generated modernity, and that still haunt our contemporary political and social life, both in positive and negative ways.

4

Between *Secular* and *Religious*
A Theological Perspective

I HAVE PRESENTED THE argument that to draw a systematic distinction between the phenomena of secularity and religion, like Taylor has done in his narrative, is extremely problematic. To accomplish a serious historical/sociological analysis of modernity and secularity, it is unhelpful to assume a definition of secularity as the sphere determined by *immanence* and *rationality* and of religion as the sphere determined by *faith, transcendence*, and *God*. Instead, it is plausible to assume a relation of inheritance and continuity between premodern theological/political mechanisms and modern secular ones. By presenting Taylor's relation to Hegelian philosophy, I have presented the argument that the rigid structure of his interpretation of society is a result of his interpretation of history as a dialectical process. Taylor himself, despite his intention to establish a connection between religion and secularity, is able to develop only a negative relation. Religion and secularity are connected through a bond of contradiction. Secularity not only operates in a different social sphere than religion, but the forms of consciousness through which operates openly negate the religious ones. In this way, we have the dichotomies between transcendence/immanence or porous/buffered selves that reveal a sharp and unbridgeable gap between what is secular and what is religious. Religion and secularism are connected purely through their dualism/opposition.

Charles Taylor interprets the concept of religion as an *aut/aut* between the transcendent and the immanent.[1] The concept of religion denotes a sense of fullness that finds its centre and source beyond this material world,

1. Taylor, *Secular Age*, 15–16.

in a supernatural source. As already introduced in the first chapter, Taylor's aim is to achieve a synthesis between religious features and secular features in our social life. Taylor adopts a language of synthesis because he analyzes the two phenomena as intrinsically different social events not only on a historical level, but also at an anthropological/social one. This feature of Taylor's philosophy becomes even more evident in the moment we examine his use of Durkheim's analytical categories concerning the religious phenomenon. As a first stage of a society, Taylor defines as *Durkheimian society* a social framework where the church and the social sacred are one.[2] Religious faith imposes its supremacy by affirming the presence of God at the level of the whole society, as the author of a Design, which society carries out. In this situation, religion embraces and determines the whole of the political structure. The *Design of God* defines the political identity of this society, which identifies itself through its religious authorities. From this stage, according to Taylor, we have reached, in our Western civilization, a second state of society called *Neo-Durkheimian*. Here a sense of sacred is maintained, but it is no longer possible to distinguish certain people, places, acts, as profane because no one church can uniquely define and celebrate the link between political society and divine providence.[3] In this stage, we have free churches, set up as instruments of mutual help whereby individuals are brought into contact with the word of God and mutually strengthen each other in ordering their lives along godly lines. They are both organized on similar principles, mobilizing to carry out the will of God. They can be seen also mutually strengthening each other. This was the case in the early U.S.A. The Republic secures the freedom of the churches, and the churches sustain the godly ethos, which the Republic requires.[4] The radical difference from the previous stage lies in the different relation between sacred and profane authorities. If in a *Durkheimian society*, the profane authorities find their legitimization in the ethos developed by a single religious authority, in the *Neo-Durkheimian* stage the public ethos is no longer linked to a

---

2. Ibid., 442. With the word Durkheimian is indicated a situation in which the church and social sacred are one—although the relation of primary and secondary focus is reversed, since for Durkheim the social is the principal focus, reflected in the divine, while the opposite is true for ultra-mundane Catholicism.

3. Ibid., 454. Taylor explain this phenomenon as an example of *denominationalism*. A denomination cannot be a national church, and its members cannot accept and join whatever claims to be the national church. Denominationalism implies that churches are all equal options, and thrives best in a régime of separation of church and state, *de facto* if not *de jure*. On another level, the political entity can be identified with the broader, overarching church, and this can be a crucial element in its patriotism, while still maintaining it politically distinguished from the religious institution itself.

4. Ibid., 453.

single sacred construal. It starts to find its own ground for legitimization. The presence of different religious authorities marks precisely the radical independence of the public ethos from them. The public ethos allows the existence of different religious authorities, not the contrary.

The contemporary stage of our society, as the third and final stage, is called *non-Durkheimian* or *post-Durkheimian*. In our present stage, we no longer possess any kind of sacred that has to be linked and communicated in society. Essentially, any individual or small group is on his or her own, there is no necessary embedding of our link to the sacred in any particular broader social framework whether church or state.[5] This will make the calls of religious institution difficult to be heard in an age modeled by such features, but, ironically, even a narrow secularism will have a hard time.[6] Taylor proposes his reconciliation between religious aspirations toward the transcendent and secular assertions of the dignity of the immanent through this interpretative path. However, despite using *Durkheimian* categories, Taylor locates himself quite in a different position than Durkheim. In *The Elementary Forms of the Religious Life*, Durkheim aims to study the most basic character of the religious life. His assumption is that religion holds to reality and expresses it, that it translates some fundamental human need, some aspects of life either individual or social.[7] We could define this a fundamental religious sentiment that pertains to human social life as such. Religious representations are collective representations, which express collective realities, so that its categories are collective representations that show the mental state of the group.[8] For these reasons, Durkheim discards both the supernatural and the divine as primary source for the religious life.[9] Instead, he believes that two fundamental features of social life constitute and are necessary for every religion, beliefs and rites. Beliefs are opinions and are constituted by representations. Rites are determined modes of action. What differentiates religious belief and rites from their nonreligious counterparts is just the class of objects involved.[10] Through the presentation

5. Ibid., 487.
6. Ibid., 504.
7. Durkheim, *Elementary Forms of the Religious Life*, 1–3.
8. Ibid., 11–16.
9. Ibid., 24–35. The supernatural, he says, is not apt as a source of the religious life, as, to be understood as a concept, it requires a concept of order of things that came to be only with positivist science. A primitive person, or in any case a person imbued in a religious society, cannot have a concept of supernatural. Divinity as well is not apt as the first source of religion, as there are religions and rites that do not involve a God or a plurality of gods (like Buddhism).
10. Ibid., 36–42.

of *A Secular Age* I have proposed in the previous chapters, then, we can see how Taylor uses Durkheimian concepts *against* Durkheim. In fact, if Durkheim aimed to trace, through the study of elementary religious forms, a fundamental religious sentiment, an anthropological constant traceable in religious and secular contexts alike, Taylor, instead, uses those same categories to reinforce further the divide between secular and religious sphere.

In the second chapter, I have presented this divide within Taylor's Hegelian perspective. I have presented the case, by way of Croce's and De Martino's work, that within the Hegelian tradition and sensibility, a different interpretation of dialectical categories and of human *existential relations* with their world is possible. This adaptation of Hegelian categories of analysis has to be freed from a deductive understanding of historical/social events. To establish suprahistorical *genera*, in our case *religion* and *secularity*, to define single historical contexts, would not allow us to notice existing areas of ambiguity between the examined social/historical structures. By contrast, I have proposed, following Croce, that an inductive method of historical/sociological analysis provides a clearer understanding of the processes involved in the development of our contemporary society. This new understanding would not be defining a general concept of religion and a general concept of secularity, and then applying them to single events analyzed according to predetermined categories.[11] Instead, it will provide an analysis of the single historical event that will proceed by analyzing the various processes, structures and contents of consciousness involved within the examined event and, only in a second moment, discusses eventual patterns of repetitions throughout history. In this way, rather than looking to apply general social categories, we search for anthropological constants within historical events.

This analytical method gives justice to the thresholds of ambiguity between a secular and a religious attitude, especially in those cases in which the events involved may not fit nicely in predetermined categories. In this way, we are able to grasp those features of human life that repeat themselves through different frameworks of reference. In my analysis so far, there have

---

11. This procedure creates unavoidable analytical problems in the moment we have to analyse single historical/social events. For example, it becomes impossible to analyse concepts like the *free market* or the *invisible hand* outside any kind of mathematic/materialistic understanding, because there is no *evident God* or *evident transcendent* involved in those concepts. However, a different analysis, that would work through broader understanding of the anthropological features underlying both religion and secularity, could argue that, even in the absence of evident religious features, concepts like free market and invisible hand have to rely, to guarantee their consistency, on principles of providential harmony and belief that surely do not fit within the category of the secular.

been recurring terms like faith, ontological security and religious sentiment. I argue that the proof of existence of such thresholds of indifference, or ambiguity, between secularity and religion lies precisely in the analysis of these concepts. Moving in this direction, Croce—in a post-Hegelian tradition—uses the concepts of religion and transcendence with much more liberality and gives them a much broader interpretation. Taylor, instead, applies his categories of analysis in an excessively schematic way. He qualifies the religious/secularity dichotomy as an alternative between belief and unbelief. In this way, the various features of secularity (or unbelief) are thought to belong to a different sphere of social reality than religious ones. On the other hand, we have seen, through De Martino's anthropological studies, that it is possible to discern common features between religious and secular frameworks. Such features, more than pertaining to specific visions of the world, are interpreted as being inherent to any kind of relation that human beings establish with the world around them. The simplicity and straightforwardness of the religious/secular divide is problematic. The divide, implies that human beings involved in different frameworks appeal to different mental resources to structure their own sense of reality. That is, different societies generate radically different human relations toward their world or centers of values, so that a secular individual is related to his world/social structure/values by appealing to a different form of consciousness then a religious individual.

In Taylor's analysis, the distinction between the secular and the religious framework is seen as a transformation in the lived experience of Western societies.[12] According to Taylor, the transition from premodernity to modernity was not just a change between theories or set of beliefs. A fundamental change in how Western populations experienced their moral/spiritual life had happened. I do agree with Taylor that a religious person and a secular person possess radically different lived experiences. However, I question the features of this *lived experience* as Taylor presents it. Taylor retains a kind of progressivism in his narrative. The simple fact that he distinguishes between naïve faith and reflected faith gives the impression that there are lived experiences that are better, or more precise than others . This follows logically from Taylor's analytical language and Hegelian structures, which depicts Western history as a progression of various epistemic gains. In this sense, then, lived experiences are epistemic instruments that allow us to grasp—in a better or worse way—our moral sources and to locate them at the center of our moral/spiritual compass. In this sense, then, the real distinction is not between lived experiences, but between moral sources.

12. Ibid., 4–10.

However, as we have seen, the concept of moral sources, especially if developed through the dichotomies religion/secularity and transcendent/immanent is not as useful as it seems in developing a proper analysis of Western history and societies. I am of this opinion because Taylor's analysis implies that to every moral source would correspond a different way in which human beings interact between them and with their world. For example, if God is the moral source of an individual, then that individual will structure his lived experience through faith, belief, and outwardness. Instead, an individual with an immanent moral source would structure his lived experience through unbelief, rationality, and inwardness. The problem in structuring the analysis through such a dichotomy becomes evident when we want to analyze those complex forms of social/existential relation that are common to both secular and religious frameworks. Features like personal commitment, zeal, or fidelity cannot be tied to a specific framework. Instead, they reveal a common human attitude toward the world and our neighbors that transcends any simple dichotomy of transcendent/immanent or belief/unbelief. We are in the presence of anthropological constants that are vital for every kind of framework.

Therefore, given the material examined so far, I would like to present this claim, which will be the driving force of the following chapters of this work: To draw a distinct line between the phenomena called secularism and religion would result in an incomplete analysis of modernity, at risk of being antihistorical. It would be more plausible to assume a relation of inheritance between premodern theological/political mechanisms and the modern secular ones. This inheritance has been possible because of some common features of human life that belong to religious as well as secular frameworks. These common features cannot be rendered effectively with the language of human flourishing or of moral sources. We are in need of better anthropological/historical categories.

In presenting this chapter, I would like to use the insights we have gathered from the previous chapters to analyze Taylor's philosophy through the thought of renowned theologians belonging to the Catholic and the Protestant traditions. My purpose is twofold: First, by analyzing what theological thought has to say about this possible blurriness between religion and secularity, I want to show how theology already possesses a certain *inductive* sensibility. Namely, the ability to separate the concept of the religious from specific human features like belief, rationality, or faith, and how they are able to discuss these features by locating them in nonreligious context as well as religious contexts. They are able to operate a distinction between the human attitude in his ontological/social relations with his surroundings, and its field of application, that can be secular or religious. Exploring this line of analysis will help demonstrate that Croce and Durkheim were quite right in presenting the possibility of a more fundamental religious sentiment. The second purpose is to show how a possible critique of Taylor's work could arise precisely from the religious field that, ultimately, he aims to preserve. In this sense, then, I will argue how, even from a theological perspective, the dichotomies through which Taylor operates result unconvincing, in a way that destabilize his whole narrative.

SECULAR ESCHATOLOGY?: A CATHOLIC PERSPECTIVE

In his theological work, Joseph Ratzinger dedicated much attention to the relation between church and secular societies. He also engaged Jürgen Habermas in a dialogue about the role of the Catholic Church in society, and, more broadly, about the features of secular societies. One of the most interesting works on this topic is the essay written by Ratzinger in the 1978, "Eschatology and Utopia." In this work, Ratzinger addresses the relation between the religious *end of history* and ideological social aims. He develops his argument through the analysis of the concepts of eschatology and utopia. According to Ratzinger, if we consider *utopia* as the highest norm by which we measure our practical actions, and *eschatology* as a pure statement of faith,[13] then any connection between the two seems impossible. In this case, we would consider utopia as an imaginative call for a human answer on the level of practical action. Eschatology, instead, would imply a specific historical dynamic that naturally tends toward a predetermined outcome; it would imply an intended result in every historical event without, or despite, human effort.[14] In this sense, then, utopia and eschatology refer to different interpretations of the meaning of human life. Utopia appeals to human reason, as it requires, to be realized, a human action guided by practical reason. Eschatology, instead, appeals to human faith, as it directs humans in the passivity of the receiver of gift. Social structures organized around either of these two concepts, by consequence, seem to appeal to different features of human life to sustain themselves. If this holds true, then, there would be an unbridgeable separation between faith and reason. However, the problem is more complex. Can an eschatological message become also a practical statement, one that is oriented to action? Can eschatology intimate/engage the practical reason?[15] Ratzinger poses this question only from a Christian,

13. That is, an act of patience in wait of the realization of the ultimate purpose of our historical time.

14. Ratzinger, "Eschatology and Utopia," 10–12.

15. Ibid., 13–14.

catholic, point of view. However, this question is relevant for any research into ideologies and their realization in society. If we assume that eschatology can engage practical reason, in a similar way as utopia, then how can we demarcate clearly the difference between them? What forbids utopia to become an eschatological statement? We hold true that it is possible to make a theoretical distinction between the two. However, in the moment we consider their social relevance and influence, how can we clearly state that utopia does not require any *statement of faith*? How can we say that utopia is only the result of a call to our rational reason?

In this sense, the doctrine of *Chiliasm*, described by Ratzinger, opens up fruitful possibilities of investigation. The name of this doctrine derives from Revelation 20, in which is said that Jesus and the saints will reign for one thousand years on earth before the end of the world.[16] Ratzinger describes chiliasm as the expectation of a meta-historical eschatology that has, nonetheless, an historical moment of realization in history and human reality

> . . . it virtually duplicates eschatology by expecting God to achieve his purpose with man and history in this world as well as in the next, so that even within history there must be an end-time in which everything will be as it should have been all along. . . . It is to be a political entity . . . but with the power, security, and success that presuppose the unmediated political activity of God himself.[17]

Chiliasm rests on a specific understanding of the relation between faith and reason, between faith and realism and—ultimately—between humanity and God. It is the expectation of a golden age, beyond all politics, given by God. However, this age has to be realized through human political means. Its possibility is guaranteed by the logic of history itself, so that it becomes right to employ political means according to a meta-political logic. Marxism, says Ratzinger, is a clear example of chiliasm, with the only difference that God has been substituted with the historical inevitability of proletarian victory.[18] The example of Chiliasm, opens the possibility of an area of blurriness between the secular and the religious. The fundamental *religious sentiment* is not limited only to historical religions. History, in fact, has presented us examples that secular ideologies rest on quasieschatological assumptions to sustain and legitimize their own claims. Of course, an immediate criticism against this possibility would suggest that such eschatological/irratio-

16. Rev 20:1–6.
17. Ratzinger, "Eschatology and Utopia," 14.
18. Ibid., 15–16.

nal claims pertain only to very specific secular ideologies—like Nazism or Communism—that had built not only a political account of society, but also a precise ontological structure regarding human life. Surely, a critic may say, this assumption about a hidden irrationality cannot be extended to secular societies generally, particular to liberal democratic ones.

To develop my hypothesis further, and with this possible criticism in mind, I would like to examine a book that Ratzinger wrote together with Habermas, *Dialektik der Saekularisierung*. In this work, Habermas addresses a most peculiar question about secular states and societies. Do they rely on normative assumptions that cannot be guaranteed naturally? Does the existence of the democratic state rest on ethical, local assumptions (of a religion or a worldview) that have prelegal, prepolitical binding character?[19]

In trying to answer to these questions, Ratzinger presents an interesting argument. We have to consider, he affirms, two main features of the problem. The first one is the formation of a global community in which political, economic and cultural powers become more and more entangled and dependent on one another. The second is the new interpretation of human possibilities that the secular framework has developed. Human beings, in the new framework, have obtained, and are described as possessing, a greater power of creation and destruction. This new dimension of human possibilities, the broader horizon in which their actions are interpreted, poses questions of the ethical and legal justifications for all of the global community. However, Ratzinger also adds a third problem that secular discourses have often ignored. In the encounter of different cultures, ethical certainties that had offered a solid foundation have largely disintegrated. The question of what the good is and why one should do the good even when it goes against his own self-interest has been left generally unanswered.[20] Ratzinger claims the answer to such a problem cannot be (and in fact has not been) provided by academic debates. A fully naturalist account of human life, that tries to investigate human life in a purely materialistic fashion, fails to maintain a consistent naturalist and materialist argument to justify and prescribe the good. Natural sciences have no interest, nor the tools, to start any kind of discussion on this subject in the first place.[21] This becomes even more evident the moment we analyze those principles that, in Western societies, are claimed to be valid and normative even before any kind of law expressed by the rule of majority. Human rights are such an example. In this particular case, we face an issue regarding the language and the sphere

19. Habermas and Ratzinger, *Dialectics of Secularization*, 21–23.
20. Ibid., 55.
21. Ibid., 55–57.

of relevance of such a concept. Can we describe human rights merely as a procedural legal matter? Is there an ethical discourse that is being developed in them? If human rights do possess an ethical value, together with their legal charge, then where does the ethical normativity of the concept come from? As counter-example, Ratzinger presents us the case that Islam has created its own set of human rights, that are different from Western ones, and that even Chinese culture is beginning to question human rights as a typical Western cultural invention. This reveals the question that, according to Ratzinger, modernity has left unanswered: What is the source of the law? Does the law stand by itself? Is it self-legitimized and self-evident? Does it come from a deeper source? Does it stand before and beyond any simple human individuality?[22]

This whole problem revolves around the concepts of *law* and *nature* as we have inherited them from Enlightenment. *Natural law* has remained the key issue of the dialogue with and within secular society. This concept implies the idea that there is a fundamental *law* that comes before any local claim because of an implicit rationality present in nature (and therefore in human nature) itself. The Enlightenment and the ethical and legal tradition developed after it, considered natural law as the foundation of any legal and ethical claim to universality. However, according to Ratzinger, with the victory of the theory of evolution, secular reason has capsized itself. The idea of evolution denies explicitly the existence of a deeper rationality within nature, as the current shape of our world has been determined just by a struggle for survival and adaptation. If there is no rationality inherent to nature itself (although we can have rational behavior in it), how can we claim the existence of a rational law that comes *from* nature?[23] In the specific case of human rights, we have to struggle with this contradiction. The concept of *human rights* relies on the assumption that by the simple fact of belonging to the human species, a human being is the subject of certain rights. Such a claim, however, is a sheer ungrounded assertion that has to rely on a fundamental ethical/ontological hypostasis about human nature and the rights it deserves. Without the support of a rational nature, human rights find themselves dangerously weakened, so that Ratzinger claims that they should be completed with a doctrine of human obligations and human limitations.[24]

Ratzinger claims that, given the tensions present in the Western tradition of rationality in itself, and the impossibility of recreating itself in a different cultural environment, we should admit that secular rationality as

22. Ibid., 58–61.
23. Ibid., 65–68.
24. Ibid., 69–72.

well should drop any claims of universality and start to seriously engage in dialogue with different cultural expressions on a position of equality.[25] According to Ratzinger, one common secular argument is that we see today, as in the past, *pathologies of religion*. That is, we see religion not being a source of positive moral action. Instead, a *moral pathology* causes people to commit violent acts. However, if this is the case, we also have to recognize that there are *pathologies of reason* as well. *Rationality* is an attitude that is not exclusive of reason, if by reason we intend the secular *faith in reason*. Instead, there is a relation between reason and faith, as well as between reason and religion. A postsecular society has to realize this social truth to strip itself of the Western *hubris* that has hitherto impeded a fruitful dialogue with different cultures.[26]

Ratzinger sees a new form of apocalypticism in modern secular ideologies. This is a clear claim that he makes in his work *Values in a Time of Upheaval*. In Marxism and positivism, Ratzinger sees forms of messianic politics, a religion for intellectuals, that has been nourished, from one side, by evolutionism, that has transformed history into a purely biological fact, and, from the other side, by the Hegelian dialectic, that has inspired a quasimythological expectation in an inevitable progress within the secular mentality. A work of demythologization is needed urgently so that politics can carry again its role in a truly rational way.[27]

Ratzinger is developing a peculiar theoretical argument. He is separating rationality from the actual scientific reason. Key concepts of modern secular ideologies, like *freedom* or *progress* are described as having a strong mythical charge that, paradoxically, reveals a deeper irrationality that presents no difference from the religious one. For Ratzinger, reason is, primarily, moral reason, a feature that guides human action. A rational attitude can be found not in the mere procedure of measuring and quantifying, but in actual ethical thought and moral struggle toward good ends through good means.[28] As Tracey Rowland has showed us, in her *Ratzinger's Faith*, Ratzinger has not written one all-encompassing comprehensive exposition of his own genealogy of modernity. He has offered us pieces of the puzzle in various books and articles. However, we can secure the general point that he has no sympathy at all for a vision of modernity as something completely new. Neither does he have any patience for the doctrine of social evolution and the Hegelian belief in constant progress to which it is closely allied.

---

25. Ibid., 72–76.
26. Ibid., 77–80.
27. Ratzinger, *Values in a Time of Upheaval*, 16–18.
28. Ibid., 24–29.

Ratzinger rejects all materialistic and deterministic theories of history.²⁹ Instead, he describes a much more complex relation between secularism and religion. It is not possible to describe secularism simply as a wholly different phenomenon. Because the two share some fundamental similarities in the ethical and moral discourse that gives them substance and social sustainability. As Rowland has showed, Ratzinger rejects all philosophies of history that would find in the historical process some dynamic outside the theodrama of God's offer of grace and the human response to this offer.³⁰

I believe the reason has to be found in this threshold of indifference between secular and religious framework, which would put them, therefore, in direct competition for the same spaces of society. This suggests that it is not possible to operate a clear distinction between transcendent moral sources and immanent moral sources, as Taylor does. Secular and religious frameworks, instead, move in a common area. Both frameworks involve transcendent and immanent sources of value and good. In determinate historical/political conditions, the two frameworks seem to exclude each other at a fundamental level. The reason, however, has not to be found in their difference but precisely in their similarity, in the sense that they try to achieve a similar outcome, namely, to give a fundamental explanation for human action and represent the ideal outcome of such action. This is the reason why Ratzinger describes secular theories of historical progress, especially Marxist and liberal ideologies, as examples of ideological optimism and a secularization of Christian hope. His genealogy of modernity does not follow the school of thinking which reads modernity as an entirely new culture, completely severed from all Christian roots. According to Rowland, Ratzinger believes that the secular discourse is entangled with the Christian heritage on a fundamental level, despite the fact that secular liberal political elites wish to deny this entanglement.³¹

For Taylor, the line between secularism and religion is clear and definite. There are specific fields that belong to secularism and other ones that belong to religion. The correct and harmonious combination of them allows creating a stable and functional society.³² It is unclear, however, what kind

---

29 Tracey, *Ratzinger's Faith*, 107.

30. Ibid., 108.

31. Ibid., 108.

32. In this sense, *open faith* becomes the fundamental moral background of a society. An underlying moral sentiment that allows people from different perspective to still share a common dialogue in a common language. It could be argued that Taylor has been deeply affected by the secular discourse of *neutral ground*. In his negation of *secularism* as *neutral ground*, Taylor proposes a search for a *new one*, instead of a work of *translations between different languages*. As a metaphor, we could say that Taylor still

of harmony would be required to achieve such a stable society. The concept of *open faith*, in this sense, does not offer any clear direction for political/social action. As introduced at the beginning of this chapter, a theological interpretation of the problem reveals features of the relation between secularity and religion that are more complex than it seems at first sight. This is why I believe we should preserve a deeper historical sensibility, to keep ourselves free from generic, deductive definitions and, instead, analyze historical/social events in their specificity. If we want to acquire a more complete comprehension of them. I believe Ratzinger's possesses this kind of disposition in his historical/social analysis. We can see the existence of a hidden *faith-oriented* attitude even in secular structures. We have seen how, according to Ratzinger, even secular ideologies possess a mythical core that allows for a process of self-legitimization. For Ratzinger, this mythical core is tied to its Christian roots at a historical/sociological level, in the sense that it is the result of a process of secularization of the previous Christian origins. Ratzinger's project, in this sense, is to recover the Christian depth and reintroduce God as the ultimate source of legitimization and ethical action.

However, there are problems with Ratzinger's approach. First, Ratzinger still relies on a dichotomy based on faith/reason that is unhelpful for the argument I wish to present. Second, Ratzinger focuses on the problem only insofar it helps him to produce an argument in favor of the Catholic position. These limitations suggest that Ratzinger's position is not enough to pursue our analytical attempt to understand the common features of human life we have assumed exist. In the hope to obtain resources to address this problem, I will now turn to the work of Johann Baptist Metz. In his theological work, Metz is alert, like Ratzinger, to the possible existence of common features between secular and religious frameworks. Moreover, in focusing on the political value of Christianity Metz is able to develop a more precise account on the features of such political value, and apply them to secular frameworks as well. We find this sensibility in his work *A Passion for God*,[33] in which Metz analyzes the path of Christian theology after the confrontation, on one hand, with Marxist ideology and, on the other, with Auschwitz. In this work, Metz argues that a postidealist paradigm for theology should start from the assumption that the Enlightenment has been unable to completely privatize religion and fully secularize politics. The result of this failure is that even politically enlightened societies have their *political*

---

looks for the *Esperanto* that would allow different cultures to communicate between each other.

33. Other works that I have found helpful toward the understanding of Metz's theology are: Metz, *Emergent Church*; Peters, *Johann Baptist Metz*.

religions through which they try to legitimize and stabilize themselves.[34] Political religions serve to politicize historical religions. Political religions not only develop their own set of ethical values and foundational codes of actions, they also lead historical religion to uphold only their strict social functionalization, which becomes another tool for the self-legitimization of the political religion. According to Metz, a new theological paradigm should criticize both religions as legitimizations myth for the political framework and theologies that, by claiming their political neutrality, are denying the inherent political value of theology.[35] Metz also analyzes how religions relate to political ideologies, and how both of them relate to modernity. It is extremely interesting that secular political bodies, once religion has been believed privatized, once the threat of totalitarianism has been defeated, fail to legitimize themselves consistently precisely on the ground of modernity *per se*, which they wish to endorse.[36]

A genuine modern politics should do without any anchoring in transcendence. It should be a politics with a purely worldly legitimization of political rule, which is separated from religious and from all religious symbolizations of political legitimacy. However, Metz affirms, modern politics has been able, in fact, to legitimize itself only through *quasireligious* symbols.[37] Metz, following an approach that has already been adopted by Agnes Heller and Jacques Derrida, affirms that modern politics needs an "empty seat of power for the sacred," for the Messiah, even though, at the same time, it knows perfectly well that this sacred seat will always be left empty. Modern politics still needs an idea of the sacred for its own stability.[38] In this sense, Metz describes secular bodies with a different language than Taylor. Metz describes them as "quasireligious systems of symbols," in relation with both society and religions, although they claim otherwise. The strong separation that Taylor creates between secular ideologies and religion is missing. Metz implies that, in the moment of creating social/political bodies, humans need a reference to some idea of the sacred.[39] This idea of the sacred, even when it is structured in immanent frameworks, still needs a quasi-cultic reference that implies some appeal to the transcendent. This transcendent needs not

---

34. Metz, *Passion for God*, 35. As examples, Metz presents both American civil religion and European bourgeois religion as forms of political religions.

35. Ibid., 35–36. It could be said, by reversing Metz's argument, that if every theology has a political value, by virtue of the failure of Enlightenment to secularize politics, than every political ideology possess also a theological charge.

36. Ibid., 136–37.

37. Ibid., 138–40.

38. Ibid., 140–41.

39. Ibid., 141–43.

be a specific God, it just needs to possess the normative power apt to impose its own rules beyond any particular political discussion. The case of human rights, on which Metz wishes to build a connection between politics and religion,[40] is exemplary in this sense.

If we follow Metz, then, it becomes extremely hard to sustain a neat and clear separation between religion and secularism. Both rely on fundamental existential features that Western modernity, despite its official rejection of them, has not been able to remove from its history. Instead, it actively needs them to stabilize and sustain itself. Metz dedicates more space to this problem in another work, *Faith in History and Society*. In this work, Metz discusses a series of questions of contemporary theology (the concept of religion, its distinction from the revelation, the features of a natural theology etc.) as problems arising during the post-Reformation era. Such problems are, mainly, reactions to the controversy about the metaphysical and historical origins of Christianity posed during the Enlightenment.[41] The Enlightenment brought two major changes in Christian structures. First, it broke the identity between faith and religious consciousness. This also allowed for the creation of a universal/fundamental concept of religion before of which Christianity had to justify itself. The second change was the breaking of the unity between religion and society. Christianity began to appear, for the first time in history, as a particular aspect of a much wider universe of social relations and historical connections. Because of the crisis of these two major structures, Enlightenment gave rise to the criticism of religion as we know it today; such criticism quickly became a criticism of ideology.[42]

However, Metz proposes a reexamination of Enlightenment and modernity as such. The simple reason being that it is extremely difficult to distinguish, in modern tradition, a real validity—in the sense of grounded in reality—for any discourse about the human being as such and his reason, autonomy, freedom and other abstract attributes that the Enlightenment claimed and advocated. Enlightenment itself, in its antireligious criticism, fell into a paradox. It recreated, in a different form, the same phenomenon it criticized. Metz, in his narrative, accepts that the Enlightenment started the process of privatization of religion,[43] followed by a loss of tradition and

---

40. Ibid., 144–45.

41. Metz, *Faith in History and Society*, 4–10. It is interesting to notice how this discourse would resonate with Cavanaugh's statements in *The Myth of Religious Violence*.

42. Ibid., 15–17.

43. Ibid., 34–36. In dealing with privatization, Metz advances ideas that are extremely similar to the one proposed by Cavanaugh. The phenomenon of privatization and religion started with the conflict between monarchs and the church. In the Middle Ages, they were not private phenomenon but actual social expression of both customs

a loss of authority by the traditional religious institutions.[44] However, Metz affirms that the Enlightenment initiated also another process, the development of a *middle-class religion*. The Enlightenment created a set of core values for a new understanding of society thanks to its criticism of the use of metaphysical reason. It revealed, on a social level, that the *reason of the time* is directly linked with the bodies of power of that time (that were, at the time of the Enlightenment, religious and political power). The metaphysical structure of the world is a process of self-legitimization of the political authorities, whose structures of power are interpreted as representing a higher order of the universe. The philosophers of the Enlightenment, by locating reason only in the study and knowledge of natural things, wanted to avoid precisely this metaphysical form of legitimization of power. In this sense, Metz agrees with Carl Schmitt's interpretation of the Enlightenment. In its attempt to escape metaphysical reason, the Enlightenment recreated precisely the same phenomenon it wanted to fight. In making reason an abstract universal value, it shaped the social body according to a specific ontological structure in which the reasonable man was the middle-class owner. The Enlightenment structured a new concept of subject, of praxis and of their social interaction so that a new elite and a new aristocracy could be created.[45] The Enlightenment, in rejecting religion, recreated a new *religio naturalis*, a religion of reason.[46] The Enlightenment, in its antimetaphysical fury, recreated a metaphysical understanding of the world.[47]

This, of course, generates strong repercussions on the social structures of political communities. As an example, we can think about Gregory Baum's analysis of middle-class religion in the American context. As Baum shows us, the idea of the United States as a middle-class society exercises a twofold influence on the way in which the single individual structures his social world. First, it cuts out those elements of society that do not *fit* in the represented image, the theory does eliminate from sight a large section of citizenry that cannot be represented through the constructed image of middle class. This allows the single individual to shape his own sense of reality according to the criteria of the middle-class paradigm. The Americans

---

and powers. It is only after the reformation that the state began to emancipate itself from religion to become an exclusive social body.

44. Ibid., 36–42. Those as well, quite classical stage in the narrative of secularization.

45. Ibid., 42–44.

46. Ibid., 44–46.

47. It will be mainly for this reason that Schmitt will claim that *modern liberalism does not know itself*. Metz seems to agree with Schmitt's interpretation of the phenomenon. The point of disagreement between the two would be the interpretation of social relations as organized by the categories of friend and foe.

regard themselves as middle-class citizens in a middle-class society, thus shaping their perceptions of their social/historical reality around that concept.[48] Second—and for this reason Gregory Baum decides to use Metz's category of *middle-class religion*—the concept offers a moral framework, a general ethos to citizens. It generates a self-symbolization of the entire nation, which acquires moral, historical and transcendental purposes.[49]

Iring Fetscher, in his "State Socialist Ideology as Religion?," offers a similar analysis on the socialist side of the argument. Using Metz's language of political religion, Fetscher describes the Marxist-Leninist ideology as a phenomenon full of religious characteristics, despite the claims of being a science. This religious character of Marxism-Leninism is found in the structure of the party and its continuous tendency to create a strong symbolic authority that, even in the language of common members of the party, must keep the theory pure. Fetscher compares this kind of position to the persecution of heretics executed by the medieval Church.[50] We are confronted here with the phenomenon of institutional Marxism in which, contrarily to intellectual Marxism, it is a specific authority—Fetscher examines the case of Stalin's organization of the party—that decides which kind of languages and which theories can be considered Marxist or not. In this way, we can define the Marxist of the period as the ones who are ready *to accept ideas that have been confirmed by the authority*, independently of their personal knowledge of the arguments mentioned.[51] The Stalinist interpretation had become a fundamental ontological structure of the world, while the Soviet communist party had become the authority that represented and was legitimized by this ontology. Fetscher, therefore, presents us the case in which an ideology, and the institution that makes itself the pure transmitter for it, not only involves an individual at the moment of procedural political decisions. It involves every moment of his life and helps in shaping all his categories and classifications of reality. In this sense, the comparison with a religion is well placed.

I suggest that, in Metz's categories of *middle-class religion* and *political religion*, we see a view comparable to the thought of Croce, discussed in the previous chapter. We see a clear distinction between the historical religions and an inherent *sentiment of the religious* that is present in secular societies as well, despite their claims to have rejected everything that is irrational. Metz's position fits in the tradition that describes human beings as

---

48. Baum, "Middle Class Religion in America," 17–19.
49. Ibid., 19–21.
50. Fetscher, *State Socialist Ideology as Religion*, 82–83.
51. Ibid., 83.

being inherently *homo religiosis*. This necessity for symbolism, for a sense of the sacred, easily escapes the dichotomy religious/secular or transcendent/immanent and refers to a deeper feature of human sociality and existence. After all, if even a self-consciously secular society produces something akin to a religion, then, where do we locate the transcendent? Can we just restrict it to the figure of a divine God?

Thinking as he does, Metz conceives a different relation between Christianity and secularity. Metz, unlike Taylor, does not rely upon an opposition of dichotomies, but on an opposition of similarities. Secular frameworks and religious frameworks compete against each other precisely because similar processes of symbolization and structuring happen in human sociality, and these frameworks compete for the same social spheres. We find another development of the question in the article "How Faith Sees the World." In this work, Metz—in agreement with Taylor—affirms that secularity is a process that could happen only by way of Christianity. It is, originally, a Christian event. However, secularity in itself is not an opposition to Christianity. He suggests, instead, it is the realization of its deeper spiritual charge. In this sense, Metz says, secularization is still imbued in a Christian framework, it operates through it and realizes, in it, a truly Christian Spirit. Western civilization, in its separation between *imperium* and *sacerdotium*, in its scientific independence, must still be interpreted as a Christian understanding of the world.[52]

Of course, we must consider the different aims of the two authors. Metz's aim is to develop a new Christian political theology for a modern church, while Taylor wants to develop a social narrative that enables the creation of a pluralist society. However, both authors address the same issue of secularization and political power.[53] In Metz, the relation between secular and religious dynamics is not described as a game of polarities, or dichotomies. For the German theologian, the boundaries between secularity and religion, between what is political and what is sacred are more blurred than we can assume at first glance. We see in Metz a reversal of the relation between Christianity and Secularism. For Taylor there is opposition and contradiction. Secularism is the answer to the inner contradictions of Christianity, an answer that aims to deny God and everything that is transcendent by relegating religion to the private sphere. The public/social sphere becomes the realm of the immanent, of secularity, regulating and

---

52. Metz, "How Faith Sees the World," 18–21.

53. To be fair, I would also say that Metz addresses the question of power in a more consistent way than Taylor does. In keeping his analysis sociological, Taylor does not really addresses the question of dynamics of power, subsuming them under the category of *cultural practices*.

restricting the languages and messages that is possible to express in it. For Metz, instead, Christianity in itself is a process of secularization. Modern secularism is the product that explicates the inner force of the Christian spirit. It has stripped mother earth of its magical character and has provided the historical separation between *imperium* and *sacerdotium*. The essence of Christianity, according to Metz, tends toward the demythologization of the world, so that this process, continued by modernity, possesses undeniable ties with its Christian predecessor. This, sometimes, has taken the forms of a rejection of the Christian understanding of the historical world, however, Metz affirms, secularism cannot deny the deep ties it has with its Christian origins, with the spirit that resides within itself.[54]

Metz develops a clear distinction between the process of secularization, which is a spiritual/cultural human process, and the secularity of the world, its worldliness. This distinction is born out of Metz's understanding of the human being as an historical actor. Every understanding of the world is always historical. For this reason, every interpretation of the world is always at odd with the world itself, as such understanding is always conditioned by the socio-historical situation in which the human being is immersed. For a Christian, the worldly quality of the world should be understood in its essential status as a creation of God, linked to him, but, at the same time, something other than him. The human being, being a creature much like the world, would always be unable to grasp a full understanding of it and always have to rely on mediated understandings of the world. In this sense, historically, Metz identifies three points of view about this quality of worldliness. First, the worldliness of the world that is yet unmediated by the historical action of Christianity, the innocent world, much like in the ancient pagan world. Second, the worldliness of the world that is released by the historical effect of Christianity, as a world with a Christian history of secularization within it. Third, the worldliness of the world that misunderstands this process and protest against its Christian origin and tries to emancipate itself from it.[55] If a process of secularization is implicit in the Christian movement toward the world, the worldliness of the world is something that keeps us at a distance. In this sense, the Christian world, with its demythologization, with its separation between the sphere of the secular and the sphere of the holy, is not a world immediately permeated by God. To be involved with the world does not necessarily imply a connection with God. Metz proposes an example; a young Christian man wants to become an engineer. This is a historical decision, namely, it is a decision made within specific

---

54. Ibid., 34–37.
55. Ibid., 40–41.

historical conditions and presupposes a relation with the world. However, such decision does not imply directly a relation with God. For the young man to live his life in a Christian way, including his decision to become an engineer, he will need an attitude of faith to catch up with his contingent history. In this way, he will establish his connection with God.[56] There is then a separation between his worldly decision to become an engineer and his faith in a Christian history. The relation with God is not immediately available to him through the world.

Such separation, implied in the process of secularization within Christianity, can be bridged with our faith. However, such bridge can never be completely developed, and the secularity of the world is always something unconquered, as not penetrated by faith. There is always a hidden implication of the Christian living in a double-truth, a silent acknowledgment that his faith in God is no longer implied directly in his historical action. For this reason, the world is truly secular, as the human historical action within it does not imply a direct link with God. Such link can only be established in a second moment, through our faith. The interesting feature of Metz's argument lies on the fact that, although he uses it in reference to the Christian religion, its application can be extended well beyond the historical concept of religion. If we do operate a distinction between secularization, as a process, and secularity as worldliness, then any form of relation between human beings and the world can be considered as a bridge of faith, an attempt to conquer the secularity of the world, even by secular social forms.[57] In this sense, any kind of ideology/system of value through which we try to orientate our lives needs a bridge of faith, as it is not implied directly in our historical action. To paraphrase Metz's example of the young man, we may see a young man that wishes to become an engineer, or a doctor, but for the young man to also recognize himself as a rational individual, or a democratic individual,[58] he will have to build a bridge of faith in which he

---

56. Ibid., 42–44.

57. After all, we could very well make the argument that science and secular ideologies have not conquered at all the world in its worldliness.

An interesting reference about this problem could be found in Edward Schillebeeckx's work. In *Church: The Human Story of God*, he affirms that the two great beliefs that, historically, proceeded with the development of secularism (that science and technology would have freed the humans from pain and suffering, and that with secularism and technology the religions would disappear) have been proved wrong by reality. Religions have not disappeared and humanity is still suffering, maybe even in a greater way than in the past. It could be argued then, that if even secular ideologies and sciences can be proved wrong by reality, then the world, in its worldliness, is still uncharted territory, even for them.

58. Or any other kind of value system/ideological qualification, like communist, capitalist, atheist, German, American, European, etc.

can inscribe his historical action. With this concept of worldliness, there is an inevitable tension between the human immediate historical action and its self-understanding.

This is precisely the kind of sensibility I have tried to outline in the previous chapter, through Croce's philosophy. Instead of the simple categories of religion and secularity and their deductive application to social realities, Metz refers to a deeper feature of human life. This feature is inherent to our existence in the world. It takes place the moment the human being enters into a relation with the objects around him and has to find some kind of structure, it has to inscribe them in a system of meaning that can *give meaning* to his immediate historical action. Such deeper religiosity as a basic feature of the human relation with the world allows Metz to develop a different description of the relation between religion and secularism. Rather than a simple opposition between transcendent and immanent, secular ideologies are fellow processes of elaboration of the secularity of the world. In this way, Metz affirms that the *Christian way of life* is not endangered by the world, in itself. Instead those ideologies that give us a falsified vision of this secularity are the real threat, as they create myths[59] that threaten to substitute the Christian understanding of the world with one equally ideological/religious. In Metz's argument, only Christianity is able to take seriously the secularity of the world, while secular ideologies always end up offering a false impression of the world, so that to Christianize the world means, for Metz, to make it truly secular.[60]

Through this process, Metz offers us a different meaning of faith, in his theology. He can describe the transition from cosmos-centrism to anthropocentrism, from religiosity to secularism, as one that has happened not against, but through Christianity precisely because he uses a different interpretation of faith. Faith is not, according to Metz, a narrowly religious sentiment, something linked with historical religions. It is, primarily, an act to bridge the separation between human historical action and the world in itself; it is the process through which we find meaning in the world and in our historical actions. This concept of faith is extremely different from the open-faith proposed by Taylor. Taylor's open faith aims to bridge the gap between transcendence and immanent, between different religions and between different social groups. It is an act of openness aimed to overcome any distinction, aimed to achieve a communal way of life. It is a moral/social sentiment for common life directed toward human flourishing. Metz's

---

59. Either the positive ones of a utopian progress on earth, or the negative ones of nihilism and scepticism.

60. Ibid., 46–51.

concept of faith, instead, comes from a very different view. It is an ontological stance toward reality, a reality perceived differently from the simple dichotomy transcendent/immanent. In his Christian understanding of the world, Metz does not derive faith from a dialectic contradiction between an immanent moral source and a transcendent one. Instead, the secularity of the world is the natural consequence of God's transcendence. Faith is the ontological stance that allows the realization of this relation between God and the world. There is, then, not contradiction, but difference between the two terms of the relation, a difference that has to be bridged through the ontological posture that we call faith. Such process happens for religious and secular interpretations of the world. As I already said, Metz still links such faith, in its perfect expression, to the Christian faith. However, I believe the application of the concept as a category for understanding historical event can be applied beyond such restriction.

FAITH AS THE CORE FEATURE OF SOCIAL LIFE: RICHARD NIEBUHR

In my argument, so far, I have suggested the existence of a fundamental human attitude that is present in both religious and social contexts. For the sake of clarity, in the previous chapter, in reference to the work of Croce and Hegel, I have called this attitude *religious sentiment*. However, this term does not help us to go beyond the secular divide. It still presupposes a *religious* approach toward reality that evokes concepts that are considered far too different from a secular attitude. The argument I propose, against the classical distinction between secularism and religion, is to use the term *faith* not to denote a *religious* attitude towards reality, but to denote the ontological relation that every social form, secular or religious, establishes with its own sense of reality. To define further the features of this ontological posture, I turn now to the work of H. Richard Niebuhr, who has developed very useful insights on what entails an *attitude of faith*. In his work *Radical Monotheism and Western Civilization*, Niebuhr proposes an interesting argument. A first important statement opens the book: "the essence of the problems of contemporary civilization is not constituted by the problem of religion; instead, the main core of these problems is faith."[61] According to Niebuhr

> We express our ultimate faith in all our social institutions and decisions, not in religion only. Furthermore, our whole culture, I believe, is deeply involved in a conflict of faiths that is to be

61. H. R. Niebuhr, *Radical Monotheism and Western Civilization*, 1.

distinguished from the collisions between religions and between religion and irreligion. In the ensuing lectures I shall try to analyze this conflict as one between radical monotheism and the other forms of human faith, polytheism and henotheism, in their modern, non-mythological guise.[62]

Faith, as a concept that indicates personal commitment, adhesion, belief or trust, is related strongly to an idea of order, may it be political or religious. When we speak of faith, we speak of an adhesion to an idea of order that is political, moral and even ontological. Niebuhr addresses the concept in different works, and always presents the problem of faith in a broader context than the religious one. For example, in *Faith on Earth*, he noticed how the concept of faith, despite being closely related, in our present society, to religious content such as God, church and creed, is, in reality, used in a much broader communicative context. Politicians not only link their discourses to a divine being, but also openly speak of *keeping faith* with those who have died in wars, or to have *faith in democracy*.[63] From this premise, Niebuhr implies that the problem of faith in itself is much more complex than the current discourse admits.

> Is not the word faith so highly equivocal or even indeterminate in meaning that it cannot be significantly used in such various connections in the course of one conversation? Now it means belief in a doctrine; now the acceptance of intuited or self-evident truths. . . Do not these meanings vary so greatly that it is an illusion to think of all these faiths as having anything in common that can be a fit subject of inquiry? It may be so . . . But it may also be that faith points to a complex structure of which now this, now that, element is focused in the attention while the remainder of the structure is implied.[64]

Faith is described as a multifaceted structure. It is a common feature of human life that reveals only specific parts of itself according to the specific context in which it appears, while implying the whole structure. Reinhold Niebuhr, Richard's brother, was very receptive to the concept of faith presented in such terms. In *Faith and Politics*, Reinhold describes how faith is related to a realm of meaning, more than to the figure of a God. In this sense, Marx, Freud and Nietzsche, in declaring the death of God, at the same time tried to project alternative *structures of meaning*. Marx was the most successful, as he was able to develop an apocalyptic materialistic vision

---

62. Ibid., 1.
63. H. R. Niebuhr, *Faith on Earth*, 1.
64. Ibid., 4.

in which a secular eschatology is unfolded through history until the final redemption, in which the working class will topple the wealthy capitalist class from its position of power.[65] In this sense then, the religious myths of creation, although disproved by science, are still valid in the inherent and mysterious need for a meaning that is expressed in them. Such need for a meaning is still present in secular ideologies as well. The Darwinian controversy during the nineteenth century is, for Reinhold Niebuhr, a clear example of this.[66]

In *Radical Monotheism*, H. R. Niebuhr offers us an analysis of the forms faith can take in our social relations. He uses the word *henotheism* to define a form of faith in which a definite social structure, political or religious in nature, becomes the object of trust and loyalty. Niebuhr describes henotheism as capable of subverting even officially monotheistic institutions such as the churches[67] to uphold its own specific set of values. For this reason, speaking from a theological view that is clearly alert to such danger, he defines henotheism as the most dangerous rival of monotheism. Faith, as a concept, is described, instead, as

> . . .the attitude and action of confidence in, and fidelity to, certain realities as the sources of value and the objects of loyalty. This personal attitude or action is ambivalent; it involves reference to the value that attaches to the self and to the value toward which the self is directed. On the one hand, it is trust in that which gives value to the self; on the other hand, it is loyalty to what the self values.[68]

---

65. R. Niebuhr, *Faith and Politics*, 3–6. However, speaking from a contemporary point of view, it is possible for us to say the same about economic neoliberalism and capitalism. The historical context did made difficult for Reinhold Niebuhr to push his thought so far but, at the same time, it could be said that, would have he used more his brother's work, he would have been able to notice the inherent weaknesses of Western culture at that time. Further evidence of this could be find, I believe, in how Reinhold Niebuhr addresses inequalities of privileges and power in *Moral Man and Immoral Society*.

66. Ibid., 6–10. In the same way, Reinhold Niebuhr states that, despite the rejection or religious myths, modern secularism still has some limits in its discourse because of the inherent mythical nature of some concepts, which makes them impossible to explicate through a naturalistic/empirical language. Things like values, the concept of creation, the unity and meaningfulness of the world are inherently mythical problems. Secular ideologies have to choose between a total discard of them or a translation of these myths in an acceptable language that, however, in the end does not negate the mythical nature of these problems; in this sense, then, we obtain rationalized myths (ibid., 15–23).

67. H. R. Niebuhr, *Radical Monotheism and Western Civilization*, 1–2.

68. Ibid., 8. It is interesting to notice how Niebuhr presents, at the same time, both

Following H. R. Niebuhr's approach, it is possible to define things such as friendship, nationalism, or the belief in a particular structure of society as forms of faith, despite being extremely different from the contemporary standard definition of the term. We can conceive faith as something like a value-centered attitude, or the commitment to a cause. The truthfulness of this definition of faith is shown when we examine severe moments of *crisis of faith*, such moments reveal the human necessity to *have faith* into something. This basic attitude of faith represents a need for a center of value that, in return, gives value to our lives. For example, we can examine what happens to a society when it meets a perceived failure. It can be the betrayal of or from the gods, a treason, the failure of an atheistic attempt to create an existentialism of self-liberation, the failure of a political ideology. All these individual/social events can easily fit the definition of *crisis of faith*.[69] In the moment of crisis, the human being faces a loss of meaning that does not involve only the things he believes in, but invest his whole world and existence.

Through these reflections on the nature of faith, Niebuhr redefines the concept of monotheism, intended as the loyalty and commitment to one specific *source of value*, a One beyond from which we derive our meaningfulness and values. Such monotheism is in constant conflict with alternative forms of faith, namely either a pluralism of sources of values, defined as polytheism, or a social faith with a specific social object, defined as henotheism. Niebuhr also redefines the concept of atheism, defined as an alternative form of faith that aims specifically to the negation of the monotheist One beyond.[70] On this note, H. R. Niebuhr says that something like true atheism, a radical negation of any source of value, would be a kind of psychological solipsism all centered on the act of negation of any value, without any positive, constructive content. In this sense, a radical form of atheism would be irreconcilable with human life. In fact, Niebuhr affirms that "to deny the reality of a supernatural being called God is one thing; to live without confidence in some center of value and without loyalty to

---

a similarity and a difference of assumptions with Charles Taylor. Niebuhr defines faith, like Taylor, as a form of connection to our ultimate values. However, unlike Taylor, we can see firstly how the relation of faith, for Niebuhr, has a nonexclusive field of application. Secondly, how this attitude is a form of relation that involves not only our evaluation of what is good, but also how the good in itself is reflected upon our self, how the self is in a relation with the evaluated good that works both ways.

69. Ibid., 9–16. Niebuhr uses here, as a primary reference, Tolstoy's work *Confession*. This theme, however, is extremely common in the whole of the Russian literature; another clear example would be Dostoevsky's *The Brothers Karamazov*.

70. Ibid., 17–18.

a cause is another."[71] Paradoxically, the atheist negation of the monotheist one-beyond does not represent an escape from the phenomenon of faith, but merely the replacement of a specific source of value with alternative sources of value.

Niebuhr's thought offer insights that are useful in criticizing Taylor's conclusions and also represent a strong foundation for the argument I am developing. The main point of difference between the two authors has to be found in the definition of faith. In Charles Taylor's *A Secular Age*, the moral source defines also the existential relation that the individual establishes with his sources of good.[72] In this way, Taylor defines the religious relation as belief (as it points toward transcendence, towards God), while secular immanentism is defined as unbelief (as it negates a transcendental source of good). In doing this, Taylor negates the possibility that an individual related to a secular framework could develop a relation of faith with his sources of good. The relation, for Taylor, is based purely on immanent grounds, while a religious individual develops a relation of faith with his sources of good. The object toward which the relation is aimed defines the existential posture of the individual. We can aim toward a religious source of good only through a relation of faith or belief, while to aim toward a nonreligious source of good we automatically establish a relation of different nature. Niebuhr, instead, interprets faith as the relational attitude of the individual (or of a society).

---

71. Ibid., 18–19; in the same way, Reinhold Niebuhr, in *The Nature and Destiny of Man*, in the first chapter, "Man as a Problem to Himself," tells us how all modern ideologies have to rest on some meaningful general assumption, a naïve faith, to give consistency to their claims.

For example: physiocratic capitalism had to rest on the assumption that nature's pre-established harmonies would stop humans from destroying themselves. While every philosophy of history has to rely on an idea of progress, in which either by a force immanent in nature itself, or by the gradual extension of rationality, or by the elimination of specific sources of evil, modern man expects to move toward some kind of perfect society (H. R. Niebuhr, *Radical Monotheism and Western Civilization*, 20–26).

72. Taylor does not openly admit this; however, I believe we can assume this strong connection from the language Taylor uses to describe religion and secularity. For example, we can analyze his affirmation that when naturalistic materialism presents itself as the only view compatible with the most prestigious institution of the modern world, like science, then it is conceivable for an individual to relinquish his faith (*Secular Age*, 28).

Another hint is the strong connection, established throughout the work, between religion as belief and secularity as unbelief. On the other hand, even more importantly, by the identification of secularity with individuality and a newfound importance for human action, even the providential social order is described, by Taylor, as an index for human action and not as an ontological statement (*Secular Age*, 541–43). In Taylor's work, ontological claims do not seem to belong to the field of secularity, while being the norm in the religious field.

He identifies the features of this relation and, then, qualifies as faith those forms of relation in which the same features are present, independently from their religious or nonreligious context. In Niebuhr's case the analysis moves from the things in which we believe to the existential attitude we assume toward them. What kind of relation are we establishing with what we consider important? What form of consciousness are we developing in this relation?

In this way, even though we can see feelings of loyalty and commitment towards intrinsically different sources of good (a definite social structure, a plurality of values or God, a unique God or value), all the existential relations that present the same features of loyalty and commitment are described as faith. We find valuable insights that help to understand this crucial difference of perspective in the work *God the Center of Value*, by Grant. According to Grant, Niebuhr understands faith as a two-moment dynamic. There is faith as *trust*, in which a source of value is experienced as that which gives value to the self and to the world around the self. After trust, there is faith as loyalty in which the individual vows an active commitment toward the source of value and vows to further promote it in his world. For Niebuhr, if trust is the passive side of faith, loyalty is the active.[73]

By comparing Niebuhr's concept of faith to Taylor's concept of faith, we see the difference more clearly. Taylor focuses only on the feature of trust toward some sources of value, and in a very partial way at that. He only focuses on the moment in which the individual enters into a relation with the source of good, but totally disregards the moment in which the value reflects back a sense of meaningfulness toward the individual and structures his whole world. In Taylor, this reciprocity of meaning is flattened to the reflective action of the pure individual subject. For this reason, Taylor is compelled to give a definition of faith only in connection to the values trusted. He does not dedicate enough attention to the second moment, in which the value, or values, structures the whole world of the subject, not just his moral compass, in a nonreflective way. This process happens in both religious and nonreligious contexts. In addition, precisely because Taylor focuses only on the trust component of faith, he completely disregards the component of loyalty. That is, the moral commitment to the value that seeks and pursues its promotion not only within the self, but also in the world. Such component of loyalty is what compels the individual to structure the world around him according to the image given by the value. In this context, something like an open faith becomes an absurd definition. It is not possible to obtain a faith that does not seek to create an external order, a totalizing

---

73. Grant, *God the Center of Value*, 43–45.

manifestation, of the value it refers, and this is true both for religious and secular faiths.[74]

Of course, there are, between the two authors, also similarities. Niebuhr and Taylor are similar, for example, in how they connect faith with lived experience. However, Niebuhr's analysis presents a limit because his system, unlike Taylor's, considers faith and its relation to ethics, a personal system.[75] Faith is, for Niebuhr, deeply personal and interpersonal. Niebuhr's ethics is pervaded by an underlying individualism. Unlike Taylor, Niebuhr is unable to conceive a social body as group. For Niebuhr, a social self is always an *individual self* alongside other individual selves.[76] It is true that Niebuhr's interest lies, ultimately, in the individual, and not in the social realities of which individuals are part. This represent a limit to how far we can use Niebuhr's analysis about faith as a criticism against Taylor who, on the contrary, is far more focused on these social realities. However, as we have noticed in the previous chapters, for Taylor as well, modernity is eminently a moment in which a strong, full concept of the self, of the individual was developed, thus allowing for the creation of a new dimension of moral and existential thought. In this sense, the two authors still align.

Regarding the status of the different forms of faith, Niebuhr believes that henotheism and polytheism were the common kind of faith present in primitive and ancient societies. These created an alternation between struggles and accommodations that shaped the different civilizations. However, according to him, the transition to a Christian society, in the West, did not lead necessarily to the triumph of monotheism and the disappearance of the other two forms of faith. In this sense, examples of henotheism and polytheism are still present in the modern world; examples of henotheism can be the various nationalisms (even the totalitarian nationalisms like Nazism and fascism), communism, or progressivism.[77] Such analysis of the differ-

---

74. Of course, we could question Niebuhr's simple polarization of trust/loyalty as active/passive sides of faith. However, Taylor himself seems to discuss the notion of trust as a more active process, a mix of belief and commitment. Of course, the reason has to be found in Niebuhr's triadic structure that composes the event of faith, and in his interpretation of loyalty as commitment.

However, a full critique of Niebuhr's would escape the main purpose of this study and, therefore, will not be pursued. In addition, while it is true that we cannot subsume Taylor's trust to a simple active/passive dichotomy, I firmly believe that we can inscribe it in a one-sided relation of individual/value.

75. Gustafson, "Christian Ethics and Social Policy," 120–21.

76. Grant, *God the Center of Value*, 28–29.

77. This, however, can create another methodological problem that Niebuhr does not address deeply enough: how is it possible to distinguish clearly about the different kinds of faith? In addition, is it correct to describe the shifts in the concept and nature of faiths throughout history only as a struggle between these different faiths?

ent forms of faith allows Niebuhr to develop a narrative of modernity that, like Taylor's, identifies the contemporary secular individual as living a moment of crisis.[78] According to Niebuhr, in modernity, with the dissolution of communal faiths we see an increased importance given to the self. Much like Taylor, Niebuhr identifies the self as the center of the moral activity in modernity. The modern self is directed toward a plurality of centers of values, which he describes as a plurality of gods, a form of polytheism. According to Niebuhr, modern polytheism is, in our contemporary society, a state of the fractured self that is turned toward a plurality of values, while at the same time being unable to settle definitively with a specific one[79]. Unlike Taylor, however, such crisis is not an experience of loss. It is actually the active call toward very different sources of values, all of each asking for commitment, which does generate the crisis. The crisis is not generated by something missing, like Taylor's loss of transcendence. The overwhelming presence of different sources of values, the plurality of different interpretations of the world, creates the fractured state of the modern self.

As a theologian, Niebuhr is more concerned regarding the state of monotheism and the dangers he perceives against it. Niebuhr defines true monotheism as *radical monotheism*. It is an act of belief and loyalty directed toward a single center of value. In the case of Christianity, the One God. Interestingly enough, Niebuhr considers radical monotheism to have always been the loser in the history of Western civilization.[80] Of course,

---

78. Ibid., 18–20.

79. Ibid., 18–26. As an Example, Niebuhr presents existentialism as a form of modern polytheism.

80. This has, of course, extremely important consequences on how a Christian should behave toward a political structure. In fact, in *Theology, History and Culture*, in the essay "Religion and the Democratic Tradition," H. R. Niebuhr addresses the problem of the relation between Christianity and Democracy, and in general, with state power.

Essentially, the form of government is totally indifferent regarding the will of God. To act according to the law of God is something that should be done regardless of the form of government in which we are. In addition, if we, to follow the will of God, are to go against the laws of the state, then we have to accept any kind of punishment and bear responsibility for our actions, as even the government of the state, as cruel it may be, is in any case an event of the will of God. Is there, however, a case in which a Christian should instead oppose openly the government? Niebuhr assumes that, when the government becomes a religion, namely, when happens what Niebuhr describe as: "The attempt of any individuals, or institutions, or whole peoples to think of themselves as powerful enough to rule without being overruled and as good enough to declare the moral law otherwise than as subjects of that law, is a great illusion which results in disaster for themselves as well as in the crucifixion of the innocent" (H. R. Niebuhr, *Theology, History and Culture*, 149).

In this case then it is right and also a duty, for a Christian, to oppose openly the

H. R. Niebuhr's point of view privileges an interpretation of this struggle as a conflict between radical monotheism and modern henotheism and polytheism,[81] or of Western Christianity against secular ideologies.[82] However, what he has been able to say about the concept of faith has relevance for the debate as a whole, independently from the specific claim one wants to defend. The actual relation that a human being, or society, develops with its idea of the good or its idea of the world is a relevant topic for religious and secular claims alike. It is fruitful to understand the characteristics that Niebuhr attributes to this relation of faith. I consider particularly important the following statement.

> Faith, as human confidence in a center and conserver of value, and as human loyalty to a cause, seems to manifest itself almost as directly in politics, science and other cultural activities as it does in religion.[83]

To support this statement, Niebuhr analyzes how it is important for the life of modern nation-states to make continuous use of a language of loyalty in their communicative structures.[84] Loyalty has assumed, in our political language, more and more the feature of *fidelity* in a political cause. Fidelity, whether practiced in the church, profession or state, has always the same general form. It is always a set of mind, a habit of devotion to a cause, and a disciplining of actions in service to a cause. It is a specific attitude that, Niebuhr claims, is clearly distinguishable from other attitudes like fearful obedience or loving attachment. At the same time, its forms of betrayal are also clearly distinguishable from other, like defiant disobedience or hatred. Fidelity in the modern state is more than simple loyalty in the community itself. It presents itself to its citizens, in political communication and propaganda, as a society pledged to the promotion of a cause that transcends the society itself. It represents itself as a *community with a mission*, significant

---

government or the society to reestablish God as the superior and almighty ruler of humankind, as well as the moral source for any kind of ethics. This, however, shows us how Niebuhr is looking at *radical monotheism* with a bias that leads him to consider Christianity as a privileged form of it.

81. H. R. Niebuhr, *Radical Monotheism and Western Civilization*, 65–84. It could be said, then, that Niebuhr himself has no desire to avoid this conflict at all, but, instead, to participate actively in it.

82. Although the two brothers uses different languages, they do share a similarity of objectives.

83. Ibid., 68.

84. Ibid., 69–73.

also for other nations and human societies, until it can encompass the whole world.[85] Following this description, Niebuhr affirms

> Three things, then, seem important when we consider the question whether faith as fidelity is present in political as well as in religious actions and communities of the West. The first is that the nation-states base their existence on the loyalty of their citizens and not only on the latter's fear and desires for benefits. The second, that the nations as communities achieve their unity and justify their existence by pledging their loyalty to transcendent causes; and third, that the loyalty expected of citizens is the double loyalty extended to the nation's cause as well as to nation as cause.[86]

The reference to transcendence is extremely important. Niebuhr is not referring specifically to some sort of metaphysical entity or idea of good. At the same time, Niebuhr's idea of the transcendent cannot be reduced to the terms of the dichotomy transcendent/immanent. Rather, he uses the term transcendence to mean *going beyond oneself*, in reference to a value that is considered of a higher order. In this sense, then, even secular ideologies can be transcendent, if they aim to achieve social structures that go beyond the simple sum of the individuals who compose it. Especially when this social structure is considered as being inherently good, because of some qualities that, despite not being fully transcendent are not very immanent either.[87] The statement that faith is an attitude inherent to human relations is essential. We are not simply talking about trust or consensus, but about a determinative, world-making, confidence, fidelity and loyalty.[88] Faith is a dynamic in which we are immersed in a web of relations with our source of value and with the other individuals who value or disvalue that source. This source may be God, but it may be as well United States, or democracy or civilization. Through this source of value, we are also in a relation with other individuals. The source of value becomes a common cause to which

---

85. Ibid., 70.

86. Ibid., 71–72.

87. Even an ideology like capitalism that has the self-interest of the individual as its core value, still aims to achieve a social structure that creates a system (the market) that cannot be reduced to the simple sum of the people composing it.

88. Ibid., 72–73. For example, even the commitment to freedom, H. Richard Niebuhr says, is not simply a materialistic confidence in the people. It also implies the presence of the assurance that there is a kind of universal government of things, a sense of how things should go, on which both nations and individuals can depend on. Without faithfulness, Niebuhr says, to an ideal or cause of truth there could be no freedom at all.

we assume our fellows will be loyal, and help us define as non-fellows those disloyal to it.[89] It helps shape also the kind of authority that represents the source of value we do consider important. We can notice how, for Niebuhr, the social/cultural struggle of Western civilization is not simply caused by conflicting ideas regarding the best way to achieve human flourishing. Contrarily to Taylor, he describes such a struggle mainly as a conflict of *different dogmas*, of different commitments toward different ideas of good and different ideas of the world. Pluralism, then, is a state of persistent moral, political and ontological struggle.

According to Niebuhr, when we express faith toward a value, we are also expressing a judgment of value. However, this process of evaluation does not exhaust its influence on our moral life. Our existence as a whole, our categories of reality are also affected. It is not only a process of creation of categories about *how things should go* but also about *how things actually are* at an ontological level. Faith is a connection to determinative categories of interpretation through which not only our lives, but also the world around us acquire a determinate meaning. Reinhold Niebuhr presents the problem in a similar way. In *Faith on Earth*, he affirms that there is a religious overtone in all political loyalties. That is, conditioned, relative and partial human institutions tend to make unconditioned claims upon the lives of individuals and to secure the acceptance of such claims. What totalitarian states do is merely an accentuation of a common process of political life since the very beginning.[90]

This feature of faith, in its existential/political feature, is well represented in another essay by H. R. Niebuhr. In *Theology, History and Culture*, in the fifth essay of the book, "The Church Defines Itself in the World," he addresses the problems related to the definition of an institution and/or of a belief, in both a practical and theoretical way. This concerns not only the institution in itself, but the problem of the definition of the institution as well, so that we have to ask: what is a definition? What kind of value has in how the humans relate between themselves and with the world? Niebuhr says that a definition is, firstly, both a descriptive and a normative statement: "it implies decision as well as perception and conception; it is a command, as

---

89. Grant, *God the Center of Value*, 45.

90. H. R. Niebuhr, *Faith on Earth*, 83–85. At the same time, Reinhold Niebuhr affirms that religious sanctification of power and its expression is something that springs naturally from the heart of the simple men. Priestly blessing may accentuate this aspect, but a natural religion, which negates priesthood, such as modern ideologies, is as well capable of fall into the same errors of the previous religious societies, generating a new religious self-glorification of power through different means (ibid., 93–96).

well as a statement."⁹¹ To define an institution, or a value, is not simply an act of description. It locates it in a web of relation with the other definitions and implies a normative prescription of the order of such relations, it involves, then, both theoretical and practical reasoning from the subject.

For example, to define an institution democratic or authoritarian is not just a descriptive operation, it also prescribes the way in which we have to relate to them and how we should locate it in our perception of the world as a whole. Niebuhr affirms that the descriptive and imperative strength of a definition—you use this term to indicate this other thing—is true for every formal statement and for every basic description of reality, and indeed has been the object of much scholarly research. However, not enough attention has been dedicated to what concerns the moment of decision present in the development of a definition, and how such decision influences all forms of social communication.⁹² It is not that decisions control definitions, however, every definition always implies a moment of decision. The two moments seem to be inextricably linked in the activity of the subject. The moments of decision that precede, or are involved with, the moments of definition act on various levels. There are decisions about purposes, distinctions and contexts or positive relations.⁹³ It takes place after the definition as a judgment of value for the definition in itself. When we define a social or historical reality, in fact, we cannot help but to reason about its purposes. We also elaborate a process to distinguish it from other social realities and, at the end, we invest it with some kind of value that orients our relation and the contexts through which we operate with said reality. While it is true that these elements are not simply arbitrary, but, instead, they are developed out of some perceived qualities of the object we are trying to define, at the same time, they are not fully objective, but involve decision, or obedience, about a situation.

For example, when we talk about the *church as the body of Christ*, we are also developing a decision about its purposes. The definition allows us to distinguish the church from what is not, and involve our decision about what the institution is, or should be, related. At this point, we can decide to accept this definition, and therefore the institution, or go against it, rejecting the given situation/institution. When we talk about definitions, therefore, we seem to face also decisional moments regarding the choice of the context of the definition, as well as with the choice of its purpose and distinction.⁹⁴

91. H. R. Niebuhr, *Theology, History and Culture*, 64.
92. Ibid., 63–65.
93 Ibid., 65.
94 Ibid., 66. The argument could also be expanded to include the analysis of *symbols* in modern political/social structures. In "Towards New Symbols," the first essay of *Theology, History and Culture*, Niebuhr introduces the problem of symbols in language

We are in presence of a decision even before the moment of establishing a definition. Niebuhr uses the term hidden presuppositions, a moment in which decisions lie before the creation of the definition in itself and that therefore, condition both the definition and the practical act following it. The decisions that follow on a theoretic definition do not follow directly from such definition only but also from the hidden presuppositions or decisions that lie at its back. Naturalistic ethics is not the simple consequent of a naturalistic definition of man but follows also from the decisions that lie at the back of that definition and have influenced it. Similarly, the definition of democracy in terms of power struggle between interest groups is not the beginning of the power-struggle ethos.[95]

Here is a very important concept. By admitting the existence of a decisional moment before the establishment of a definition, we acknowledge that, on a social level, the formation of a discourse is influenced by the social relations, conflicts, and accordance with other groups, as well as by the discourse in itself. We also admit the existence of a deeper, unseen, influence in the development of a discourse that lies where the establisher of the definition attempts to apply, in his act of establishing a new definition, his decisional power.[96] It is not plausible that Niebuhr would be describ-

---

and their vitality in human societies. With symbols, we must intend what we use, in our cultural relation, to indicate specific things. It is evident that every culture use symbols to indicate its core values, but how these symbols change and die?

Niebuhr affirms that symbols change and disappear because they become *weak*, they experience a loss of *symbolic vitality*, and this is achieved in two cases: Firstly, when the relation between the symbol and the meant reality become so strong that the symbol *is* the reality. This leads towards the end of the relation between speaker and hearer, and their relation to the reality meant by the symbol. Secondly, when the symbol is imposed in a dogmatic way, this also leads to an end of human and cultural relation, making the symbol lose its vitality in the long run.

It is interesting to notice how this analysis on symbols could be easily adapted to *any symbolic language* and not solely to the religious one. It is a shame, however, that Richard Niebuhr dedicated so few pages to present his point of view on such a topic; at the same time, this means that, starting from his assumptions, it would be possible to further expand his analysis to a more comprehensive context. An attempt of this kind will be introduced in the next chapter.

95. Ibid., 67.

96. We can also find more information in the third chapter of *Faith on Earth*, "Believing and Knowing." In this chapter, Niebuhr describes the problematic relation that exists between belief and knowledge, particularly scientific one.

Analysing the tradition of logic and epistemology since Kant, Niebuhr affirms how our contemporary knowledge rests on a complex web of belief and trust in authorities and direct observation. Niebuhr analyses how, of the five ways in which we attain knowledge described by logics (first is tradition, second is authority, third is self-evident truth, fourth is persuasion and fifth is through reasoning) three of them rests in an indirect knowledge obtained through trust into persons whom we believe.

ing only the establishment of moral discourses. The sense we receive from his work is that, in the process of establishing a discourse, a definition, not only codes of practical action are developed, but also existential categories that allow us to classify reality in itself, categories from which, then, we derive our moral codes. We see an example of this decisional power coming into social practice in the case of American denominationalism. As Harry Stout has written, Niebuhr strongly believed that the social factors of the American continent were a fundamental cause for the diversified state of the Christian churches. It was the way religion was defined and the way it ought to be practiced.[97] The definition of religion reflected a set of hidden suppositions at a social level that were proper of the American historical context and determined the successive development of the various Christian denominations.

If we relate Niebuhr's theory of description as a decision to Taylor's work, two things become clear. Against Taylor, we can no longer consider secularism simply as the resolution of the inner contradictions of Christianity. In this way, we would also have to ignore the decisional moment in which the secular discourse has been developed and applied. However, with Taylor, we can still admit the persistence of an ideal moment that, together with the material historical causes, contributes to the development of the discourse. Such ideal causes, however, must be considered more complex that we earlier assumed.[98] To clarify further the nature of the problem, I

What we know is something we have been taught, either since childhood or by people that we believe hold higher knowledge than us, so that, even with objective knowledge we establish, in reality, a relation of belief. For this reason, Niebuhr affirms explicitly: "In the actual human experience, a believing enters into all our knowing and a knowing into all our believing" (*Faith on Earth*, 34). Again, it would be extremely interesting to apply these insights to an analysis of our ontological perception of the world and of our relations with other human beings.

97. Stout, "Historical Legacy of H. Richard Niebuhr," 84–85.

98. The problem, in this sense, would be to establish precisely what Taylor considers as ideal causes in history. As an Anglo-Saxon Hegelian, he admits the dialectic persistence and coexistence of contradictions in history, which have to be resolved through a synthesis. At the same time, however, he rejects the existence of a Hegelian cosmic *Geist* that would rule over the whole of existence, the transcendence; the metaphysical being sought by Taylor has to be identified fully with the Christian God. The core of the matter, at this point, would be to establish, finally, if the contradiction in Taylor's historical account is also a moment that persists on an ideal level.

If that would be the case, the material introduced in the first chapter of this work could be of some help in the current state of the problem. In establishing a direct accordance between metaphysic and political structures, Schmitt is implying an accordance between the two phenomena that goes beyond simple material/ideal distinctions. While Cavanaugh, in rejecting the definition of religion, is also rejecting a purely dialectical process for the distinction between secularism and religion, as the cultural

have to address how Niebuhr understands the features of this structure of faith and its social relevance. In *Faith on Earth*, Richard Niebuhr describes faith as a multifaceted attitude that relate human beings with a multiplicity of realities, not just religious ones. Questions about faith seem to arise in every area of human existence. Though the word, as we understand it today, seems to imply a connection to concept such as God, church and creed, we use it, in our everyday life, in many other connections.[99] In the relation of faith, according to Niebuhr, we develop a personal interaction of the self with other persons, which appear in the act of believing to others. In this act, the *I*, the individual self, acknowledges the existence of a *You*, another self. The individual recognizes the existence of different others and through this recognition is able to build knowledge of himself. However, Niebuhr notices that in this *I-You* relation there is a feature insufficiently noted in social studies. When we interact with others, we do not simply engage in analogical communication. There is always something being assumed, an unspoken object, or statement, by virtue of which we can engage in actual meaningful communication with the others.[100] For the *I* to be able to communicate with the *You*, a third element is needed in the relation, an *It* that stands in between them, a common object that allows for meaningful communication between different selves.[101] Regard this, Niebuhr states clearly

> We have community with each other and can communicate with each other just because we are not only present to each other, but have a common co-presence, some object with which and about which we can communicate. Apart from such common objects we do not communicate but have only mutual awareness of or feeling for each other. "I," "Thou" and "It" form a triad in such a way that all knowledge of the "It" depends on a self's relation to other selves. . . . I know you or acknowledge you in my act of believing your statement about a common third.[102]

There is also a second important feature in this relation, in establishing the *I-You* relation about a common third, the selves also enter into a relation

---

process that came up with the distinction in itself was already imbued with hidden presuppositions that made the distinction in itself functional to the legitimization of a specific metaphysical interpretation of the world.

Regarding also the problem of the *discourse* in itself, I do believe it would be extremely valuable to link it to Foucault's *Archaeology of Knowledge* to obtain more insights on the problem of the *definition* and of its creation.

99. H. R. Niebuhr, *Faith on Earth*, 1–2.

100. Ibid., 43–44.

101. Ibid., 46–48.

102. Ibid., 47.

of faith between each other. The belief in this common third does not exhaust itself in the relation with the object of faith, but is also projected in the social life of the believer. It allows him to build relations and communities of faith with other social selves. The self not only acknowledges the other as another knower of this third element, but also as a fully developed self, which possess the freedom to be bound to the source of value, or to reject it. Faith is present here in the reciprocal act of faith between the selves in which an *I* trusts a *You* and so acknowledges him as a person with—or without—fidelity and, therefore, as a moral personality. Trust is a response to and an acknowledgement of this fidelity.[103] At this point, for Niebuhr, great importance falls on the *It* previously introduced. The relation *I-You* is never a simple dyad, it always involves a third element, that is the common object that stands as a guarantee of the relation of faith between individuals. This common object may not necessarily be of religious nature, in the sense we understand the concept today. In fact, Niebuhr proposes examples like the university, where the common object is *knowledge and truth*. An object that structures the relation of faith between professor and student; or the nation, in which fellow citizens stand in a relation of fidelity between themselves precisely by having the common cause as central object that structures their relation.[104] For this reason, Niebuhr proposes a concept of faith community that goes beyond the simple context of religious groups: whenever we have the presence of this triadic character of faith, we can, and should, speak of faith communities.[105] The triadic character of faith relation established by Niebuhr implies that, not only we are in a relation with the other selves and our common cause, but also the common cause in itself is in a relation with us. The greatest difference between Charles Taylor and H. R. Niebuhr is founded in this reciprocal character of faith relation between individuals and with their object of loyalty.

We have seen that, according to Charles Taylor, communities develop around sources of good and around social imaginaries, in this sense, every social order is also a moral order. This is particularly evident in the chapter that Taylor dedicates to social imaginaries, in *A Secular Age*.[106] A moral order, a social imaginary, Taylor admits, always presents also an ontic component, it also tries to identify features of the world that make the moral norm realizable.[107] However, for Taylor, the modern moral order stopped identify-

103. Ibid., 47.
104. Ibid., 48–52.
105. Ibid., 53.
106. Taylor, *Secular Age*, 159–211.
107. Ibid., 64.

ing features of the world and relied, instead, on claims about human beings that could be deduced from within the social structure. The modern social imaginaries, according to Taylor, stopped linking social realities to other realities. It did no longer identify features of the world to structure their own claims.[108] For this reason Taylor describes social imaginaries as involving only social realities, because the actual foundations of social imaginaries may, or may not, possess an ontic foundation outside themselves. In this sense, Taylor makes the claim that secularism, although useful in developing the understanding of our self, the importance of normal human flourishing, is creating, by trying to cast away any kind of religious remains, a world where human life is empty, cannot inspire commitment, offers nothing worthwhile.[109] In its attempt to recover from the loss of transcendence, Taylor defines contemporary secularism as a dangerous struggle, because religion answers to the human need of meaning.[110] As an overcoming of the problem, Taylor affirms that we should interpret experience of the divine in a different way.[111] No more as a distinct moment separate from the observed and the observer, instead we should perceive the three of them as a whole that, by opening to a deeper reality, brings a life-changing fullness to our own life.[112] So Taylor affirms that the landscape of faith, today, is one of a faith that is not identified in a specific code, because the code, be it religious or secular, roots in us as an answer to some of our deepest metaphysical needs, that for meaning, for instance, or that for a sense of our own goodness. The code can rapidly become the crutch for our sense of moral superiority.[113]

However, if we follow Niebuhr's description of faith as fidelity, we have to admit that secular societies also share a basic constitutional attitude that we can call faith. In addition, this faith, in being an attitude of fidelity, loyalty, asks precisely for a code, a rule of conduct. In addition, in Niebuhr's analysis we can see how the relation of faith, in aiming toward a source of value, still projects meaning in features of the world that have to act as foundation for the realization of the code. Like in Niebuhr's example of modern nationalism as a faith, the nation is projected as a community with a mission, such mission transcends the simple social event and develops ontological claims about the world in itself, in which determined

108. Ibid., 165–66.
109. Ibid., 717.
110. Ibid., 718.
111. Ibid., 729–30.
112. Ibid., 730.
113. Ibid., 743.

features are identified that legitimize the claim of the nation. As I will show in the next chapter, modern social imaginaries have not given up ontological claims about the world itself, or history. The affirmation that modernity has only provided ontological claims about human beings can be defined as an historical misinterpretation on Taylor's part. Niebuhr greatest difference from Taylor is precisely the acknowledgement of this existing code tied with ontological claims. Once we are aware of the existence of different codes within the same society, of conflicting ideas of the world (not only of moral action), then we face the problem of their possible, or impossible, coexistence. However, the negation of the existence of this multiplicity of ontological interpretation of the world risks becoming, in Taylor's narrative, a naïve negation of the problem. It was precisely for this reason that Connolly could easily accuse Taylor of being unable to cope with the problem of difference within society.

Moreover, I suggest that Niebuhr's definition of faith is more precise regarding to what faith has actually been, as a phenomenon, in human societies. By admitting his definition of faith, we have to admit that the attitude defined as faith is something that embraces a whole constellation of different fields and values that cannot be restricted to religion only. The fact that faith identifies itself with some kind of present or past order would be, then, one of the features inherent in the very concept of faith. Not just a moral risk as Taylor implies. However, Niebuhr's analysis is not enough to develop a complete analysis of this relation of faith because of a vital missing component. As I have already introduced, Niebuhr considers a relation of faith only as a personal and interpersonal social phenomenon. The social individual, for Niebuhr, is always a determined individual, a subject; in this sense, Niebuhr's analysis rests on a strong individualistic interpretation of human social actions. As I already have presented, then, if Niebuhr has correctly grasped the depth, the ontological claims and commitment involved in a relation of faith, unlike Taylor, the second has, however, correctly grasped its social importance and relevance, its communitarian value.

In *Faith and Ethics*, James Gustafson, has correctly interpreted this fundamental individualistic nature of Niebuhr's ethics as being founded, primarily, on a strong concept of the person as a unity.[114] The unity of Niebuhr's ethics is founded on the unity of the person, there cannot be ultimate separation of the religious and the moral, the social, the political because these things cannot be extracted from the person that reasons and acts morally.[115] In this sense, there are two strong motifs, in Niebuhr's eth-

---

114. Gustafson, "Christian Ethics and Social Policy," 120.
115. Ibid., 120–21.

ics, that determine the individualistic nature of his interpretation of faith. One is, as we already said, the personalist value of morality. Moral decisions can only be radically personal; the reason of the moral decision is always the reason of the heart of the serious person.[116] Another motif in Niebuhr's ethics is response. Moral actions are always responsive and responsible actions. The moral individual responds in the light of the total context of action, such response is always a self-conscious personal relationship to institutions, persons, facts, principles and Being itself. The moral act must be fitting, responsible toward this complex web or relations in which the individual is embedded.[117] This allowed Niebuhr to grasp the seriousness with which relations of faith are lived by the individual, the existential and ontological relevance of the claim expressed in a statement of faith" At the same time, however, for the same reason he has been unable to grasp the social relevance of the relation of faith. Those moments in which we are embedded in a relation of faith, which we could also define as a narrative or a framework. In these social relations, it can be extremely hard to define sharply a boundary in which the person is still a self-conscious, responsible self and not, instead, embedded in a web of social influences.

I believe we have reached, in this chapter, a fundamental acknowledgment. By admitting that religious and nonreligious social forms share common dilemmas toward reality and common attitudes toward it, common relations of faith, we may be able to truly create a meaningful discussion between the two and finally compare, with honesty, the respective ways in which each form of life structures the world and human moral action within it. The risk of considering faith as a purely religious or transcendental attitude is that it leads us to misunderstand completely the kind of relations that human beings build with the world around themselves. In this case, communication would really die and every group would merely pursue its own path toward flourishing in total disregard of the opinions and objections of other groups. This would further break human communities and would risk of generating such tragedies that Heidegger's statement "Only a God can save us" would become dangerously even truer.

---

116. Ibid., 121.
117. Ibid., 121–22.

5

Secular Faiths Today

THE LAST CHAPTER OF *A Secular Age* is titled "Conversions."[1] In this chapter, Taylor discusses what he denotes as *self-authenticating experiences*,[2] or at least impressions inspired by great people (saints, prophets, charismatic leaders) that have been so strong to convince people that a turning toward a religious language may be a valid road to fullness. This becomes extremely important especially in our secular age, where, according to Taylor, experiences of conversions are evidence of the necessity of the return to a transcendental source of value, to articulate our moral life. Contemporary conversions to a religious outlook are described as a *paradigm shift*, a moment in which we move from an immanent perspective to a spiritual one, in which God, good and evil are taken as serious realities. It is a moment in which the internal economy of the immanent framework, which is internal to the human mind, is disrupted and this leads to the realization of something transcendent.[3] It is a moment in which the set parameters of the time are deeply unrooted and put into discussion, even if only at a personal level. According to Taylor, all great reconversions toward Christianity of the last two centuries possess two tendencies in common; on one side they are accompanied by a sense that the immanent order of psychological or moral self-understanding are deeply flawed, on the other side, they also indicate an awareness of a larger order which can alone make sense of our lives. This

---

1. Tayor, *Secular Age*, 728–72.
2. Ibid., 729.
3. Ibid., 731–32.

order is divinely ordained and tied to transcendental sources of value, the realization that turns us toward that order has to be seen as a *path to faith*.⁴

However, I am of the opinion that the traits that Taylor identified in such conversions cannot be described as pertaining only to *religious turns*, or to turns toward the transcendent. In fact, my argument throughout the book has been that we can see also in secular/immanent frameworks traits and attitudes that we can denote with the term *faith*. In the first chapter, I introduced a short historical review of the interpretations of the concept to introduce the theoretical background that motivated the book you have been reading so far. I have shown how the concept of faith denoted a much larger sphere of events of the social, political and ontological consciousness of human beings, before modern consciousness restricted its field of application to religious meanings.

In the second chapter, I have presented the argument, through an analysis of Schmitt's and Blumenberg's works, that there are narratives of secularity that offer a different interpretation of the transition from Western premodern frameworks to the modern one. In addition, through Schmitt's approach, I have argued that it is viable to use a language of *inheritance* between theological and secular structures to describe the transition to modernity. Schmitt developed a philosophical/sociological interpretation of legal concepts to theorize similarities between religious and secular structures. His sociology of concepts also aimed to demonstrate that there was a connection between the political/bureaucratic structure of a society and its social conceptual/metaphysical self-representation.⁵

In the third chapter, I presented the argument that Hegel's strong influence on Taylor's philosophy shapes Taylor's definitions of secularity and religion as opposites. I presented the case that Taylor, through a strong application of dialectics in his historical analysis, reinforces the sense of radical difference between religion and secularity and undermines his attempt to achieve a synthesis between the two. Modernity becomes a necessary step and a necessary improvement of Western civilization. In addition, with the category of *buffered self*, Taylor implies that not only the framework and the lived experience of individuals changed, but also their epistemic perception of themselves as human being has been improved. However, through Croce's criticism of Hegelian dialectics, I presented the argument

---

4. Ibid., 744.
5. Schmitt, *Political Theology*, 45–48. Such connection is not described necessarily as a causal connection. That is, Schmitt's sociology of concepts has no interest in tracing a historical cause between the ideals of a society and its pragmatic forms. Rather, it simply aims to show that there is a strong connection between the two and that it is impossible to properly examine one without taking into account the features of the other.

that this kind of historical analysis benefits only partially from the application of a dialectic methodology. Croce aimed to complete the Hegelian model with a *dialectic of distinct concepts* that develops not through *opposition* but through *induction*. According to Croce, it is not possible to apply universal concepts to particular historical events. Instead, his philosophical interpretation derives general concepts from the study and comparison of single historical events. This does not abolish the use and application of general categories. However, it allows the development of a more precise and historically consistent narrative, as we obtain the categories of definition from historical facts themselves. In our specific case, Croce's historical interpretation does not abolish the categories of religious and secular. Such categories can be used as analytical instruments to allow us to distinguish between historical/sociological phenomena. What does change is the content implied by the concepts. We can no longer consider religion simply as the realm of faith or transcendence. While the secular sphere would be the realm of the immanent or unbelief. I have also presented the case, through Ernesto De Martino's anthropological work, that the category of buffered self is just another ontological/sociological structure developed so that the modern framework could sustain itself; it would not be, then an entirely new product but the reproposition, in a different historical form, of a fundamental human attitude. In this sense, the *buffered self* is not a different stage of the human self, but just a different construct through which the Western civilization copes with its ontological fears of nonexistence.

In the fourth chapter, I have tried to find a definition for this fundamental attitude of faith by presenting theological analyses on the problem of religion/secularity. Through the analysis of Ratzinger and Metz, I have argued that secular social forms share a fundamental religiousness in shaping their own structures, they rely on ultimate claims that cannot be grounded on practical/immanent sources of value.[6] In searching for a proper definition for this attitude of faith, I have presented H. R. Niebuhr's analysis on faith, a concept that Taylor, in his own narrative, has simplified and overlooked.

Niebuhr proposed an interpretation of the concept less tied to its religious features and more focused on its normative/existential features. In this interpretation, faith can be expressed in nonreligious contexts as well as religious ones. Faith designates the relational commitment toward a source of value, a cause that, in return, gives meaning to our lives. Unlike Taylor,

---

6. As we have seen through Ratzinger's work, things like *human rights* have to rely on an almost-transcendent source of legitimacy and, as he has presented us, they have become, in the current global balance of powers, a tool for the Western understanding of human life to impose itself on different cultural forms.

Niebuhr presents this form of relation as working in both directions. It is not only an act of trust from the individual to the source of value, the source of value itself projects a realm of meaning toward the individual and his relations. In return, this source of value allows us to have meaningful relations with other individuals. The value in which we have faith becomes the standard through which we can consider our neighbours trustworthy or worthy of loyalty. However, this is possible only insofar as we are willing to pursue our commitment to the cause to which we have adhered, to work toward its realization in our life and the society around us. Faith, then, for Niebuhr, independently from its context of appearance, always calls for the creation of a structure to uphold and develop further the sources of values to which it refers.

In this way, Niebuhr has been able to grasp an important feature of faith that has eluded Taylor's analysis. Faith, as an existential form of relation, appears in secular and religious contexts alike. Such contexts are not just frameworks that provide us directions for our moral compass, these frameworks project meaning unto our lives. In the face of this provided meaning, we are not only asked to trust in our source of value, but also to uphold it, to spread and realize it in our life and social context. We are asked to be loyal. In this sense, a definition like Taylor's *Jamesian open space* becomes an impossible statement. Faith is never just an open act; it creates boundaries, rules and codes of conduct. In swearing loyalty to my source of value, in committing myself to its promotion, I am also implicitly affirming that I will relinquish those alternative sources of value that conflict with the one at the centre of my realm of meaning. I will not accept them. Even the most liberal system, after all, has to rely on some fundamental non-negotiable principles to sustain itself, while rejecting those principles that are considered as hostile.

As introduced at the conclusion of the previous chapter, however, there are features of this relation of faith that Niebuhr himself has overlooked. Taylor has been able to address the component of trust and the social reality of the framework, while Niebuhr has been able to grasp the component of loyalty and structure. However, there is a third feature of faith, a feature which I have addressed in the third chapter, through Ernesto De Martino's work. The modern buffered self, despite being the affirmation of modern individuality, is still embedded in a framework that provides the sources of goods through which the individual establishes his moral compass. Taylor attempts to find a way through so that the different goods can coexist in a liberal society. Niebuhr, instead, presents the relation of faith as a form of connection between individuals. The individual enters into a relation with the source of value; in so doing, he also enters into different relations with other single individuals. Society is the result of such complex webs of relations.

Taylor has clearly understood the social value of the framework as a social body—that is, a source of influences that transcends the single individuals composing it. However, he conceives the relations we establish within such frameworks in a much too optimistic way. Niebuhr, on the other hand, has grasped the seriousness and depth of the relations with which we establish our sources of values, but is not interested on how they act on and within the social body. The result is that both authors have been able to present only partially how the framework—the relation of faith—provides meaning to an individual and a society. However, as I have argued at the beginning of this book, the framework exercises a much deeper influence on the individual and the social body, an influence that goes beyond the ethical/moral compass. Ernesto De Martino, with his concept of *culturally conditioned nature*, presented a concept that is similar to what I would like to propose in this last chapter. With this concept, Ernesto De Martino indicates the given ontology through which a culture/society/civilization is able to sustain its own social structures, to cope with its existential fears. It is not only a hidden understanding about *how things should go*, but also about *how things are* on the ontological level. It is the acknowledgment about a fundamental structure present in the universe, which allows the single individual to make sense of the social practices around him. In this fashion, the relation of faith refers to a sense of higher order. However, unlike Taylor, I do not believe that this higher order must be necessarily transcendental or divine. In addition, this order is not only the source of legitimization, but also the source of sense for things that happen socially, individually, and physically.[7]

A relation of faith is not just a relation of trust, or an epistemic position, like Taylor implies. In addition, it is not just a triadic relation, as Niebuhr presents it. Instead, a relation of faith always presents four terms: We have the individual subject, the value/good/institution in which he has faith, the social body/companion to which he is related and this final level of ultimacy, a hidden hypostasis that acts as the guarantee for the establishment of all the previous steps. We do not establish relations of faith just because we have a sense of how things should go but also because we have a precise idea of how the world in itself is structured. It is because the world is a certain way, because it possesses a specific ontological structure, that the things around us make sense. The framework, then, as the connection to

---

7. In this sense, social practices, institutions and moral claims make sense only insofar as they are grounded on this fundamental ontology, on these fundamental claims about the nature of the things of the world.

this given ontology, is not merely a filter that changes our perceptions of the world. It constitutes those experiences of the world. Following De Martino, every image of *nature* is always culturally conditioned. There is a *Weltanschauung*, a comprehensive worldview, implied in the framework, which allows the framework to make sense. In this sense, every framework—or social imaginary—relies on a worldview that provides the fundamental ontological hypostasis to ground its own social/ethical claims. We are literally talking about *realms of meaning*, in the sense that every relation of faith is attached to a whole sense of how existence in itself (and not just my existence or the existence of the community) works. The change of a framework, therefore, represents quite literally the historical moment in which a world dies and a new world is created in its stead. Faith, therefore, represents the connection that a society and the individuals that compose it establish with such a world.

For the reason of providing a consistent argument for this claim I have presented, this chapter proposes a thought experiment that mirrors Taylor's chapter on "Conversions." Through this experiment, I wish to propose the possibility of considering faith as an attitude related to a *Weltanschauung*, and, for this reason, as a dynamic present in all social contexts: religious and secular alike. Therefore, I wish to show instances in which modern discourses retain this existential attitude that we can define as faith. They not only provide a realm of meaningfulness for individuals, or social groups, to which they refer, but they also draw on an implicit ontology, a hidden hypostasis that is the foundation and legitimization of their claims. The presence of such fundamental *Weltanschauung* in modern social forms is the main motivation for my use of faith as a philosophical/anthropological category for a broader scope of analysis. Can we describe social processes and structures that take place in secular ideologies as faith? I will propose analytical examples to show how the vocabulary of faith retains a strong descriptive power for such structures and phenomena. For this operation, I will present some examples from economic theory, political propaganda and philosophical inquiry.

ECONOMIC FAITH

Giorgio Agamben, in his book *The Kingdom and the Glory*, has presented the case that the forms through which Western society has been structured are linked to Christian theology through two fundamental paradigms. These paradigms are political theology, which developed into political philosophy and the theory of sovereignty, and theological economy, which developed into theory of government as *oikonomia*, the active attempt to create an immanent order—intended as domestic order, not political in a strict sense—in society.[8] Agamben develops his argument through the Christian premodern concept of *Trinitarian economy*.[9] The Trinitarian economy is founded on the Greek concept of *oikonomia*, interpreted as an administrative function assessed only in the context of the aims pursued. This was the solution of early theologians to questions like, *how can God be one if he is also three?*

The term *oikonomia* was used to explain how God administrates his household into three different persons while maintaining a singular ontology. Agamben interprets the Pauline expression of *economy of mystery* as an attempt to define and solve the ontological problem of the Trinity through an administrative paradigm. Hippolytus and Tertullian, however, developed a radical change in the interpretation of the economy of mystery. They operated an inversion of the theological device such that *economy of mystery* became the *mystery of economy*. With this inversion, the term *oikonomia* stopped being just an analogy for the divine household and became a technical theological term to designates the Trinitarian articulation of divine life. At this stage, the term *oikonomia* started to designate not only God's organization of the holy Trinity, but also his organization of his influence on the divine and the material sphere. The width of his administrative influence was suddenly expanded to encompass the whole of creation.[10] The term *oikonomia* started, therefore, to designate the governmental function of God's influence and, by consequence, the organizational functions of secular powers. It is through this reversal that Agamben wishes to consider the threshold of indeterminacy between politics, economics and theology.[11]

8. Agamben, *Kingdom and the Glory*, 1. Political theology attempted to found the transcendence of sovereign power on the One God; theological economy replaced such transcendence with the idea of an *oikonomia*, that is, an immanent ordering of both divine and human life.

9. Ibid., 12–16.

10. Ibid., 18–37.

11. It is important to note here the fundamental difference between Agamben and Foucault: Foucault traced the genealogical origins of modern governmental structures in the concept of *pastoral care*, developed by the church during the Middle Ages. Agamben, while accepting Foucault thesis, pushes further back this origin into the theological debates of early Christianity, in which the concept of *Trinitarian economy* and *divine economy* were created. A noteworthy description of Agamben's presentation of the problem can also be found in Rasmus Ugilt's work *Giorgio Agamben: Political Philosophy*.

In addition, it should be noted that Agamben is not theorizing that, before this theological transformation, God was considered as having *no influence* on the world. It was the character of this influence that was culturally transformed and started to be interpreted as *administration*.

The roots of this threshold of indifference rest on the fact that the theological mechanisms of the Trinitarian economy, articulated after Hippolytus and Tertullian, generated a principle of anarchy in the divine influence on the earthly sphere. It gradually removed the principle of sovereignty from the divine being and assigned it to secular authorities. This dynamic is made clear in the theological claim according to which *God has created the world to work as if it is without him, and govern it as if it would be able to govern itself.* Agamben claims that liberal thinkers like Hume and Smith could develop their political/economic ideas because their major assumptions rested on an immanent principle of natural order connected historically to this theological mechanism of divine anarchy.[12]

Rasmus Ugilt is, then, correct when he describes Agamben's history of theological economy not as a story of prefiguration of modern liberalism in Christianity, but exactly the opposite. Modern liberalism should be seen as a specific formation of power, which is reminiscent of the formations of power of early Christianity.[13] It inherited some fundamental concepts and theoretical structures through which it could articulate its own ontology. If God, as a central figure of power, disappears to leave the space to his economic influence over the world, then, in the human society, it is not the sovereign (nor the sovereign people) that are in power, but rather the administrator, the one that manages political and economic resources.

Flowing from this assumption, Agamben proposes an interpretation of Smith's image of the invisible hand as the representation of the action of an immanent principle of order. Such a principle originally belonged to the bipolar mechanism of the theological *oikonomia*. In such a mechanism, there is no conflict between divine providence and naturalism, because the mechanism functions precisely by correlating a transcendent principle to an immanent order.[14] Modern liberalism represents the modern tendency that pushes to an extreme the supremacy of the pole of the *immanent order-government*, to the point that it almost eliminates the *transcendent God-kingdom* pole. In so doing, it seeks to play off one side of the theological mechanism against the other. When modernity abolishes the divine pole, the economy that is derived from it will not thereby have emancipated itself from its providential paradigm. It will have created a new mechanism that,

---

12. Ibid., 285–87.

13. Ugilt, *Giorgio Agamben*, 88–90.

14. Agamben, *Kingdom and the Glory*, 286. As an example, the *economy of nature* described by the physiocrats is entirely in agreement with this premise. Yet, it is extremely curious that there has not been sufficient reflection about the circumstance that modern sciences of economics and government were developed through strong connection with the paradigm of the divine/providential *oikonomia*.

despite not being related to a superior divine being, is still theological and providential in its own inherent nature.[15] At this point, however, in trying to describe the genealogical link between modern government/economics to the Trinitarian *oikonomia*, Agamben does not dedicate enough attention to the status of this new, modern form of economics, in which the immanent pole has rejected the transcendental pole. It is evident that the presence of an immanent principle of order, which certainly displays how economics can easily be described as a theological mechanism, does not satisfactorily explain what makes its application on a social level a phenomenon of faith.

I find an example of this attitude of faith in economics in the presentation delivered by Milton Friedman, on 10 October 1974. It was delivered at the University of Chicago and entitled *Free Market for Free Men*. Friedman outlined the following assumption:

> You can say with great certainty that free markets make free men and that controlled markets destroy free men . . . my proposition is far more obvious for the more material components of freedom—the freedom to decide how to spend your money, what to do with your time, where to work, what job to take, where to live. Those material aspect of freedom are all associated with free markets, and they are no less important to most people than freedom of thought, of speech, of political persuasion . . . the absence of free market destroys free men, and presence of free markets makes free men.[16]

The free market is described, historically, as the result of *lucky accidents*. Such accidents tended naturally toward the realization of free markets; they were not the product of political choices. According to Friedman, the preservation of free market in the U.S. was the unavoidable result of the inevitable failure of the alternatives to free market.[17] The natural impossibility to establish an alternative order of society allowed free market to become the obvious choice. Building on this assumption, Friedman describes the American free man more as the product of the mechanism of free market than its agent. This allows Friedman to assume that, the more a market is free, the more the human individuals within it can be free and enjoy various liberties. In this sense, then, the mechanisms of the free market represents a principle of harmony, inherent to human history and society, which quickly assumes moral and ethical qualities.

---

15. Ibid., 285–86.

16. Friedman, *Free Markets for Free Men*.

17. Thus, I would ask myself how *lucky* those accidents could be if they were realizing a *natural* tendency of human history and sociality.

In *Free Market for Free Men*, we can discern the presence of all the characteristics that constitute a phenomenon of faith. There is trust in the free market, as the source of good, its framework resting upon its perceived successes as a consistent past. Because the alternatives to the free market failed, free market policies were necessarily implemented, thus allowing the society as a whole to develop institutions and values that allowed the freedom of its citizens. We also see the loyalty to the market as a source of value. An expansion of the free market is a promise for the future. It is not only materially, but also morally desirable, as it will increase the amount of freedom for the people. Built upon the trust for the perceived past successes, Friedman affirms with profound confidence that the processes started by free market will increase the amount of freedom for the people stretching into the future. He asks for a commitment towards the free market and for its actual enforcement in human societies. In addition, there is the ontological hypostasis, the hidden implication of an ontological structure, the awareness of the existence of an immanent and necessary order that allows and substantiates the activity of free markets. The failures of alternatives to free market policies, despite being described as accidents, are also deemed as *necessary*. They were intrinsically destined to fail, as they went against a greater order, order of which the free market is the most consistent worldly representation. Its institutions represent the best political/social organization. The free market becomes the only possibility that can be countenanced.

It would be unfair, and incorrect, to limit our analysis just to Friedman's neoliberalism. In reality, many different economic schools had to rely on some principle of *immanent order*, and to *promise* a *foreseeable* better future, that was both morally and materially desirable. Two main examples, in total contrast to Friedman neoliberalism, can be advanced here: Marxism and Keynesianism. Marx described the capital not as a thing, but more as an inevitable process, immanent in history, through which social classes are separated and through which they conflict between each other. For example, we can read, in the third volume of *Capital*:

> ... capital is not a thing. It is a definite interrelation in social production belonging to a definite historical formation of society. This interrelation expresses itself through certain thing and gives to this thing a specific social character. Capital is not the sum of the material and produced means of production.... Capital means not merely the products of the laborers made independent of them and turned into social powers, the products turned into rulers and buyers of their own producers, but also the social powers and the future ... form of labor, which antagonize the producers in the shape of qualities of their products.

> Here, then, we have a definite and, at first sight, very mystical, social form of one of the factors in a historically produced process of social production[18]

Capital, therefore, is not really a specific thing or concept; it is more like an immanent principle that underlies all of historical processes and contributes to the historical development of classes. As Steven Lukes already acknowledged, the various interpretation of Marxism face a great paradox: for on one hand, Marx always dismissed any moral discourse as mythological and result of historical circumstances, on the other, however, his description of the historical process of capitalism always lead to the necessary conclusion of a *superior state of humanity*. The last state of humanity, once capitalism has faced its ultimate crisis, will be one in which begins the development of human energy, the true realm of freedom. In which is possible to achieve the "development of the richness of human nature as an end in itself."[19] Such a society is described, by Marx, in terms of *true freedom* and *real liberation*. It is the final overcoming of *alienation* and the realization of human essence and nature. The important thing to notice, however, is that such process and final result, in Marx's economic construction, is deemed as *necessary* and *inevitable*. Much like Friedman's final victory of free markets.

Much like Marx and Friedman, Keynes had to postulate a principle of *immanent order* to develop his economic theory and a *theological discourse* to propose it as desirable and viable. In his 1930 essay "Economic Possibilities for Our Grand-Children," he tries to describe the economic process as a principle of immanent order that, although leading (in his present) to moral distasteful attitudes, it was nonetheless naturally prone to reach, in a foreseeable future, a "state of economic bliss."[20] Of course, these are only few among countless examples that could be selected.[21] However, the present study does not wish to focus only on the debates on economic theories.[22] Much more interesting and telling will be, in this sense, the analysis of political discourses and propaganda.

18. Marx, *Capital*, 3:555.
19. Lukes, *Marxism and Morality*, 9.
20. Keynes, *Essays in Persuasion*, 330–31.
21. For more information regarding a possible religious interpretation of economics, I suggest the work from Nelson, *Economics as Religion*. In this work, Nelson presents the case that economists, in lobbying and producing claims for their economic mechanisms, have developed moral and historical discourses that seem suspiciously theological.
22. In this sense, the present study can be considered more as an earnest invitation for scholars in economics to dedicate more attention to the foundational assumptions of their subject and the kind of dialogue and relation current economics (of every theory and school) establishes within them.

POLITICAL FAITH

Political discourses developed in the twentieth century are excellent examples of how faith takes place in political discourse. However, I wish to focus the attention not on the more evident examples (like Nazism or Communism), but on the political discourses developed within Western societies in the Cold War, where we identify the establishment of *secularity* and the disappearance of religion. Walter L. Hixson, in his work *Parting the Curtain*, presents an excellent analysis of the propaganda warfare waged by United States and Soviet Union in the period 1945–1961. Hixson shows how this war of information stepped up, in its intensity and the scope covered, after 1950, when President Truman launched his *campaign of truth*.[23] This initiative was intended to break through the *Iron Curtain* and conquer the hearts and minds of people under the influence of Soviet propaganda. It was described, by many senators of the time, as a psychological and spiritual offensive against the Kremlin.[24] Such maneuvers were executed mainly through the programs aired on the radio station *Voice of America*. The *VOA* scheduling focused mainly on the weaknesses and evils of imperialistic communism. However, they also emphasized the virtues of democracies, as well as the inevitability of the ultimate triumph of democratic America. The strategy of *VOA* was to target the Soviet intelligentsia, and so sought to depict an image of the suffering of the people in the Soviet Union so as to create a contrast between "what is and could be in Soviet Union if there were no communist government."[25] Once the United States Information Agency began to play a major role in the propaganda warfare, the tone of the message focused more on the positive aspects of U.S. freedom, capitalism, and democracy. An excellent example of this is the exhibition named *People's Capitalism*. Such operations, starting from 1956, were designed to translate the principal facts of U.S. economic life into popular terms. It highlighted the economic achievements of United States economy over 180 years and tried to build up a sense of impending success in the immediate future and beyond. The exhibits carried headlines such as "Class Lines Begin to Disappear," "Almost Everybody Became a Capitalist," "Education for All," "Machines Were Invented to Do Heavy Work." The final summary presented America as an exciting and constantly changing, innovative society. Despite its flaws, the American system promised to fulfill man's old dream of a life

---

23. Hixson, *Parting the Curtain*, 14–18.
24. Ibid., 15.
25. Ibid., 38–39.

free of want, with each individual free to develop to the fullest those talents and abilities given to him by the Creator.[26]

Leo Bogart, in his *Premises for Propaganda*, offers another remarkable analysis of U.S. propaganda during the Cold War. In analyzing the intended aims of the USIA, Bogart shows that United States foreign policy was perceived as "promising people things that they had usually been led to expect from only God and Luck."[27] From this basis, Bogart reached the conclusion that the actual aims of the USIA were, in some cases, confused. They shifted constantly from the desire to fight against communism, to fight against the Soviet Union to supporting the positive role of the United States. As Bogart says, the agency's actions were governed by feelings more than scientific discipline.[28] Another important quality of U.S propaganda was the differing emphases through which the USIA tried to project America to the rest of the world. One of the major points of emphasis was to show that the "American life has a spiritual quality."[29] In addition, it clearly assumed in all of its own programs and activities a very specific anthropological model. They never questioned that the people with whom they were communicating were driven by their own self-interest.[30] Of course, the final aim of USIA was to inspire political action, but how to inspire such action was a matter of debate. One of the main branches of thought within USIA was one which held the long-term objective of changing the inner workings of people's minds, so as to create a climate of opinion favorable to the U.S.[31] Reinhold Wagnleitner, in his work *Coca-Colonization and the Cold War*, presents a similar point. He affirms that no analysis of U.S. foreign policy can ignore the doctrine of Manifest Destiny, the conviction that the United States based their activities on the hidden conviction that their nation possessed a special destiny, a particular mission, which sets them aside from every other nation in the world.[32] This can be seen in how, after World War II, the cultural war against communism and Soviet Union quickly led to the strong identification of the United States with *freedom*. Intellectual and political freedom became identified with the American way of life, and the few domestic critics were labeled as anti-American. The faith in the American liberal system generated, paradoxically, a return to forms of conservative and nationalistic

26. Ibid., 138–41.
27. Bogart, *Premises for Propaganda*, 12–13.
28. Ibid., 13.
29. Ibid., 90.
30. Ibid., 106.
31. Ibid., 16.
32. Wagnleitner, *Coca-Colonization and the Cold War*, 48–49.

power.³³ In this sense, the cultural activities of the United States assumed more and more the characteristics of "a government-directed effort to integrate others into a new Pax Americana."³⁴

It was, then, not merely a process of spreading positive news regarding U.S. policies, but the creation of a whole framework of peace and freedom, in which people could frame and reframe their own ideas and sphere of actions, so that when unfavorable details about the U.S. arose, people would find it harder to believe them. It is remarkable how the U.S. propaganda tried to foster, in the people beyond and within the Iron Curtain, those forms of consciousness that I have associated with faith. In fact, U.S. Cold War propaganda showed evidence of a sense of trust in the American civilization, built upon the perceived past economic and cultural successes, and the development of a framework in which the American way of life and its political freedom became the new source of good for society. This framework also relied on loyalty and reciprocal promises. The United States actively asked the targets of their information system to take up the challenge and commit themselves to the idea of liberal freedom. In return, they promised to reciprocate with a commitment to the well-being and comfort for those people that refused the evil of communism and tried to change it, or flee from it. In addition, there was the awareness of an immanent order, a deep ontology of the world, which revealed the United States as the natural outcome that God, history or nature had provided for the world, while communism represented an evil against this harmonious natural order of things. U.S. propaganda had the purpose of shaping the idea of a *community with a mission*, a manifest destiny whose effects were relevant not only for the United States, but for all the nations of the world. It was not just the attempt to create trust toward specific institutions or push for some certain political actions. It was the deliberate attempt to shape a new framework of reality and, in so doing, reshape those frameworks perceived as hostile. There was the active attempt to connect a specific institutional/political reality—the conflict between U.S. and Soviet structures of power—to a higher realm of values and meaningfulness relevant for all human life. It aimed to shape an ontological background to provide consistency for its realm of meaning. To be fair, the purpose of propaganda has to be interpreted purely as military/political; the people producing and spreading did not necessarily have to believe in it. Still, this does not change the value of the example proposed. Propaganda, as a form of communication, has the fundamental and primary

33. Ibid., 57–58. The author presents, as examples, McCarthy's personal war on Communist spies and the troubled relations that United States had with UNESCO until the 1990s.

34. Ibid., 65.

purpose of shaping and developing determinate forms of consciousness in the people it targets. It aims to generate feelings, images and thoughts into the minds of the people it touches to direct them toward specific values and beliefs. It aims to develop categories of meaning and their, allegedly, *correct* interpretation. In this case, U.S. propaganda aimed to develop a sense of certitude, truthfulness and inevitability of the American way of life into the people beyond the Iron Curtain. It aimed to generate faith in and toward the American system of meanings.

FAITH AS A PHILOSOPHICAL NARRATIVE

Economics and politics are not the only fields in which faith is present. Philosophical narratives also reveal this attitude, a connection to a deeper *Weltanschauung*, an ontology of the world. A great example, in this sense, is Francis Fukuyama's work *The End of History and the Last Man*. The reason I am presenting Fukuyama's narrative, and not Taylor's, as an example, rests on the fact that the analyses presented in the course of this book already provide enough material to trace an attitude of faith in Taylor's work. Fukuyama is not only a different author,[35] but also presents in his work this attitude of faith very clearly. In his work, Fukuyama analyzes the state of Western democracies in the period immediately after the fall of Soviet Union. Fukuyama proposes a linear and simple narrative. In the last part of the twentieth century, all forms of totalitarian regimes, both left and right, were facing crises that led to their failures and falls. The Soviet Union was the last and greatest of these failures. Fukuyama calls, then, for an analysis of liberal democracies to uncover the reasons for their successes.[36] He develops an analysis in which liberalism and democracy, although related, are separate concepts. If liberalism is the concept that recognizes certain individual rights of freedoms from government control, democracy is the concept that claims the right of the citizens to share the political power, that is, the right to vote and participate in politics.[37] Fukuyama admits that, on a pragmatic level, democratic forms of government show defects and problems. However, he insists, nonetheless, that the formal definition of democracy remains the most viable way to describe a state as democratic.[38]

---

35. A fact that allows me to present this attitude of faith in philosophy in a broader context.

36. Fukuyama, *End of History*, 8–22.

37. Ibid., 42–43.

38. Ibid., 43. Fukuyama rejects strongly, then, the substantivist critique against democratic forms of government. He claims that formal democracies, in the long term,

After having defined his interpretation of democracy, Fukuyama discusses the presence of a pattern in world history that tends toward the global affirmation of democratic governments. In this reading, the shortcomings and failures of market economies of democratic processes do not constitute a radical questioning of this process:

> ... the fact that there will be setbacks and disappointments in the process of democratization, or that not every market economy will prosper, should not distract us from the larger pattern that is emerging in world history ... of the different types of regimes that have emerged in the course of human history ... the only form of government that has survived intact to the end of the twentieth century has been liberal democracy.[39]

The real victor, however, is not just liberalism as a practice, but also liberalism as a system of values.[40] This victory of liberal and democratic values, at the end of twentieth century, is the result of an inevitable historical process.[41] If one looks at the whole scope of history, Fukuyama argues, we will see that liberal democracies occupy a special place. If it is true that, before 1776, no democracy ever existed, after 1790 (with France, Switzerland, and U.S. as the first democracies) a historical pattern of constant increase of democratic forms of government takes place.[42] Fukuyama presents this as the evidence that there is a fundamental process at work. Such processes dictate a common evolutionary pattern for all human societies. This function as something like a *universal history* of humanity in the direction of liberal democracies.[43] To discuss the failures of democracy in a specific historical context, or in a specific state would reveal, for Fukuyama, a narrowness of view that is unable to accept that the principles of democracy and liberty are not accidents or the result of specific cultural context. "Liberty and equality are discoveries about the nature of humanity as such, whose truth does

---

are more likely to develop substantive democracies. At the same time, he admits that there are liberal governments that are not democratic, and democratic governments that are not liberal.

39. Ibid., 45.
40. Ibid., 45.
41. Ibid., 46–48.
42. Ibid., 48. I personally find it amazing that Fukuyama discards the democracy of Periclean Athens, because it did not systematically protect individual rights; and yet admits U.S. in 1790 as a liberal democracy, where slavery was a reality for a great number of people. This reinforces the impression that there is an active attempt to create an ontological background for an historical framework, not just a series of relatively humble claims about an architecture of government.
43. Ibid., 48.

not diminish but grows more evident as one's point of view becomes more cosmopolitan."[44]

If Fukuyama's narrative is accurate, then, the question that must be addressed becomes: Is history directional, and is there reason to think that there will be a universal evolution in the direction of liberal democracy? The question aims to discriminate between those cyclical or random views of history, as opposed to the assumption of a unique direction toward history, which, according to Fukuyama, reveals the reasonableness of his position.[45] Fukuyama wishes to begin his analysis by considering modern natural science. Science, he claims, does not proceed cyclically. We can only proceed forward with our scientific and technical knowledge. Moreover, modern natural science produces historical change that is both directional and universal. Military competition and progressive conquest of nature are the two main structures through which, according to Fukuyama, science has brought change for all humanity in a specific direction. That is, the rationalization of labor and the concept of defensive modernization.[46] However, Fukuyama is still not placing any moral or ethical calculation on the historical directionality implied by modern science[47] although he claims it is irreversible.[48] Another feature that reveals the mono-directional character of this democratic *Universal History* is the triumph of capitalism as a global form of economy. Capitalism, Fukuyama claims, has proved to be far more efficient than centrally planned economic systems in developing and utilizing technologies, and in adapting to rapidly changing conditions under the conditions of a mature industrial economy.[49] Evolution in the direction of decentralized decision-making and markets becomes a virtual inevitability for all economies that hope to achieve the same amount of success.[50] The complexity of modern economies proved to be beyond the capabilities of noncapitalistic governments, whose bureaucratic organizations were simply

---

44. Ibid., 51.

45. Ibid., 71–73.

46. Ibid., 72–81.

47. It could be argued, however, that the vocabulary used by Fukuyama (process of rationalization of labor, satisfaction of desire, control of nature, *more efficient* economic development) already implies a strong moral charge.

48. Ibid., 82–88. Modern science and scientific thinking is, for Fukuyama, an irreversible process. It would be impossible to *uninvent* science as well as its grip on contemporary human societies, only the total annihilation of the human race would be able to actually *destroy* science. Anything short than this, he claims, would be unable to question the grip that science has on humans, it is now part of their very own being.

49. Ibid., 90–91.

50. Ibid., 92–94.

unfit to sustain the weight of modernity. Therefore, Fukuyama claims, societies possess a degree of freedom to the extent that they regulate and plan capitalist economies. No other path has proven to be equally efficient and rational in achieving the same result.[51] Capitalism was an inevitable phenomenon for advanced countries. However, for Fukuyama, this trajectory cannot just be a history of economy, or of technical sciences. A universal history of humanity that aims to understand how the triumph of liberalism in the modern age has been possible has to also take into account its premodern origins and influences, as well as the primary motor behind any kind of human history.[52] The source, for Fukuyama, is provided by a constant struggle for recognition, inherent in the human being, and that leads to increasing amounts of liberty through the unfolding of history.[53]

As Williams, Sullivan, and Mathews, in their introduction to Fukuyama's work, *Francis Fukuyama and the End of History*, have shown, Fukuyama creates a strong Hegelian ontology of liberalism through which its inner superiority is revealed to the public. Fascism and Nazism were destined to fail because of their internal contradictions, which would have led them to fail even in a scenario where they triumphed World War II. Communism had to face the same destiny; pressured by its own internal contradictions, it was bound to meet the moment of its end. Liberal democracy, instead, is free of any internal contradiction, even if it meets some short-term difficulties. In the long-term, it is destined to succeed.[54] This ontological difference becomes evident in Fukuyama's account of war. He claims that war will not disappear from the world in the near future, not because of an internal deficiency of liberalism, but because there are still states that are not yet liberal democracies. Those states, those civilizations, are still *in history*, and therefore are embedded in historical struggles, while liberal democracies tend naturally to free themselves from their own historical conditions.[55] They are posthistorical. This generates a sense of *threat from history* for liberal democracies. Fukuyama divides such threats into three categories. The first category is comprised of those states from the undeveloped world. Iraq or Syria are prime examples. Of course, such threats are not ideological, but merely military and economic; since the ideologies and social forms of these states are considered inherently weak. The ideology of liberalism, in itself, is

51. Ibid., 95–97.
52. Ibid., 133–35.
53. Ibid., 135–36.
54. Williams et al., *Francis Fukuyama and the End of History*, 74–75. Another interesting work that I consider useful for an understanding of Fukuyama's philosophy is: Bertram and Chitty, *Has History Ended?*
55. Ibid., 107–8.

considered invincible and above challenge by any other ideology. Fukuyama claims that any individual with the right understanding of the functions of these "inferior" societies cannot deny that these states are merely police states bent on the interest of their rulers.[56] The states of the second category also do not represent a strong threat against liberal democracies. This group is comprised of those states that, although developed, possess a resentment toward liberal democracies. Examples include states of the Islamic world, in which the law is based on Islamic fundamentalism. However, according to Fukuyama, to possess any kind of religious sensibility in our contemporary world is an antihistorical act in itself. While religion possessed an instrumental function at some point in history, to facilitate the road toward progress, today religious societies are an empty shell that represent an obstacle toward further progress. They are destined to fail as well.[57] The last category of threat is represented by authoritarian and paternalistic states. Even though these systems may possess human rights and regular elections, or a capitalist system, there is little actual change over time in those who wield power. Although they possess a multiparty system, most of the time they function as a one-party benevolent dictatorship.[58] Although these systems do not represent an ideological threat to liberal democracies, they still represent a political challenge.

The end of history, therefore, the process through which all alternatives to liberal democracy will disappear, will truly be achieved when these political challenges are addressed and when existing liberal democracy resolves the final two issues they present. The first issue is the ongoing debate between individualism and communitarianism, and the second is the ongoing process of evolution in which they are still embedded.[59] Fukuyama's criticism of political realism reveals the hidden ontology, the *Weltanschauung* inherent to his philosophy. Realism states that the fundamental element in foreign policy is, and always must be, the interest of the State. Power is the factor that is always decisive in our analyses about what a state ought to do, while moral considerations do not figure in these calculations. For Fukuyama, legitimacy, and not force, should be recognized as the central category for modern national and international politics. Liberal democracies, in this sense, possess the truest legitimacy, as their power is based on the consent of the wider number of people of the nation. The moral ground

---

56. Ibid., 109.
57. Ibid., 109–10.
58. Ibid., 110–12.
59. Ibid., 113.

on which liberal democracies develop their claims is inherently stronger.⁶⁰ This certifies the truthfulness of liberal ideology. Since liberal ideology is true, all other ideologies are false, and unworthy to survive in the posthistorical world.⁶¹

Fukuyama's universal history, therefore, reveals all the features of the relation of faith, and is connected to a deeper *Weltanschauung*, a constitutive ontology of the world that allows the values and institutions of liberal democracy to make sense. Such *Weltanschauung* connects the perceived past successes to the legitimate expectations toward the future. There is the trust in the perceived past successes of liberal democracies and capitalist economies. Since the universal history of humanity aims naturally toward the realization of liberal democracies, all of the previous history is interpreted as the inevitable process that leads to that outcome. In this sense, Fukuyama's narrative is similar to Hegel's system. In a narrative of this kind, even predemocratic and precapitalist successes are interpreted as the successes of democracy and capitalism, as the path of universal history naturally draws these social forms into being. This contributes to the development of trust in the values and in the institutions that represent them. We see the presentation of an *objective spirit* of liberal democracy, immanent and inherent in history, which aims for more and more perfected forms of expression. We also see the loyalty and commitment required to realize future successes of democracy and capitalism, successes that possess a relevance for the whole of humanity. In this sense, liberal democratic states are *communities with a mission*, relevant for all humanity and expressing claims that are considered as inherent to human nature. In Fukuyama's narrative, there is also the claim that such future is approaching its final realization. The final promise of freedom is about to be fulfilled. The humans living in liberal democracies have already reached their posthistorical age. They are outside history and their struggle. The final obstacle to be overcome is the spreading of the values of liberal democracy to those populations that live still in history. By experiencing the inevitable destiny of humanity to live in democracy and capitalism, humanity has fulfilled its quasi-eschatological promise. We can only experience quantitative improvements of our conditions, but not qualitative ones. The past successes, the future expectations and the present forms of the values of liberal democracies make sense due to the awareness of a higher order, an inevitable historical pattern inherent to human nature and history itself that leads toward the inevitable outcome of the victory of democracies. This awareness is tied to the fundamental ontological hypostasis about the world and human existence, a *Weltanschauung* that

60. Ibid., 116–20.
61. Ibid., 122.

allows the institutions representing the values of democracy and liberalism to make sense, to be invested with meaning. Democracy has not triumphed just because of contingent historical events. It was the only possible outcome of the history of humanity.

The examples proposed in this chapter demonstrate that every narrative, whether political, historical or economic is not just an epistemic structure. We are not talking about a simple framework of interpretation, which can be progressively improved to obtain a better grasp of reality. A narrative that believes frameworks are just epistemic structures has to rely on an interpretation of history as a necessary progress. The successive epochs represent a better understanding of problems and principles, or a better expression of values and patterns, that are inherent to human history and society. We have seen this progressive character of history in the examples proposed in the previous pages. Taylor's and Blumenberg's narratives also had to rely on this natural progressive character of human history to give consistency to their theories. Instead, every framework implies a whole sense of reality, an ontological structure that sustain and legitimizes the claims of the narrative. In this sense, historical change is not brought about by an epistemic improvement of our categories of understanding. Instead, it is a conflict between worlds, between *Weltanschauungen*; a continuous strife between ontologies of the world that seek their own expression at the expense of rival theories. The presence of an implicit ontology, of an unproven and unprovable understanding of the world that precedes any claim expressed by a narrative, is confirmed by this attitude of faith present in the various contexts presented so far. The narratives that I have briefly presented here had to rely, at some point, on an irrational connection to their sense of things. There was a belief, a faith, according to which the values and institutions advocated made sense, were right, because of deeper reasons. It might be a sense of ultimacy, the belief of a pattern inherent in history, or a fundamental trait of human nature. A *Weltanschauung* may also be constituted by all these things at the same time.[62] Still, whether there is one or many worldviews involved, this attitude of faith, this need for belief in a sense of consistency that cannot be identified clearly on an immanent level, reveals itself as an anthropological constant.

---

62. In this sense, it would be interesting to address what kind of *Weltanschauung* lies behind the narratives I have presented in the previous pages. Do those economic, political and historical narratives imply the same *Weltanschauung*? Or does every field of knowledge rely on a different *Weltanschauung*? Are there thresholds of indifference between them?

These are just some of the questions that my line of inquiry opens up as scholarly investigations; such questions will surely be addressed in future research.

Conclusion

Faith and *Weltanschauung*, the Need for a New Theoretical Framework

AT THE CONCLUSION OF *Il Mondo Magico*, Ernesto De Martino affirmed that the modern fight against any form of alienation of the products of human work presupposes, as a historical condition, the acknowledgment of the fundamental human struggle behind such fight, namely, the wish to guarantee our presence in the world.[1] However, contemporary academic debate have never really focused on determining the qualities and features of such *presence*. This lack of analysis was one of the thing De Martino criticized the most in the anthropological studies of his time and, sadly, scholarly pursuits after him have not deemed the problem worthy of more investigations. Every culture, epoch, and framework of reference is an existential situation that is historically determined. As such, it also shares the historical drama of the *culturally conditioned nature*, the need for fundamental categories of reality that constitute ontologically the world, a fundamental *Weltanschauung* that substantiates and legitimizes social/political claims. This book had two main purposes, connected to this interpretation. The first purpose was to propose, through my criticism of Taylor, that the current interpretation of the controversy between religion and secularity is unable to address properly the historical drama of the development of categories of reality. As in Taylor's analysis, the general interpretation of the debate understands religion and secularity as wholly different forms of consciousness. This interpretation of their difference goes beyond the simple understanding of their historical difference and reaches the conclusion that the two phenomena appeal to different spheres of human life, almost as if they appeal to different anthropological sources.

---

1. De Martino, *Il Mondo Magico*, 222.

I have examined others narratives, besides the one proposed by Taylor, that imply such fundamental differences between religion and secularity, thus revealing that the prejudice is not something limited to few authors, but has to be interpreted as a fundamental category of contemporary Western consciousness. As I have presented, all these narratives rely on interpretations of history as an inevitable story of progress and improvement of human culture, in which modernity represents the current peak historically known. To develop this argument, I have discussed Blumenberg's criticism of secularization theory and provided a comparison with Taylor's interpretation of the problem. Through this comparison, I have proposed the argument that Taylor, despite his attempt to develop a different theoretical framework, proposes a narrative that is similar to the one proposed by Blumenberg, in which modernity is represented as the negation of the predominant feature of the previous, religious, age. According to Blumenberg, in *The Legitimacy of Modern Age*, modernity is the second overcoming of Gnosticism and the reflected and mature rejection of the premodern religious answers to the same problem, answers that were considered untenable and contradictory. For Taylor, modernity still represents a moment of loss, the loss of transcendence, and the overcoming of the inner contradictions of the previous religious framework. Both authors provide a description of modernity as a solution, an overcoming, to a fundamental historical problem that relied on a negative moment. In this way, modernity becomes an historical and ontological improvement in a one-directional history of progress.

However, I have strongly rejected such an interpretation. The drama of historical existence, and the social/psychic realities involved therein, cannot be understood as long as we rely on the modern presuppositions of an absolute individual, independent from other human beings and from the form of consciousness of its society of reference. Such presuppositions are what has constituted the belief of the inherent difference between religion and secularity, in the modern framework. It is born out of a cultural assumption that spatial and temporal separations are an absolute that has to be taken for granted. In this sense, Schmitt's studies on political theology have been the perfect example to introduce a historical sensibility that understands modernity as a process of transformation and transposition. In addition, Schmitt has been the author that has allowed this book to introduce the argument that a specific cultural framework does not just produce moral/epistemic structures, as Taylor implies. Instead, every cultural framework always develops a metaphysical image of the world, which helps the society to structure its own political institutions. The ontology of the world goes hand in hand with what a society consider acceptable as political/ethical organization. Through Schmitt, we have been introduced to a criticism of the secular divide, as well as to the implication that faith plays a role in a how a society structures its own paradigms, independently from its being religious or not. However, Schmitt acknowledged the lack of a proper theoretical framework to develop his analyses beyond the field of legal studies. The debate on modernity, religion and secularity is already framed in an *a priori* understanding of these concepts. This constitutes an obstacle to any attempt to develop a historical narrative that would escape the secular divide; we have seen proof of this through Löwith's failed attempt. A possible theoretical method to escape this *a priori* understanding has been provided by Croce and De Martino. Their analytical method does not focus directly on the concepts that constitute the secular divide. Instead, they focus on the historical conditions that gave birth to the specific interpretation of those concepts. By understanding the historicity and contingency of the cultural paradigms through which our current debate is framed, we have the possibility to understand what cultural needs have determined the development of a specific understanding of a concept. In this way, we obtain full possession of the history of the concept, thus, the possibility to alter its contemporary and future understanding. An analysis focused on the origins of the concept, as I introduced in the first chapter of the book, allows us to call into question the specific and contingent cultural needs that determined its specific, local understanding. In this way, we are freed from any *a priori* understanding of our concepts of analysis. This approach allows us to address consciously the realities that the concepts attempted to signify. In this way, we are able to operate honest comparisons between different ages and societies, with the aim of grasping more precisely what are the similar features, and where the differences do really lie.

The second purpose of this book was to show that it is possible to identify, through an analysis of the phenomenon of faith, a common anthropological constant that transcends the separation between religion and secularity. This anthropological constant represents the existential relation that a society, and the individuals that compose it, establish with the fundamental *Weltanschauung* of their society; the categories of reality that allow them to structure and make sense of their institutions and customs. I have presented the case that secular social forms engage in an activity of *worldmaking*, which they share in common with religious social forms. I have identified such activity with the concept of faith, which I have presented as bound up with fundamental features that occur historically, whenever a society tries to structure its own foundational values. In this sense, faith, as an existential/historical phenomenon happens in religious and secular contexts alike. It is not an irrational attitude, but a prerational one. Faith is the acknowledgment of a sense of order that precedes even the categories through which we establish the rationality/irrationality of a position in specific social contexts. It is the attitude that allows us to make sense of those categories. In this light, a thought that relies on *a priori* presuppositions, as the secularity/religion dichotomy does, is the worst enemy of any investigation oriented in this direction. De Martino's analyses, which I believe should be developed further by the scholarly community, are to be understood precisely in this fashion, as the fundamental criticism of any *a priori* supposition in the study of human history.

Benedetto Croce, in his review of *Il Mondo Magico*, harshly criticized De Martino's attempt to historicize the categories of historical analysis. The affirmation that primitive people possessed different categories of reality and, therefore, should have been studied through different categories of analysis was the critical point upon which Croce centered his attack.[2] Such criticism was enough to convince De Martino to halt his studies in this line of inquiry and to not develop consistent studies regarding the *culturally conditioned nature*. However, our contemporary situation calls for a renewal of such a line of studies. The analyses I have presented on Taylor's narrative, and on other philosophers and thinkers that share similarities with him, reveal how the use of *a priori* categories, and the reliance on an optimistic concept of progress, are damaging to any accurate comprehension of the human phenomena that constitute the history of our Western civilization. The use of absolute historical categories, and of a given ontology of the human and of the world, considered as universal, provides a false understanding of how our Western civilization has been able to structure its own institutions and cultural paradigms.

In proposing a new understanding of the concept of faith as an anthropological constant, I aimed to abandon precisely any *a priori* thought or any arrogant attempt to establish our categories of reality as the universal categories for every culture, society and history of the world. In this sense, then, this line of inquiry opens up new fruitful scholarly investigations: What are the constitutive terms of our Western *Weltanschauung*? Is there actually one, fundamental, Western *Weltanschauung* implied in our cultural forms? Alternatively, is our Western contemporary civilization in itself a fragmented whole of different worldviews? In addition, is it possible to develop a consistent theoretical framework about the concept of faith as an anthropological phenomenon, as a human constant that appears beyond the simplistic schematizations of religion/secularity? In particular, these last two questions are the most urgent line of scholarly inquiry that should be promptly addressed, before being able to address the more complex

---

2. Croce, *Intorno al Magismo come età Storica*.

questions regarding the fundamental *Weltanschauung* of our Western civilization. I presented the case that faith, as an anthropological constant, is strongly connected with a need for meaning and sense. Faith is the human relation that express this need to structure fundamental categories of our reality. In this way, society, and the individuals within it, are able to find meaning and, most importantly, to make sense of customs and institutions in which they are involved. In this sense, the successive inquiry that naturally follows from the work I presented is an investigation of this need for a sense, the human necessity to make sense of customs, institutions and daily events. We severely need a consistent theoretical framework to discuss the phenomenon of faith in a philosophical/anthropological way, without being influenced by the religion/secularity schematization.

At the same time, however, this book should not be understood as endorsing a religious irrationalism or a cultural relativism. These lines of thought, in fact, share with dogmatic realism and progressive Hegelianism the same methodological limits. They oversimplify the cultural/historical problems in which human societies are involved in their historical conditions, particularly our Western one. Like De Martino, I never intend to question the fundamental values of our Western societies, neither have I questioned the fact that we consider those values universal. What I question, however, is whether the secular universal values of Western civilization rest on suprahistorical claims, and in so doing, they ground themselves on roots that can be found only outside history, while the public common discourse rejects the suprahistorical roots of alternative cultural forms. Our universal values have been formed historically and rest on categories of reality that we have created historically. While it is expected that we consider our values important, even universal, it is not possible to believe, for a serious scholar, that such values rest on an objective reality, which is not influenced by historical events. For this reason, I am of the opinion that, today, we are in dire need for a return to an absolute historicism in historical, sociological, philosophical and theological thought.

Bibliography

Abbey, Ruth. *Charles Taylor.* Cambridge: Cambridge University Press, 2004.
Adamson, Walter L. "Benedetto Croce and the Death of Ideology." *Journal of Modern History* 55, no. 2 (1983) 208–36.
Adorno, Theodor W. *Hegel: Three Studies.* Translated by S. W. Nicholsen. London: MIT Press, 1993.
Agamben, Giorgio. *Homo Sacer: Sovereign Power and Bare Life.* Translated by Daniel Heller-Roazen. Stanford, CA: Stanford University Press, 1998.
———. *The Kingdom and the Glory: For a Theological Genealogy of Economy and Government.* Translated by Lorenzo Chiesa (with Matteo Mandarini). Stanford, CA: Stanford University Press, 2011.
———. *State of Exception.* Translated by Kevin Attell. London: University of Chicago Press, 2005.
Angus, Ian. "Recovery of Meaning? A Critique of Charles Taylor's Account of Modernity." In *Aspiring to Fullness in a Secular Age: Essays on Religion and Theology in the Work of Charles Taylor,* edited by Carlos D. Colorado and Justin D. Klassen, 243–61. Notre Dame, IN: University of Notre Dame Press, 2014.
Aquinas, Thomas. *An Apology for the Religious Orders, by Saint Thomas Aquinas, Being a Translation of Two of the Minor Works of the Saint.* Edited by John Procter. London: Sands and Co., 1902.
———. *Summa Theologiae.* New York: Blackfriars, 1964.
Augustine. *De Vera Religione,* 1–10. Translated by John H. S. Burleigh. In *Augustine: Earlier Writings,* edited and translated with introductions by John H. S. Burleigh, 218–83. Library of Christian Classics 6. Philadelphia: Westminster, 1953.
Baum, Gregory. "Middle Class Religion in America." In *Christianity and the Bourgeoisie,* edited by Johann Baptist Metz, 15–23. Concilium 125. New York: Seabury, 1979.
Berger Peter. *The Heretical Imperative: Contemporary Possibilities of Religious Affirmation.* New York: Anchor, 1979.
Bertram, Christopher, and Andrew Chitty, editors. *Has History Ended?: Fukuyama, Marx, Modernity.* Sydney: Avebury, 1994.
Blumenberg, Hans. *The Legitimacy of the Modern Age.* Translated by Robert M. Wallace. Studies in Contemporary German Social Thought. London: MIT Press, 1983.
———. *Work on Myth.* Translated by Robert M. Wallace. Studies in Contemporary German Social Thought. Cambridge, MA: MIT Press, 1985.
Bogart, Leo. *Premises for Propaganda: The United States Information Agency Operating Assumptions in the Cold War.* New York: Free Press, 1976.

Borsari, Andrea. *Hans Blumenberg: Mito, Metafora, Modernità*. Studi per le scienze della cultura 1. Bologna: Il Mulino, 1999.

Botterwick, G. Johannes, and Helmer Ringgren, editors. *Theological Dictionary of the Old Testament*. Translated by John T. Willis. Grand Rapids: Eerdmans, 1974–2004.

Brown, Colin, editor. *New International Dictionary of New Testament Theology*. Vol. 1, A–F. Exeter: Paternoster, 1975.

Bubbio, Paolo D. "God, Incarnation, and Metaphysics in Hegel's Philosophy of Religion." *Sophia* 53, no. 4 (2014) 515–33.

Buber, Martin. *Two Types of Faith*. Translated By Norman P. Goldhawk. London: Routledge & Kegan Paul, 1985.

———. *Zwei Glaubensweisen*. In *Werke*, 1:651–82. Munich, Koesel, 1962.

Caird, Edward. *Hegel*. Cambridge: Scholars, 2002.

Calderone, Salvatore. *Pistis-Fides, Ricerche di Storia e Diritto Internazionale dell'Antichità*. Rome: Università degli Studi di Messina, 1965.

Calhoun, Craig. Review of *A Secular Age* by Charles Taylor. *European Journal of Sociology* 49, no. 3 (2008) 455–61.

Carroll, Jerome. "'Indirect' or 'Engaged': A Comparison of Hans Blumenberg's and Charles Taylor's Debt and Contribution to Philosophical Anthropology." *History of European Ideas* 39, no. 6 (2013) 858–78.

Casanova, José. *Public Religions in the Modern World*. Chicago: University of Chicago Press, 1994.

———. "A Secular Age: Dawn or Twilight?" In *Varieties of Secularism in a Secular Age*, edited by Craig Calhoun, Jonathan VanAntwerpen, and Michael Warner, 265–81. Cambridge, MA: Harvard University Press, 2010.

Cavaliere, Renata V. *Saggi sul Futuro; la Storia come Possibilità*. Firenze: Le Lettere, 2015.

Cavanaugh, William T. *Being Consumed: Economics and Christian Desire*. Cambridge: Eerdmans, 2008.

———. *The Myth of Religious Violence: Secular Ideology and the Root of Modern Conflict*. Oxford: Oxford University Press, 2009.

———. *Theopolitical Imagination*. London: T. & T. Clark, 2002.

Connolly, William E. *Identity/Difference: Democratic Negotiations of Political Paradox*. London: University of Minnesota Press, 1991.

Cotroneo, Giovanni. *Croce Filosofo Italiano*. Firenze: Le Lettere, 2015.

Croce, Benedetto. "Fede e Programmi." *La Critica* 9 (1911) 390–96.

———. "Intorno al Magismo come età Storica." In *Il Mondo Magico: Prolegomeni ad una Storia del Magismo*, by Ernesto De Martino, 242–53. Torino, Bollati Boringhieri, 2007.

———. *La Storia come Pensiero e Azione*. Bari: Laterza, 1966.

———. *Storia dell'età Barocca in Italia*. Bari: Laterza, 1946.

———. *What Is Living and What Is Dead of the Philosophy of Hegel*. Translated by Douglas Ainslie (1915). Ontario: Batoche, Kitchener, 2001.

De Cusa, Nicolas. "De Pace Fidei." In *Unity and Reform: Selected writings of Nicholas De Cusa*, edited and translated by John Patrick Dolan. Notre Dame, IN: University of Notre Dame Press, 1962.

De Martino, Ernesto. *Il Mondo Magico: Prolegomeni ad una Storia del Magismo*. Torino, Bollati Boringhieri, 2007.

De Wilde, Marc. "Fides Publica in Ancient Rome and Its Reception by Grotius and Locke." *Tijdschrift voor Rechtsgeschiedenis / Revue d'Histoire du Droit / The Legal History Review* 79, nos. 3–4 (2011) 455–87.

Descombes, Vincent. "Is There an Objective Spirit?" In *Philosophy in an Age of Pluralism: The Philosophy of Charles Taylor in Question*, edited by James Tully with the assistance of Daniel Weinstock, 96–118. Cambridge: Cambridge University Press, 1994.

Dines, Jennifer M. *The Septuagint*. Edited by Michael A. Knibb. London: T. & T. Clark, 2004.

Dupré, Louis. *Passage to Modernity: An Essay on the Hermeneutics of Nature and Culture*. London: Yale University Press, 1993.

Durkheim, Emilé. *The Elementary Forms of the Religious Life*. Translated by Joseph Ward Swain. London: Allen & Unwin, 1957.

Fahr, Wilhelm. *Zum Problem der Anfaenge des Atheismus bei den Griechen*. Hildesheim and New York: Olms, 1969.

Faraguna, Michele. "Pistis and Apistia: Aspects of the Development of Social and Economic Relations in Classical Greece." *Mediterraneo Antico* 15, no. 1 (2012) 355–74.

Feil, Ernst. *Religio: Die Geschichte eines neuzeitlichen Grundbegriffs vom Frühchristentum bis zur Reformation*. Goettingen: Vandenhoeck & Ruprecht, 1986.

Ferrarin, Alfredo. *Hegel and Aristotle*. Modern European Philosophy. Cambridge: Cambridge University Press, 2001.

Fetscher, Iring. "State Socialist Ideology as Religion?" In *Christianity and Socialism*, edited by Johann-Baptist Metz and Jean-Pierre Jossua, 82–87. Concilium 105. New York: Seabury, 1977.

Fransens, Piet. "A Short History of the Formula "Fides et Mores."" In *Hermeneutics of the Councils and Other Studies*, edited by H. E. Mertens and F. de Graeve, 287–318. Bibliotheca Ephemeridum Theologicarum Lovaniensium 69. Leuven: Leuven University Press, 1985.

Friedrich, Gerhard. *Theological Dictionary of the New Testament*. Translated by G. W. Bromiley. Vol. 4. Grand Rapids: Eerdmans, 1972.

Friedman, Milton. *Free Markets for Free Men*. Selected Papers 45. Graduate School of Business, University of Chicago, October 10, 1974. Online at https://www.chicagobooth.edu/~/media/917BA065D1914F8F8DF7536680FD7EE7.pdf.

Fukuyama, Francis. *The End of History and the Last Man*. London: Penguin, 1992.

Fuerstenberg, F. "What Do We Learn from an Analysis of Religion in Terms of the History of the Concept?" In *On the Concept of Religion*, edited by Ernst Feil, translated by Brian McNeil, 51–55. Binghamton, NY: Academic Studies in Religion and the Social Order, 2000.

Gelven, Michael. *A Commentary on Heidegger's Being and Time*. Dekalb, IL: Northern Illinois University Press, 1989.

Grant, C. David. *God the Center of Value: Value Theory in the Theology of H. Richard Niebuhr*. Fort Worth: Texas Christian University Press, 1984.

Gregory, Brad S. *The Unintended Reformation: How a Religion Revolution Secularized a Society*. London: Harvard University Press, 2012.

Gustafson, James. "Christian Ethics and Social Policy." In *Faith and Ethics: The Theology of H. Richard Niebuhr*, edited by Ramsey Paul, 115–35, New York: Harper, 1965.

Habermas, Juergen, and Joseph Ratzinger. *Dialectics of Secularization: On Reason and Religion*. Edited by Florian Schuller, translated by Brian McNeil. San Francisco: Ignatius, 2006.

Harris, R. Laird, editor. *Theological Wordbook of the Old Testament*. 2 vols. Chicago: Moody, 1980.

Hart, William D. "Naturalizing Christian Ethics: A Critique of Charles Taylor's *A Secular Age*." *Journal of Religious Ethics* 40, no. 1 (2012) 149–70.

Hauerwas, Stanley. *Against the Nations: War and Survival in a Liberal Society*. Minneapolis: Winston, 1985.

Hausmaninger, Herbert. *Die Bona Fides des Ersitzungsbesitzers im klassischen romischen Recht*. Vienna and Munich: Herold, 1964.

Hegel, Georg W. F. *Elements of the Philosophy of Right*. Translated by H. B. Nisbet. Cambridge: Cambridge University Press, 1991.

———. *Phenomenology of Spirit*. Translated by Arnold Vincent Miller. Oxford: Oxford University Press, 1977.

Heidegger, Martin. *Being and Time*. Translated by John Macquarrie and Edward Robinson. Oxford: Blackwell, 1962.

Hixson, Walter L. *Parting the Curtain: Propaganda, Culture and the Cold War 1945–1961*. New York: St. Martin, 1997.

Holder, Rodney D. "Quantum Theory and Theology." In *The Blackwell Companion to Science and Christianity*, edited by Stump J. B. and Alan G. Padgett, 220–32. Oxford: Blackwell, 2012.

Janz, Paul D. "Transcendence, 'Spin,' and the Jamesian Open Space." In *Aspiring to Fullness in a Secular Age: Essays on Religion and Theology in the Work of Charles Taylor*, edited by Carlos D. Colorado and Justin D. Klassen, 39–70. Notre Dame, IN: University of Notre Dame Press, 2014.

John Paul II, Pope. *Fides et Ratio: On the Relationship between Faith and Reason*. Rome: Libreria Editrice Vaticana, 1998.

Keynes, John Maynard. *Essays in Persuasion*. London: Macmillan, 1972.

Klassen, Justin D. "The Affirmation of Existential Life in Charles Taylor's A Secular Age." In *Aspiring to Fullness in a Secular Age: Essays on Religion and Theology in the Work of Charles Taylor*, edited by Carlos D. Colorado and Justin D. Klassen, 13–38. Notre Dame, IN: University of Notre Dame Press, 2014.

Laitinen, Arto. *Strong Evaluation without Moral Sources: On Charles Taylor's Philosophical Anthropology and Ethics*. Berlin: de Gruyter, 2008.

Lombardi, Luigi. *Dalla Fides alla Bona Fides*. Milan: Giuffré, 1961.

Löwith, Karl. *Meaning in History: The Theological Implications of the Philosophy of History*. Chicago: University of Chicago Press, 1957.

Lukes, Steven. *Marxism and Morality*. Oxford: Clarendon, 1985.

Luther, Martin. *A Commentary on the Galatians, by Martin Luther, with the Life of the Author*. Originally published, Chester: Jones and Crane, 1796. Eighteenth Century Collections Online. Gale, University of Aberdeen.

Marcos, Natalio Fernández. *The Septuagint in Context: Introduction to the Greek Version of the Bible*. Translated by Wilfred G. E. Watson. Boston: Brill, 2000.

Marx, Karl. *Capital: A Critique of Political Economy*. Translated by by Samuel Moore and Edward Aveling. 3 vols. Chicago: Charles H. Kerr, 1909.

Marder, Michael. *Groundless Existence: The Political Ontology of Carl Schmitt*. New York: Continuum, 2010.

Metz, Johann Baptiste. *The Emergent Church: The Future of Christianity in a Postbourgeois World*. Translated by Peter Mann. London: SCM, 1981.
———. *Faith in History and Society: Toward a Foundational Political Theology*. Translated by David Smith. New York: Seabury, 1980.
———. "How Faith Sees the World." In *Theology of the World*, translated by William Glen-Doepel, 16–51. New York: Seabury, 1969.
———. *A Passion for God: The Mystical-Political Dimension of Christianity*. Translated by James Matthew Ashley. New York: Paulist, 1998.
Milbank, John. *Theology and Social Theory: Beyond Secular Reason*. Cambridge, MA: Blackwell, 1991.
———. *The World Made Strange: Theology, Language, Culture*. Oxford: Blackwell, 1999.
Morgan, Michael L. "Religion, History and Moral Discourse." In *Philosophy in an Age of Pluralism: The Philosophy of Charles Taylor in Question*, edited by James Tully with the assistance of Daniel Weinstock, 49–66. Cambridge: Cambridge University Press, 1994.
———. Review of Charles Taylor's *A Secular Age*. *Notre Dame Philosophical Reviews*, August 8, 2008. https://ndpr.nd.edu/news/a-secular-age/.
Morgan, Theresa. *Roman Faith and Christian Faith: Pistis and Fides and in the Early Roman Empire and Early Churches*. Oxford: Oxford University Press, 2015.
Mynarek H. "A Critique of Ernst Feil's Conception of Religion and Faith." In *On the Concept of Religion*, edited by Ernst Feil, translated by Brian McNeil, 86–93. Bringhamton, NY: Academic Studies in Religion and the Social Order, 2000.
Nelson, Robert H. *Economics as Religion: From Samuelson to Chicago and Beyond*. University Park: Pennsylvania State University Press, 2001.
Nicholls, Angus. *Myth and the Human Sciences: Hans Blumenberg's Theory of Myth*. London: Routledge, 2015.
Niebuhr, H. Richard. *Faith on Earth: An Inquiry into the Structure of Human Faith*. New Haven, CT: Yale University Press, 1989.
———. *Radical Monotheism and Western Civilization*. Lincoln: University of Nebraska, 1960.
———. *Theology, History and Culture*. New Haven, CT: Yale University Press, 1996.
Niebuhr, Reinhold. *Faith and Politics*. New York: George Braziller, 1968.
———. *The Nature and Destiny of Man*. Vol 1. London: Nisbet, 1941.
Nietzsche, Frederick. *Writings from the Late Notebooks*. Edited by Rüdiger Bittner, translated by Kate Sturge. Cambridge: Cambridge University Press, 2003.
Peluso, Rosalia. *Lessico Crociano*. Napoli: La Scuola di Pitagora, 2016.
Peters, Tiemo R. *Johann Baptist Metz: Theologie des vermißten Gottes*. Mainz: Grünewald, 1998.
Ratzinger, Joseph. "Eschatology and Utopia." In *Joseph Ratzinger in Communio*, vol. 1, *The Unity of the Church*, 10–25. Cambridge: Eerdmans, 2010.
———. *Values in a Time of Upheaval*. Translated by Brian McNeil. San Francisco: Ignatius 2005.
Reardon, Bernard M. G. *Hegel's Philosophy of Religion*. London: Macmillan, 1977.
Scheuerman, William. *Carl Schmitt: The End of Law*. Lanham, MD: Rowman & Littlefield, 1999.
Schillebeeckx, Edward. *Church: The Human Story of God*. Translated by John Bowden. London: SCM, 1990.

Schmitt, Carl, and Hans Blumenberg. *Briefwechsel 1971–1978 und weitere Materialien.* Edited by Alexander Schmitz and Marcel Lepper. Frankfurt am Main: Suhrkamp 2007.

———. *Political Theology.* 1922. Translated by George Schwab. Chicago: University of Chicago Press, 1985.

———. *Political Theology II: The Myth of the Closure of Any Political Theology.* Translated by Michael Hoelzl, and Graham Ward. Cambridge: Polity, 2008.

———. *State, Movement, People.* Translated by Simona Draghici. Corvallis, OR: Plutarch, 2001.

———. *Theory of the Partisan: Intermediate Commentary on the Concept of the Political.* Translated by G. L. Ulmen. New York: Telos, 2007.

———. "Three Possibilities for a Christian Conception of History." *Telos* 147 (2009) 167–70.

———. *La Tirannia dei Valori.* Edited by Paolo Becchi .Milan: Adelphi, 2008.

Seidl, Ernst. "Pistis in der griechischen Literatur bis zur Zeit der Peripatos." PhD dissertation, University of Innsbruck, 1952.

Singer, Peter. *Hegel.* Oxford: Oxford University Press, 1983.

Skinner, Quentin. "Modernity and Disenchatment: Some Historical Reflections." In *Philosophy in an Age of Pluralism: the Philosophy of Charles Taylor in Question*, edited by James Tully with the assistance of Daniel Weinstock, 37–48. Cambridge: Cambridge University Press, 1994.

Stagaman, David. "Piet Fransen's Research on Fides et Mores." *Theological Studies* 64 (2003) 69–77.

Stepelevich, L. S. "Hegel and Roman Catholicism." *Journal of the American Academy of Religion* 60, no. 4 (Winter 1992) 673–91.

Stout, Jeffrey. *Democracy and Tradition.* Princeton, NJ: Princeton University Press, 2004.

Stout, Harry S. "The Historical Legacy of H. Richard Niebuhr." In *The Legacy of H. Richard Niebuhr*, edited by Ronald F. Thiemann, 83–100. Minneapolis: Fortress, 1991.

Taglia, Angelica. *Il Concetto di Pistis in Platone.* Firenze: Le Lettere, 1998.

Taubes, Jacob. *The Political Theology of Paul.* Translated by Dana Hollander. Stanford, CA: Stanford University Press, 1993.

Taylor, Charles. *Dilemmas and Connections: Selected Essays.* London: Belknap, 2011.

———. *Hegel.* London: Cambridge University Press, 1975.

———. *Hegel and Modern Society.* London: Cambridge University Press, 1979.

———. *Modern Social Imaginaries.* London: Duke University Press, 2004.

———. *A Secular Age.* London: Belknap Press of Harvard University Press, 2007.

———. *Sources of The Self: The Making of Modern Identity.* Cambridge: Harvard University Press, 2001.

Toulmin, Stephen Edison. *Cosmopolis: The Hidden Agenda of Modernity.* New York: Free Press, 1990.

Tracey, Rowland. *Ratzinger's Faith: The Theology of Pope Benedict XVI.* New York: Oxford University Press, 2008.

Ugilt, Rasmus. *Giorgio Agamben: Political Philosophy.* Penrith: Humanities-Ebooks, 2014.

Wagnleitner, Reinhold. *Coca-Colonization and the Cold War: The Cultural Mission of the United States in Austria after the Second World War.* Translated by Diana M. Wolf. London: University of North Carolina Press, 1994.

Weijers, Olga. "Some Notes on Fides and Related Words in Medieval Latin." *Archivum Latinitatis Medii Aevi* 40 (1977) 77–102.

Williams, Howard, David Sullivan, and E. Gwynn Matthews. *Francis Fukuyama and the End of History.* Cardiff: University of Wales Press, 1997.

Woodford, Peter. "Specters of the Nineteenth Century: Charles Taylor and the Problem of Historicism." *Journal of Religious Ethics* 40, no. 1 (2012) 171–92.

Yunis, Harvey E. *A New Creed: Fundamental Religious Beliefs in the Athenian Polis and Euripidean Drama.* Göttingen: Vandenhoeck & Ruprecht, 1988.

www.ingramcontent.com/pod-product-compliance
Lightning Source LLC
Chambersburg PA
CBHW051641230426
43669CB00013B/2390